CHANGING
MINDS

The Art and Science of Changing
Our Own and Other People's Minds

Howard Gardner

HARVARD BUSINESS SCHOOL PRESS
BOSTON, MASSACHUSETTS

No part of this publication may be reproduced, stored in or introduced into a retrieval system, or transmitted, in any form, or by any means (electronic, mechanical, photo-copying, recording, or otherwise), without the prior permission of the publisher. Re-quests for permission should be directed to permissions@hbsp.harvard.edu, or mailed to Permissions, Harvard Business School Publishing, 60 Harvard Way, Boston, Massa-chusetts 02163.

1-4221-0329-3 (pbk ISBN 10)
978-4221-0329-6 (pbk ISBN 13)

Library of Congress Cataloging-in-Publication Data
Gardner, Howard.
    Changing minds : the art and science of changing our own and other peoples minds / Howard Gardner.
    p. cm.
Includes bibliographical references and index.
ISBN 1-57851-709-5
  1. Change (Psychology) 2. Persuasion (Psychology) 3. Influence (Psychology) I. Title.
    BF637.C4G37 2004
    153.8'5—dc22

                                                        2003019437

CHANGING
MINDS

Leadership for the Common Good

The Leadership for the Common Good series represents a partnership between Harvard Business School Press and the Center for Public Leadership at Harvard University's John F. Kennedy School of Government. Books in the series aim to provoke conversations about the role of leaders in business, government, and society, to enrich leadership theory and enhance leadership practice, and to set the agenda for defining effective leadership in the future.

To Courtney Sale Ross-Holst

Contents

Preface

NO MATTER HOW LONG YOU WORK on a book, and how much you try to anticipate its reception, there will always be surprises. This was certainly true in the case of *Changing Minds*. As it went to press at the beginning of 2004, I conceived of the book as a synthesis of my own studies in cognitive psychology, with special reference to the issue of how one goes about changing minds. The primary audiences were readers in business, a new audience for me, and readers in education and psychology, audiences that I had long addressed.

The first surprise came even before the book was published. I received a phone call from the office of Ralph Nader, who was launching his campaign for president. The campaign had not been going well, and the caller said that Nader was interested in changing the minds of the press and the public with respect to his candidacy. More surprises followed. The first three invitations that I received to speak about the book came from an advertisement agency (clearly in the business of changing minds); an academic-corporate collective seeking to change the fast-food eating habits of obese Americans; and a high-level commission on national security, charged with altering the beliefs and work habits of five thousand intelligence officers. While writing the book, I had not given a moment's thought to any of these audiences.

In April 2004, the month that the book was published, I gave a talk at the Barnes & Noble bookstore located in Rockefeller Center, in New York City. The talk went reasonably well; then I opened up the floor for questions. The only question that I remember was asked by twelve-year-old Danny. He queried: "I want to know why anyone would want to vote for John Kerry, since he changes his mind all the time, on so many issues." I was taken aback by the confidence of the questioner, the presupposition of the question (that it was necessarily bad to change one's own mind), and the political urgency of the topic. Had I in fact written a book for a political season?

In the ensuing months, the topic of my book—though not, to be sure, the book itself—became a major issue in the presidential election. As I came to see it, the election pitted John Kerry, who was seen as "flip-flopping" on urgent issues, against George W. Bush, who was seen as often wrong but always resolute. Cover stories serenaded the "swing voter." In the weeks before the election, I was inundated by requests to appear on the broadcast media or to answer questions posed by print reporters. Clearly, the serendipity of the book's publication date and the personae of the major candidates combined to make me an instant expert on presidential politics. Had the book appeared in April 2003 or April 2005, its positioning would likely have been quite different.

These unanticipated reactions have taught me two related things. First of all, events in the real world—in this case, a heavily fought presidential election—can provide an unexpected thrust to the title, the presumed contents, and even the sales of a book. Second, when a book sports a general title or theme, readers will project onto it their own personal concerns, ranging from their body weight, to their desired customers, to their presumed enemies. I am pleased that the wide tent of mind-changing has attracted a broad readership in many countries.

As I leaf through the pages of the book, two years after its initial publication, I am struck by the ephemerality of some examples and the timelessness of others. Writing at a time when George W. Bush was popular, I did not fully anticipate the costs of his obstinacy or of his unwillingness ever to admit a mistake. Reflecting on the conversation between Harvard President Lawrence Summers and Harvard Professor Cornel West, I had hoped that Summers would learn to weigh his words more carefully; he was either unwilling or unable to monitor his public and private statements, and this situation eventually contributed to his resignation in February 2006. John Chambers remains in charge of Cisco, but his once-hyperbolic triumphalism has been replaced by cautious, almost muted forecasts. In characterizing my cognitive approach, I wish that I had contrasted it with "evolutionary psychology" rather than an increasingly anachronistic sociobiological approach. And while I recognized the resistance to Darwinian ideas 150 years after they were first enunciated, I had not anticipated the continuing skepticism about evolution among the American public and its willingness to countenance notions of "intelligent design" and creationism. Resistance to the findings of human science is never far from the surface, particularly on American soil.

My discussion of changing minds was couched in terms of "significant changes of mind"—a characterization that rings true to me. I wish that I had more sharply made two distinctions. First, there is a difference between the original formation of mind, as in a young child's initial ideas about the composition and motions of world, and what it takes to change a mind, once formed. Second, there is a difference between a deepening of mind—as occurs when one learns more about a subject or enhances one's skills—and a genuine transformation of mind, when one's knowledge or skill veer in a new direction.

In presenting the arguments of the book, I have found it useful to distinguish graphically (see the following figure) among the three factors involved in mind change: (1) the four entities of mind change (stories, theories, concepts, and skills); (2) the six arenas of mind change (ranging from the large arena of a nation to the intimate arena of one's own family and one's own soul); and (3) the seven levers of mind change, all conveniently beginning with the letters RE. In any given effort to change minds, one should identify the specific entity, the particular arena, and the most suitable lever of the seven. In total, as the figure illustrates there are 168 possibilities—$4 \times 6 \times 7$. I don't think that we will ever have a formula or algorithm for picking the optimal lever for each specific entity and arena. These decisions will always have contextual and fortuitous components. But evidence will continue to accumulate about which levers, on the average, are more likely to be effective in specific circumstances.

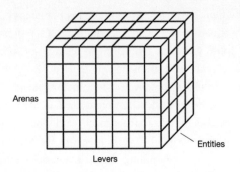

Arenas

Entities

Levers

When I teach classes or give talks on this subject, engaged members of the audience often nominate additional levers beginning with "re." Among the most popular candidates are *re*ligion, *re*lationships, and *re*spect. A plausible case could be made for each of these levers, and no doubt others—for example, "passion," "charisma," or "trust." I make no claim that my seven levers are the only ones. They do represent my effort to identify a variety of factors that can lead to mind change and to encourage aspiring mind-changers to examine their own *re*pertoire and, perhaps, alter or enlarge it.

The factor that continues to intrigue me the most is the degree of *re*sistance that most efforts encounter. If I could dispense just one morsel of advice to mind changers, it is to spend less time trying to convince individuals of a new perspective, and more time trying to understand and thereby to neutralize the resistances. On this score, I was pleased to learn about the extent to which my ideas about mind changing and its resistances had been anticipated by no less an authority than British economist John Maynard Keynes. Note his insightful words, courtesy of the (Wikipedia):

> *When the facts change, I change my mind. What do you do, sir?*

> *A study of the history of opinion is a necessary preliminary to the emancipation of the mind.*

> *Practical men who believe themselves to be quite exempt from any intellectual influences are usually the slaves of some defunct economist.*

The difficulty lies, not in the new ideas, but in escaping from the old ones, which ramify, for those brought up as most of us have been, into every corner of our minds.

There is one point that I wish I had explored further in the original publication—the relationship between the personal and the organizational arenas. As a trained psychologist, I think naturally in terms of individual psyches—how one mind changes itself or alters the minds of other persons. Even when the mind changer is working with large-scale organizations or political entities, I tend to think of the thousands or millions of individual minds to be changed. But as I've thought more about organizational or institutional cultures, I have come to appreciate the extent to which changes in mental models or patterns of behavior may reflect procedures that are invisible to most actors. Individuals think and behave differently depending on whether the culture of their organization is flat or hierarchical; whether it mandates the same requirements for all members, or is flexible and individualized; whether it regards cognate organizations as mortal enemies or as potential collaborators, or ignores peer organizations altogether. Should the organization change with respect to one or more of those parameters of institutional culture, members may well find that they think and act differently even if nothing has been explicitly stated, nothing new has been mandated. Of course, the psychologist within me points out that such changes are difficult to effect, difficult to sustain, and come about only if dedicated individuals strive to initiate them.

Changing Minds concluded with a discussion of three factors that are likely to influence mind changing in the future. Turning first to *wetware*, our knowledge of the brain continues to accumulate at an impressive rate; this knowledge is already being mobilized in efforts to change individual minds in arenas arranging from the products that we buy to the political candidates that we support. Direct efforts to alter brain structure or gene expression are sure to follow. Advances in *dryware*—computational and information systems—are equally striking. Increasingly, sources of information are being personalized; systems are designed to provide each user with the references, sources, and tools that are most likely to help her achieve her specific goals. Already, intelligent computational systems can successfully mimic intelligent human beings. Clearly, by drawing on information about the users, such targeted informational systems could also be used to alter views—perhaps surreptitiously.

Throughout my writings, I have made it clear that analytic schemes are not moral devices; each of the human intelligences can be used positively or negatively: creative individuals may use their powers to build or destruct; leaders can use their skills to catalyze utopias or dystopias. This amorality extends to mind changing. For every Nelson Mandela, who uses his skills to bring about a more harmonious community, there is, alas, a Slobodan Milosevic, who changes minds in a divisive way.

Aware of this situation, I have in recent years been studying *goodware*—a third way in which to change minds in the future. Through the collaborative GoodWork project, I have sought to understand those precious individuals who use their skills at mind changing to help bring about a better world. This work has recently led me to a consideration of the nature of trust and of trustees, two terms that do not appear in the index to *Changing Minds*.

No community can exist without a measure of *trust*. We trust drivers not to move while the light is red; we trust the government to pay our social security when it is due; we trust our bosses to let us know if the business is in trouble. When any of these trusts is abused, our more general sentiments of trust are undermined. In my view it is also desirable to have *trustees*, individuals in one's community who are assumed to see the big picture clearly; who are concerned with the long-term welfare of the society; and who, most importantly, are expected to behave in a disinterested way—that is, to recommend and to do what is right, rather than what improves their own lot or advances their own interests.

As I consider the currently stipulated levers of mind change, it seems to me that trust falls most comfortably under the aegis of resonance: when one trusts a person (or group or institution), one feels at ease, one resonates with that entity. By the same token, a loss of trust—in a parent, a lover, a boss, a president, a company a medium of information—signals a diminution or disappearance of resonance, and a correlative rise in resistance. Much of one' capacity to change the minds of other hinges on whether or not one is trusted, seen as trustworthy, deemed to be a trustee.

As with integrity, honesty, truthfulness, trust is not a property that can be faked in the long run. Trust is earned, and must periodically be confirmed. If I were to rewrite *Changing Minds*, I could discuss trust under the aegis of resonance or even of resistance. I could adhere to the "re" rule, by invoking "*re*liability." But because of its importance in the promotion of good ware and GoodWork, I would address directly the issue of trust.

Howard Gardner
March 2006

CHAPTER 1

The Contents of the Mind

WE TALK ALL THE TIME about changing minds. The meaning of this exceedingly common metaphor seems clear enough: We have a mind set in one direction, some operation is performed, and—lo and behold—the mind is now set in another direction. Yet clear as this figure of speech may seem on superficial consideration, the phenomenon of changing minds is one of the least examined and—I would claim—least understood of familiar human experiences.

What happens when we change our minds? And what exactly does it take for a person to change her mind and begin to act on the basis of this shift? These questions have engaged my own curiosity: I have thought about them as a psychological researcher, while realizing that some aspects of mind changing are likely to remain an art for the foreseeable future. I present my own answers in the pages that follow.

Minds, of course, are hard to change. Yet so many aspects of our lives are oriented toward doing just that—convincing a colleague to approach a task in a new way, trying to eradicate one of our own prejudices. Some of us, even, are involved professionally in the business of changing people's minds: the therapist who affects his patient's self-concept; the teacher who introduces students to new ways of thinking about a familiar topic; the salesperson or advertiser who convinces consumers to switch brands. Leaders almost by definition are people who change minds—be they leaders of a nation, a corporation, or a nonprofit institution. Certainly, then, rather than taking the phenomenon of mind changing for granted, we can benefit from a better understanding of its many fascinating puzzles—of what, exactly, happens when a mind shifts from a seemingly intractable state to a radically different viewpoint.

At the outset let me state what I mean—and do not mean—when I use the expression "changing minds." To begin with, I am speaking about *significant* changes of mind. In a trivial sense, our minds change every moment that we are awake and, in all probability, while we are dozing or sleeping as well. Even when we grow senile, our minds are changing, though not in ways that are desirable. I shall reserve the phrase "changing minds" for the situation where individuals or groups abandon the way in which they have customarily thought about an issue of importance and henceforth conceive of it in a new way. So if I decide to read the sections of the newspaper in a different order, or to lunch at noon rather than at one o'clock, these do not qualify as significant changes of mind. If, on the other hand, I have always voted the straight Democratic ticket and decide that from now on I will actively campaign for the Libertarian Party; or if I decide to drop out of law school in order to become a pianist at a bar, I would consider these to be significant changes of mind. (Granted, there is always the odd bird for whom switching lunch time represents a bigger shift than changing careers.) The same contrast obtains when someone else is the agent of change—the person who brings about a mental shift. A teacher who decides to give tests on Thursday rather than Friday and who thereby affects my weekly study calendar is bringing about at most a modest change in my mind. But a teacher who turns me on to learning, and thereby stimulates me to continue pursuing a topic even after the course is over, has affected my mind more substantially.

I focus on changes of mind that occur *consciously,* typically as a result of forces that can be identified (rather than through subtle manipulation). I survey an ensemble of agents who sought to bring about a change of mind and who did so in a straightforward and transparent manner. My examples include political leaders like Prime Minister Margaret Thatcher, who altered the direction of Great Britain in the 1980s; business leaders like John Browne, now Lord Browne, who changed the operations of the British oil giant BP in the 1990s; the biologist Charles Darwin, who transformed the way in which scientists (and, eventually, laypersons) think about human origins; the spy Whittaker Chambers, whose own tumultuous changes of mind altered the political landscape of the United States in the early 1950s; and less well-known school teachers, family members, professional colleagues, therapists, and lovers who changed the minds of those around them.

My focus falls primarily on agents who succeed in changing minds, but I will also consider failed efforts by political leaders, business leaders, intellectuals, and other aspiring mind-changers. Except incidentally, I am not going to treat changes that occur through compulsion, nor changes that come about as a result of deception or manipulation. I introduce seven factors—ranging from reason to resistance—that operate either individually or jointly to bring about or thwart significant changes of mind; and I show how they work in a variety of specific cases. I am of course aware that changes do not always occur because of the intentions of the change agents or the desires of the person whose mind has been changed; some effects will be indirect or subtle or long-term or unintended or even perverse.

Often artists are the first to scout out terrain that is eventually explored in a more explicit way by scholars. As it happens, the novelist and essayist Nicholson Baker presents a charming example of mind change *and*—more revealingly—offers a thoughtful intuitive account of how such mind changing may come about.[1] Baker recalls a bus trip that he took from New York City to upstate Rochester. The co-occurrence of two events on that trip stimulated Baker to ruminate about the process of mind changing.

First of all, at a scheduled stop en route, the driver of the bus noticed a stray shoe. He asked whether the shoe belonged to anyone. When no customer responded, the bus driver tossed the shoe into a nearby trash can. At a later point on the trip, a rather pathetic-looking passenger asked the driver whether a shoe had been discovered. The driver informed the passenger that he was too late and that the shoe had already been discarded in the vicinity of Binghamton.

Baker contrasts the decisiveness of the shoe tossing with a much more gradual instance of coming to a decision—in fact, a change of his own mind. While on the same bus trip, the writer began to fantasize about how he might furnish an apartment. In particular, he thought about an imaginative way in which to seat people: he would purchase and install rows of yellow forklifts and orange backhoes in his apartment. Visitors could sit either on slings hanging between the forks of the forklifts or on buckets of the kind used in excavating backhoes. Baker had been in the process of calculating how many forklifts a floor would sustain when the hapless passenger inquired in vain about the whereabouts of his shoe.

Baker reflects on what happened in the five years since he had first envisioned this exotic form of furnishing: "I find that, without my knowledge, I have changed my mind. I no longer want to live in an apartment furnished with forklifts and backhoes. Somewhere I jettisoned that interest *as irrevocably as the bus driver tossed out the strange sad man's right shoe* [Baker's italics]. Yet I did not experience during the intervening time a single uncertainty or pensive moment in regard to a backhoe."[2]

Baker proceeds to reflect on the peculiar nature of these gradual changes of mind—such changes as the drifting apart of two friends, a shift in artistic taste, an alteration of political consciousness or persuasion. As he sees it, a mind change most often results from a slow, almost unidentifiable shift of viewpoint rather than by virtue of any single argument or sudden epiphany. Moreover, such so-called jolting insights are usually things we point to only after the fact, becoming stories that we eventually tell ourselves and others to explain our change of mind. He concludes his meditation with a characterization that encompasses just the kinds of mind changes that I am trying to understand: "I don't want the story of the feared-but-loved teacher, the book that hit like a thunderclap, the years of severe study followed by a visionary breakdown, the clench of repentance: I want each sequential change of mind in its true, knotted, clotted, viny multifariousness, with all of the colorful streams of intelligence still taped on and flapping in the wind."[3]

From a phenomenological point of view, Baker has captured well the experience that all of us have had with respect to two varieties of mind changing: on the one hand, an apparently abrupt decision, like the tossing of a shoe out the window; on the other hand, a decision we come to gradually, perhaps even imperceptibly, over a longer period of time, like a shift in one's taste. I believe that Baker is correct in asserting that even those changes that erupt dramatically in consciousness often mask subtler processes that have jelled over a lengthy period of time. Still, such cases of personal mind-changing are but a subclass: In many cases, other agents—leaders, teachers, media personalities—play a decisive role in helping to bring about a change of mind, be it sudden or emergent.

All these forms of mind changing call for an explanation. What is enigmatic to the novelist or provocative for the essayist can and should be explicated by the social scientist. In this book, I identify (1) the various agents and agencies of mind change, (2) the tools that they have at their disposal, and (3) the seven factors that help to determine whether they succeed in changing minds. And I seek to show the power of my cognitively based account, as compared to rival rationales: for example, one based on biological factors or one that focuses on cultural or historical factors.

Before we launch into the specific agents and tools that can create a change of mind, let me define what I am talking about when I speak of what happens in the "mind." Though both Nicholson Baker and I speak about changing minds, it is clear that what I am writing about (and perhaps what he is writing about as well) ultimately involves changes of behavior. Changes that occur "within the mind" may be of academic interest, but if they do not result in present or future changes of behavior, then they are not of interest here.

Why, then, not simply speak of behavior? Why bring the mind into the discussion at all? Because a key to changing a mind is to produce a shift in the individual's "mental representations"—the particular way in which a person perceives, codes, retains, and accesses information. Here we run smack into the history of psychology—and a way of thinking about the human mind that will allow us to answer the question: What does it take to change a mind?

A PSYCHOLOGY OPEN TO "MIND" TALK

A century ago, in the earliest days of scientific psychology, researchers relied heavily on self-reports (introspection) and displayed no hesitation in speaking about ideas, thoughts, images, states of consciousness, even the Mind. Unfortunately, human beings are not necessarily accurate observers of their own mental life, and introspective accounts of experience did not satisfy strict scientific standards. As a reaction against this overreliance on personal, Nicholson Baker–style reports, a generation of psychologists decided to eliminate from their fledgling discipline all personal testimony—all reference to mental phenomena. They called instead for an exclusive emphasis on observable behaviors—acts that can be objectively seen, recorded, and quantified. Their approach—which held sway in the United States and some other countries for half a century—was called behaviorism. The tenets (and limits) of behaviorism are well conveyed in an old joke: Two behaviorists make love. The first then says to the second, "Well, it was great for you. But tell me, how was it for me?"

Whatever its virtues, behaviorism died during the second half of the twentieth century. There were various accessories to the fact but the principal executioner was the computer. By the 1950s and 1960s, it had become clear that computers were capable of problem solving of a sophisticated sort. To effect such problem solving, the computers required information—data—on which various operations were then performed in sequence. Often the computers went about computations in ways that appeared similar to those employed by human beings. As evidence accrued that manmade objects could think, it seemed absurd to deny mental activity to those entities—human beings—who built the hardware, created the software, and modeled the processes by which computers operated.

Thus was launched the cognitive revolution.[4] This intellectual current swept through a number of disciplines fifty years ago and gave rise to an interdisciplinary field called cognitive science. Rejecting the strictures of behaviorism, cognitive scientists revisit the questions and concepts that were considered fair game during the first years of psychology (and, indeed, in the great philosophies of the past). Cognitivists have no hesitation in speaking about images, ideas, mental operations, and the Mind. In doing so, they rely heavily on the analogy and terminology of the computer age. And so, like mechanical or electrical computing devices, individuals are said to take in information, process it in various ways, and create diverse mental representations. It is possible to describe these mental representations in plain English (or French or Swahili)—as I will often do. But ultimately it is preferable if these mental representations can be described as precisely as the objects and operations of a programming language. Indeed, a new field called cognitive neuroscience posits that one day these mental representations will be explicable in purely physiological terms. We may be able to point to the set of neural connections or networks that represent a particular image, idea, or concept and observe changes thereto directly. And if the future techniques of brain transplants or genetic engineering achieve their potential, we might even be able to change minds by operating directly on the neurons or nucleotides (more on this in the closing chapter of the book).

To pursue the present inquiry I appropriate the language of cognitive science and speak about the ways in which mental representations change, or are changed. Of course, in a modest way our mental representations change all the time. Indeed, you could not have gotten this far in the first chapter if you had not undergone voluntary changes in representation—perhaps changes in the ways in which you understand the history of psychology or think about the common phrase "changing my mind." Moreover, unless you read works of social science purely for pleasure, you are presumably plowing through this book in the hope that your mental representations of "changing minds" will undergo further changes, and that those changes will prove useful to you at home, at the work place, or at your favorite watering hole.

So what is the stuff of mental representations? Let's start with an example.

MENTAL REPRESENTATIONS: THE 80/20 PRINCIPLE

Consider a change of mind that many individuals have experienced over the years. From early childhood, most of us have operated under the following assumption: When confronted with a task, we should work as hard as we are able and devote approximately equal time to each part of that task. According to this "50/50 principle," if we have to learn a piece of music, or master a new game, or fill out some role at home or at work, we should spread our effort equally across the various components.

Now consider another perspective on this issue. Early in the last century, the Italian economist and sociologist Vilifredo Pareto proposed what has come to be known as the "80/20 principle" or rule. As explained by Richard Koch in a charming book, *The 80/20 Principle,*[5] one can in general accomplish most of what one wants—perhaps up to 80 percent of the target—with only a relatively modest amount of effort—perhaps only 20 percent of expected effort (see figure 1-1). It is important to be judicious about where one places one's efforts, and to be alert to "tipping points" that abruptly bring a goal within (or beyond) reach. Conversely, one should avoid the natural temptation to inject equal amounts of energy into every part of a task, problem, project, or hobby; or to lavish equal amounts of attention on every employee, every friend, or every worry.

Why should anyone change his or her mind from operating under the 50/50 principle to believing Pareto's apparently counterintuitive proposition? Let's consider some concrete instances. Studies show that, in most businesses, about 80 percent of the profits come from 20 percent of the products. Clearly it makes sense to devote attention and resources to the profitable products while dropping the losers. In most businesses, the top workers produce far more than their share of profits; thus one should reward the top workers while trying to ease out the unproductive (and unprofitable) ones. Complementing this notion (and with a nod to pessimists), 80 percent of the trouble in a workforce characteristically comes from a small number of troublemakers—who, unless they are relatives of the boss, should promptly be excised from the company. (In corporate America this philosophy has been explicitly adopted by companies like GE that single out the top 20 percent for reward and the bottom 10 percent for oblivion.) The same ratio applies to customers: The best customers or clients account for most of our successes, while the vast majority of clientele contribute little to our bottom line. With respect to almost any product or project, one can accomplish the basic specifications and goals with only about one-fifth of the customary effort; nearly all remaining efforts are then expended simply to reach perfection or to satisfy our own obsessive streak. In each case, one must ask: Do we truly desire such perfection? What are the opportunity costs of devoting significant energy to just one of a raft of possible endeavors? The 80/20 principle even crops up in current events. According to the *New York Times,* 20 percent of baggage screeners at airports account for 80 percent of the mistakes.[6] Responding to this need, an aviation expert named Michael Cantor designed a simple perceptual task that "screens out" the least able screeners.

FIGURE 1-1

The 80/20 Principle

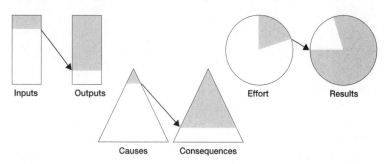

From Richard Koch, *The 80/20 Principle* (New York: Currency/Doubleday, 1998). Reprinted by permission of Random House.

By now, even if you have never heard of this principle, you have probably gotten the gist of it (maybe even 80 percent thereof!). You'll have a sense of whether this is familiar territory for you ("Pareto was just talking about 'cutting your losses'"), or whether it represents a genuinely new way of thinking about things ("I am going right down to the director of human resources and see how we can get rid of the most moribund 20 percent of our team"). You'll probably have some questions—for example, is it always 80/20? How do you know which 20 percent to focus on? Do we really want our pilots, our surgeons, our scientists, or our artists to practice 80/20 triage? And if you are a bit irreverent, you may ask: "How could someone named Koch write a 300-page book on the 80/20 principle?" Quick answer: It's a good read.

In other words, by this point, chances are that you're beginning to change your mind about previous beliefs and accept the plausibility of Pareto's proposition—in theory, at least. Indeed, from one perspective, the 80/20 principle seems easy enough to state, understand, absorb. Human beings could have been designed as the kinds of creatures who can readily learn to think about choices in such a new way. In reality, however, nothing could be further from the truth. One of the most entrenched habits in human thought is the belief that one should operate according to a rival 50/50 principle. We should treat everyone and everything fairly and equally—and expect the same from others (particularly our parents!). We should spend the same amount of time on each person, each customer, each employee, each project, each part of each project. Evolutionary psychologists go so far as to claim that this "equity principle" is part of the mental architecture of our species. But there is no need to invoke a biological explanation. There is ample cultural support from earliest childhood for the notion that one should devote attention equivalently: "Now children, let's share the candy so that each of you gets exactly the same amount." And so even individuals who ardently wish to operate on a basis other than 50/50—be it 80/20, 60/40, or 99/1—find it challenging to do so: It's easy enough to state or tout the 80/20 principle; changing one's mind and henceforth operating in accordance with it proves much harder.

The 80/20 principle is perhaps best described as a concept. Human beings think in concepts, and our minds are stocked with concepts of all sorts—some tangible (the concept of furniture, the concept of a meal), others far more abstract (the concept of democracy, or gravity, or the gross national product). As concepts become more familiar, they often seem more concrete, and one becomes able to think of them in almost the same way that one thinks of something one can touch or taste. Thus on a first encounter, the 80/20 principle may seem abstract and elusive, but after one has used it for a while, and played with it in various contexts, this principle can become as familiar and cuddly as an old stuffed teddy bear.

Moreover, the more familiar a concept, the easier it is to think of in various ways. Which brings me to an important point: Presenting multiple versions of the same concept can be an extremely powerful way to change someone's mind. So far, we have described the 80/20 principle in words and numbers—two common external marks (readily perceptible symbols that stand for concepts). But the principle need not be confined to linguistic or numerical symbolization—and it is the possibility of expression in a variety of symbolic forms that often facilitates mind changing. In figure 1-1, I already presented one graphic depiction of the principle.

Consider now three contrasting figures contained in Koch's book. Each of these figures presents data about the consumption of beer that is relevant to the 80/20 principle and each might help convey the same general point—either to the same or to different kinds of audiences. Figure 1-2 is an ordered list of 100 beer drinkers, each represented by the number of glasses of beer consumed per week. The first 20 beer drinkers consume about 700 glasses; the remaining 80 drinkers consume 300 glasses, and, of those, the 20 least indulgent drink a mere 27 in total.

Figure 1-3 is a Cartesian grid plotting the number of glasses per person drunk per week against the cumulative percentage of total beer drunk. Here one can see both the number of glasses drunk by each person (the vertical stripes) and the cumulative percentage by cohort (the line that rises sharply on the left side of the grid and then slowly levels off across the top).

Figure 1-4, the simplest in most respects, features a pair of bar graphs. This idealized portrayal contains no information about individual drinkers. However, one can readily see that a relatively small percentage of bibulous individuals (20 percent) drink most of the beer (about 70 percent).

These various ways of thinking about Pareto's principle brings us to an important point about mental representations: They have both a content and a form, or format. The *content* is the basic idea that is contained in the representation—what linguists would call the *semantics* of the message. The *form* or *format* is the particular language or system of symbols or notation in which the content is presented.

Each of the three ways of viewing the 80/20 idea essentially conveys the same content or semantic: a relatively small percentage of people in any group drink most of the beer. However, the graphic means employed—the form, format, or (more technically) the syntax—is distinctive, and different people may well find one form of reportage easier to decode than the others. Note that from a formal point of view, each of these graphic systems could denote anything from the number of sunny days in Seattle during September to the rate of brain cell loss during each decade of life. Only when labels have been affixed to these visual aids is it possible to appreciate the specific meaning that the graphic artist is trying to convey.

Essentially the same semantic meaning or content, then, can be conveyed by different forms: words, numbers, dramatic renditions, bulleted lists, Cartesian coordinates, or a bar graph. At first encounter, one may find it possible to think of the 80/20 principle only with reference to a numerical ratio (4:1). Over time, however, one can think of it in terms of

FIGURE 1-2

The 80/20 Principle Applied to Beer Drinkers

Rank	Name	Glasses drunk	Cumulative
	Our top 20 beer drinkers		
1	Charles H	45	45
2	Richard J	43	88
3=	George K	42	130
3=	Fred F	42	172
5	Arthur M	41	213
6	Steve B	40	253
7	Peter T	39	292
8	Reg C	37	329
9=	George B	36	365
9=	Bomber J	36	401
9=	Fatty M	36	437
12	Marian C	33	470
13	Stewart M	32	502
14	Cheryl W	31	533
15=	Kevin C	30	563
15=	Nick B	30	593
15=	Ricky M	30	623
15=	Nigel H	30	653
19	Greg H	26	679
20	Carol K	21	700
	Our bottom 20 beer drinkers		
81=	Rupert E	3	973
81=	Patrick W	3	976
81=	Anne B	3	979
81=	Jamie R	3	982
85=	Stephanie F	2	984
85=	Carli S	2	986
87=	Roberta F	1	987
87=	Pat B	1	988
87=	James P	1	989
87=	Charles W	1	990
87=	Jon T	1	991
87=	Edward W	1	992
87=	Margo L	1	993
87=	Rosabeth M	1	994
87=	Shirley W	1	995
87=	Greg P	1	996
87=	Gilly C	1	997
87=	Francis H	1	998
87=	David C	1	999
87=	Darleen B	1	1000

From Richard Koch, *The 80/20 Principle* (New York: Currency/Doubleday, 1998). Reprinted by permission of Random House.

FIGURE 1-3

80/20 Frequency Distribution Chart of Beer Drinkers

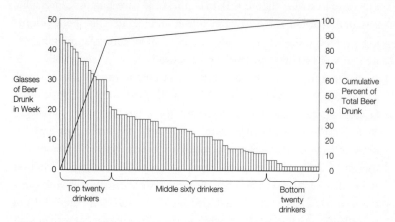

From Richard Koch, *The 80/20 Principle* (New York: Currency/Doubleday, 1998). Reprinted by permission of Random House.

FIGURE 1-4

Beer/Beer Drinking Ratios

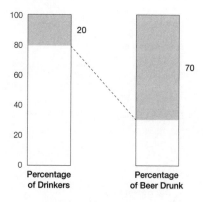

From Richard Koch, *The 80/20 Principle* (New York: Currency/Doubleday, 1998). Reprinted by permission of Random House.

spatial images, verbal metaphors, bodily states, or even musical passages. Indeed, one effective way of conveying the 80/20 principle is through the use of a cartoon (figure 1-5). In contrast, the same linguistic or graphic system of marking can be used to convey an indefinite number of meanings, so long as the syntactic rules that govern the particular marking system are followed and the labeling is appropriate.

Again, I argue here that multiple versions of the same point constitute an extremely powerful way in which to change minds. But what other factors might cause an individual to shift his or her perspective and begin to act on the basis of that principle—for instance, abandoning a 50/50 point of view and espousing instead an 80/20 perspective on various sectors of life? Would they be the same factors that persuaded Nicholson Baker that he did not, after all, want to furnish his apartment with forklifts and backhoes? I have identified seven factors—sometimes I'll call them levers—that could be at work in these and all cases of a change of mind. As it happens, each factor conveniently begins with the letters "re."

FIGURE 1-5

Quick and Dirty Diagram

This diagram shows the process of "Quick and Dirty." Note that the center figure is a circle with holes in it. This is because in doing "quick and dirty" you cut all corners and there are things that are left out.

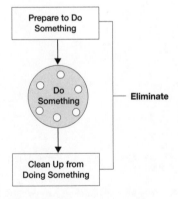

G. Robert Michaelis, *The Quick & Dirty Official Quick & Dirty Handbook* (San Jose: Writer's Showcase, 2000). Reprinted by permission.

Reason

Especially among those who deem themselves to be educated, the use of reason figures heavily in matters of belief. A rational approach involves identifying of relevant factors, weighing each in turn, and making an overall assessment. Reason can involve sheer logic, the use of analogies, or the creation of taxonomies. Encountering the 80/20 principle for the first time, an individual guided by rationality would attempt to identify all of the relevant considerations and weigh them proportionately: Such a procedure would help him to determine whether to subscribe to the 80/20 principle in general, and whether to apply it in a particular instance. Faced with a decision about how to furnish his apartment, Baker might come up with a list of pros and cons before reaching a final judgment.

Research

Complementing the use of argument is the collection of relevant data. Those with scientific training can proceed in a systematic manner, perhaps even using statistical tests to verify—or cast doubt on—promising trends. But research need not be formal; it need only entail the identification of relevant cases and a judgment about whether they warrant a change of mind. A manager who has been exposed to the 80/20 principle might study whether its claims—for example, those about sales figures or employee difficulty—are borne out on her watch. Naturally, to the extent that the research confirms the 80/20 principle, it is more likely to guide behavior and thought. Writer Baker might conduct formal or informal research on the costs of various materials and on the opinions of those who would be likely to visit his newly furnished apartment.

Resonance

Reason and research appeal to the cognitive aspects of the human mind; resonance denotes the affective component. A view, idea, or perspective resonates to the extent that it feels right to an individual, seems to fit the current situation, and convinces the person that further considerations are superfluous. It is possible, of course, that resonance follows on the use of reason and/or research; but it is equally possible that the fit occurs at an unconscious level, and that the resonant intuition is in conflict with the more sober considerations of Rational Man or Woman. Resonance often comes about because one feels a "relation" to a mind-changer, finds that person "reliable," or "respects" that person—three additional "re" terms. To the extent that the move to forklifts and backhoes resonates for him, Baker may proceed with the redecoration. To the extent that 80/20 comes to feel like a better approach than 60/40 or 50/50, it is likely to be adopted by a decision maker in an organization.

I note that rhetoric is a principal vehicle for changing minds. Rhetoric may rely on many components: In most cases, rhetoric works best when it encompasses tight logic, draws on relevant research, and resonates with an audience (perhaps in light of some of the other "re" factors just mentioned). Too bad rhetoric has that "h" as a second letter.

Representational Redescriptions (Redescriptions, for Short)

The fourth factor sounds technical but the point is simple enough. A change of mind becomes convincing to the extent that it lends itself to representation in a number of different forms, with these forms reinforcing one another. I noted previously that it is possible to present the 80/20 principle in a number of different linguistic, numerical, and graphic ways; by the same token, as I've shown, a group of individuals can readily come up with different mental versions of Baker's proposed furnishings. Particularly when it comes to matters of instruction—be it in an elementary school classroom or a managerial workshop—the potential for expressing the desired lesson in many compatible formats is crucial.[7]

Resources and Rewards

In the cases discussed so far, the possibilities for mind changing lie within the reach of any individual whose mind is open. Sometimes, however, mind change is more likely to occur when considerable resources can be drawn on. Suppose that a philanthropist decides to bankroll a nonprofit agency that is willing to adopt the 80/20 principle in all of its activities. The balance might tip. Or suppose that an enterprising interior decorator decides to give Baker all of the materials that he needs at cost, or even for free. Again, the opportunity to redecorate at little cost may tip the balance. Looked at from the psychological perspective, the provision of resources is an instance of positive reinforcement—another "re" term. Individuals are being rewarded for one course of behavior and thought rather than the other. Ultimately, however, unless the new course of thought is concordant with other criteria—reason, resonance, research, for example—it is unlikely to last beyond the provision of resources.

Two others factors also influence mind changing, but in ways somewhat different from the five outlined so far.

Real World Events

Sometimes, an event occurs in the broader society that affects many individuals, not just those who are contemplating a mind change. Examples are wars, hurricanes, terrorist attacks, economic depressions—or, on a more positive side, eras of peace and prosperity, the availability of medical treatments that prevent illness or lengthen life, the ascendancy of a benign leader or group or political party. Legislation could implement policies like the 80/20 rule. It is conceivable that a law could be passed (say, in Singapore) that would permit or mandate special bonuses for workers who are unusually productive, while deducting wages from those who are unproductive. Such legislation would push businesses toward adopting an 80/20 principle, even in eras where they had been following a more conventional 50/50 course. Turning to our other running example, an economic depression could nullify Baker's plans for refurnishing his apartment, whereas a long era of prosperity could make it easier. (He could even purchase a second "experimental" flat!)

Resistances

The six factors identified so far can all aid in an effort to change minds. However, the existence of only facilitating factors is unrealistic. Indeed, in chapter 3 I will introduce the major paradox of mind changing: While it is easy and natural to change one's mind during the first years of life, it becomes difficult to alter one's mind as the years pass. The reason, in brief, is that we develop strong views and perspectives that are resistant to change. Any effort to understand the changing of minds must take into account the power of various resistances. Such resistances make it easy, second nature, for most of us to revert to the 50/50 principle, even after the advantages of the 80/20 principle have been set forth convincingly. Baker, for example, might elect to retain his current pattern of apartment furnishing, even when reason, resonances, rewards, and the like issue their Circean song. The hassle of moving, the possibility that he or others might become disenchanted with the extra backhoes and forklifts might overpower several pushes toward the new furnishings.

I've now introduced the seven factors that play crucial roles in mind changing. As we look at individual cases of successful or unsuccessful changes of mind, we can see these various factors at work in distinctive ways. For now, I will only say that a mind change is most likely to come about when the first six factors operate in consort and the resistances are relatively weak. Conversely, mind changing is unlikely to come about when the resistances are strong, and the other factors do not point strongly in one direction.

Changes of mind, of course, occur at a number of different levels of analysis, with the aforementioned seven factors being brought to bear on entities ranging from a single individual to a whole nation. In chapters 4 through 9 of this book I examine six realms, or arenas, in which changes of mind take place:

1. Large-scale changes involving heterogeneous or diverse groups, such as the population of an entire nation
2. Large-scale changes involving a more homogeneous or uniform group, such as a corporation or a university
3. Changes brought about through works of art, science, or scholarship, such as the writings of Karl Marx or Sigmund Freud, the theories of Charles Darwin or Albert Einstein, or the artistic creations of Martha Graham or Pablo Picasso
4. Changes within formal instructional settings, such as schools or training seminars
5. Intimate forms of mind changing involving two people or a small number, such as family members

6. Changes within one's own mind, such as those that took place in Nicholson Baker's musings about furniture.

Finally, let me introduce some basic terminology that I'll be drawing on.

CONTENTS OF THE MIND:
IDEAS, CONCEPTS, STORIES, THEORIES, SKILLS

Most of us use the word *idea* to denote any mental content—and that's perfectly appropriate. There are many kinds of ideas, of course, but (in addition to concepts like the 80/20 principle or a new type of apartment furnishing) I will focus on four others that prove of particular importance for a study of mind changing: concepts, stories, theories, and skills.

A *concept,* the most elementary unit, is an umbrella term that refers to any set of closely related entities. When we denote all four-legged furry household pets that bark as dogs, we are revealing our concept of canines. Even young children know hundreds of concepts—ranging from automobile to zebra—though they may not delineate the boundaries between concepts—say "dog" and "cat"—in the same way that grown-ups do. Grown-ups also have more abstract concepts—gravity, democracy, photosynthesis, pride—which elude young children.

Stories are narratives that describe events that unfold over time. At a minimum, stories consist of a main character or protagonist, ongoing activities aimed toward a goal, a crisis, and a resolution, or at least an attempt at a resolution. (In his essay about mind change, Baker tells two very short stories—the man and the shoe, the author and his fantasized apartment.) Human beings like to hear stories and are also natural storytellers. By the time individuals enter school, they know dozens of stories, gleaned from their family, the media, and their own observations and experiences. And by the time they are grown, individuals know many hundreds of stories, though these stories may well be constructed on the bases of a smaller number of plots. (Remember, there are only six basic jokes!)

Theories are relatively formal explanations of processes in the world. A theory takes the form "*X* has occurred because of *A, B, C*" or "There are three kinds of *Y*, and they differ in the following ways" or "I predict that either *Z* will happen or *Y* will happen, depending on condition *D*." Pareto's principle captures a theory about how to operate efficiently in daily life. From an early age, young children develop theories about how things work in the world. They will also encounter theories that are held by others in their culture. And once they begin disciplinary study in the schools, they will also encounter formal theories. And so, to take just one example, all youngsters in rainy climates develop theories about thunderstorms. At first they may think that these weather events represent the anger of their parents or a temper tantrum of the gods or the scheming of a wicked witch. Later on, observing the predictable order of events, they will hypothesize that the lightning causes the thunder to occur. In most cases, they will not discover the explanation of thunderstorms, and the relation between lightning and thunder, unless they study meteorology in school and learn about air currents, changes in temperature, electrical charges, and the differing speed of light and sound.

The example of the thunderstorm helps to clarify the relation among the three kinds of content that I've mentioned so far. At first, a child may have only a concept of a thunderstorm—an undifferentiated amalgam of wetness, a bolt of lightning, a shattering sound. Then she may well develop a story that satisfies her: "The god of food is angry at me because I misbehaved at supper. And so he makes a noise that frightens me." This story can evolve into a lay theory: Lightning causes a storm, and the storm is noisy. A course in meteorology may lead to a more sophisticated theory: thunderstorms understood as air currents within a cloud churning up moisture and building up electric charges that yield lightning.

Which leads to our fourth and last content of the mind—the *skills* (or practices) of which an individual is capable. Stories and theories are by their nature propositional. Individuals can state these stories or theories in strings of words, though they may well be represented mentally in other formats (such as a silent film or video sequence). In contrast, skills (or practices) consist of procedures that individuals know how to carry out, whether or not they choose to—or even can—put them into words. Skills will range from the mundane—eating a banana or catching a ball—to the complex—playing a Bach sonata on the violin or solving differential equations by hand. Often the facility of these skills changes gradually, as a result of practice, on the one hand, or disuse, on the other. But skills can also be subject to more dramatic forms of change, and when they are, we find ourselves centrally in the terrain of "mind changing" under study here. For example, consider an experienced performer who typically learns a new piece of music by starting at the beginning and mastering it a measure at a time. If, as a result of any or all of the factors that I have identified, she becomes convinced that pieces are better learned backward, or by mastering the ending and the beginning first, or by first playing the piece through in its entirety with no regard to accuracy, then there has been a significant change in mind. (Note: The more gradual improvements that occur through repetitive practice also represent changes of mind, but they are of less interest here because of their ordinariness and predictability.)

The relation between content and form unfolds somewhat differently in the case of such skilled practices. One cannot simply state the content—like the 80/20 principle—in one symbol system and then show how it is basically preserved, but slightly altered, when captured in another symbolic form. The current status of the practice *is* both its form and its content—to recall poet William Butler Yeats's famous query, "How can one tell the dancer from the dance?" The content and the form of the procedure can and do change—but by and large they change together. It may well be the case that the change of a practice has effects on other practices; for example, if one learns to write prose in a new way, one may also come to speak (or even compose music) in a new way. In such a case, we could say that a particular change in content reverberates (or, more technically, "transfers") across various formats.

One might ask whether it is possible to stipulate the contents of the mind: to state all of the concepts, stories, theories, and skills in the mind of a particular human being—or indeed all human beings. In a sense, this question is a setup. Human beings constantly create or construct new mental representations, and so the content of the mind is by its nature an open, infinitely expandable category. At the same time there are serious attempts to itemize and categorize the principal contents: Think of dictionaries, encyclopedias, yellow pages, and search engines. In any event, there is no question that certain concepts, stories, theories, and skills carry a large proportion of the cognitive weight in our lives. Consider these examples:

Prevalent sets of concepts: living entity/dead entity; virtue/vice; pleasure/pain; plant/animal

Prevalent stories: Girl meets boy; hero is defeated by a tragic flaw; good triumphs over evil; the prodigal son returns home

Prevalent theories: Those who look like us are good, others are evil; if two events occur in close proximity, the first causes the second; might makes right

Prevalent skills: Dividing resources equally; conserving energy in preparation for a high-stakes performance; finishing assignments just before a pressing deadline.

There, then, we have the major kinds of content that inhabit the human mind. All of us possess—or, if you are a thoroughly modern mentalist, all of us *are*—our ideas, concepts, stories, theories, and skills. Cognitive scientists argue vociferously about whether we are born with this content—to use the lingo, whether there are such things as *innate ideas* (in which case all humans would be born knowing the 50/50 principle), or whether we are equally capable of learning every conceivable idea (were this the case, one could design cultures where 77/23 were as easy to master as 50/50 or 100/0), or whether certain ideas are learned easily because we are predisposed to acquire them (in which case it is much easier for humans to learn the 50/50 than the 80/20 rule). Full disclosure: I favor this latter hypothesis. The major job for cognitive scientists is to identify these ideas and explain how they come to be.

In the chapters that follow, I endeavor to show how these various kinds of ideas change: to see at work the several factors that either induce or thwart significant changes of mind. First, however, having introduced the major contents of mind, we must turn our attention to the various forms in which these contents can be manifest.

CHAPTER 2

The Forms of the Mind

A MEETING THAT CHANGED MY MIND

When I was a graduate student in psychology at Harvard in the late 1960s, behaviorism was still prevalent (Professor B. F. Skinner's office in William James Hall was a few floors below mine—somewhat more spacious, to be sure), but the cognitive approach was on the rise. As a "Young Turk," I found myself sympathetic to the newly minted cognitive approach, favored by one of my mentors, Professor Jerome Bruner. Yet, one property characterized both of these warring camps: a lack of interest in the brain and the nervous system. Neither camp actually denied the importance of the brain; that would have been downright foolish. But the behaviorists were interested in modifying behavior; they felt that all-important goal could be accomplished by precisely calibrated manipulation of the environment. The remaining "black box" was to be left unopened. For their part, cognitivists sought to explicate how various mental operations were represented and carried out. They believed that these operations could be analyzed in their own terms: It simply did not matter whether an operation like computing an 80/20 ratio happened to be carried out via paper and pencil, by a mainframe computer (the personal computer did not yet exist), or within a chunk of nervous tissue situated between the two ears.

Though I had enjoyed biology as an undergraduate, had considered attending medical school, and had audited a course on human physiology, I shared this psychologists' prejudice; during graduate study, I rarely took the brain seriously. I had already embarked on an idiosyncratic research career—trying to understand the development of human cognitive capacities, with a particular focus on artistic skills and understandings (the arts were the idiosyncratic part). My ultimate (admittedly grand) goal was to unravel the mysteries of artistic creation. As far as I was concerned, there was little reason to become interested in the neurons and synapses that, at a microscopic level, were surely accomplishing cognitive feats like composing a melody or recognizing an artistic style. (At the time, no one I knew was thinking much about the genes that give rise to everything.)

One of the principal assertions of this book is that, after the early years, minds rarely change quickly. But I can pinpoint one major change of one mind—my own!—that coalesced one afternoon in the fall of 1969. As a graduate student, I had begun two years earlier to work at Harvard Project Zero. Founded by the eminent philosopher Nelson Goodman, Project Zero was a basic research group that was investigating human artistry and arts education. Goodman and I had become intrigued by a finding that was just beginning to enter public consciousness: despite their mirror appearance, the two halves of the brain carry out distinct mental activities. Moreover, a principal difference between the left and the right hemispheres apparently mapped directly on a distinction that was occupying Goodman and me: the possibility that there exist two fundamentally different kinds of symbols and symbol systems (what I termed "external marks" in chapter 1). Brain research suggested that the left hemisphere deals with digital types of symbols—like numbers and words—while the right hemisphere deals with more holistic or analog types of symbols—like those embodied in painting, sculpture, dance, and other artistic realms.[1]

It so happened that neurologist Norman Geschwind, a leading researcher in this field, taught at the Harvard Medical School across the Charles River and so we invited him to come and speak to our little group one afternoon. As audience members, we were mesmerized.

Geschwind spoke about the startling cognitive profiles that one sees from time to time in a neurological clinic: patients who can write words and name objects but lose the ability to read words (though they can still read numbers); patients who cannot remember ever having visited a setting but can still find their way with ease around that apparently unfamiliar setting; hearing patients who cannot understand what is being said but can speak fluently and can appreciate music. And he described for us the remarkable findings about the cortical representations of different abilities in the brains of normal people, the left-handed, and occasional geniuses or "freaks" of various sorts. Geschwind also mentioned certain artists who had become aphasic; for example, the composer Maurice Ravel, who lost the ability to speak or compose but could still perform certain of his own pieces and also point out flaws in the performances of others. He spoke of the French artist Andre Dérain, whose painting had been seriously compromised by brain damage; as well as of other visual artists whose work had remained competent, or even improved (or so it was said), following the loss of language.[2]

Though it was supposed to last only two hours, the meeting continued over dinner and until late in the evening. By the time this marathon encounter with Geschwind had concluded, I had experienced a change of mind that amounted to a pivotal career decision. I was going to seek postdoctoral funds to work on a neurological unit with Geschwind and his associates. At the very least, I would have the opportunity to interact with a fascinating mind and personality and learn about the human brain. At best, I would acquire an entirely new set of biological and clinical perspectives from which to examine issues of cognition and artistry.

Though postdoctoral study seemed a reasonable possibility, I had no idea at the time that I would end up spending two decades working at the Aphasia Research Center of the Boston Veterans Administration Medical Center and the Boston University School of Medicine (where I still hold an appointment). I learned a great deal about the operation of the brain (I used to quip that I would make a credible neurologist "from the neck up"), the ways in which various human abilities are represented in the "normal" brain, and how they are compromised by various forms of pathology. At the same time, I also continued my work in developmental psychology, coming to know children of different ages and talents, studying their developing mental abilities, even teaching in the public schools and giving private piano lessons.

With the benefit of the hindsight that has led me to write this book, I now realize that such "lightning changes of mind," as I felt I'd experienced after Geschwind's talk, do not occur like a thunderbolt—no matter how much they may feel that way. After all, I had a long-standing interest in biology. I loved to learn new things and had been thinking about what kind of a postdoctoral fellowship might rescue me from embarking on a standard teaching trajectory that held little appeal. I have always been attracted to scintillating thinkers—and Geschwind was one of a kind.

But here's the most important reason for my own mind-changing experience: I had become stymied in pursuing my own research agenda. (Indeed, a feeling of "hitting a dead end" often primes one for a change of mind.) I felt that I needed to understand how skills are organized in the extremely fluent mature artist. But I'd found out two disturbing things: (1) such exquisitely developed abilities prove extremely difficult to dissect, and (2) the most creative artists do not welcome probing by a psychological researcher who is still wet behind the ears. Through his delineation of how fluent skills break down under various forms of brain damage, Geschwind presented a "royal road" to the elucidation of artistic skills. Thus, while the decision to work with Geschwind erupted almost instantly into consciousness, this "change of mind" had long been in the works in the subterranean recesses of my mind.

In terms of the seven factors or levers of mind change, I could see at work several factors that induced me to take the study of the brain much more seriously. There was *reason:* this novel scientific perspective could answer questions in which I was interested. There was relevant *research:* Neurological findings were enriching our understanding of numerous facets of the human mind. There were *real world* factors: brain research was becoming much more important (and much better funded, the *resources* were ample!). There was *resonance:* working with Geschwind on issues about the mind felt right to me, and I identified with this respected, luminous role model. Perhaps most important, the *resistances* did not amount to much. While studying neurology seemed like a detour to my more career-minded peers, I did not much want to enter the ranks of the professoriat at this point in my life.

But I indulge in this autobiographical reflection for one more reason. When I began my research in psychology almost forty years ago, I had no scholarly interest in the issue of human intelligence. Like most individuals raised in the Western intellectual and pedagogical tradition, I assumed that there was a single kind of intelligence, that it developed (or emerged) over the course of childhood, and that it could be compromised by senescence or trauma. Exposure to Geschwind's line of thinking, in conjunction with my own studies of children, gradually undermined my belief in this orthodoxy. If intellect were truly of a piece, did it really make sense that one kind of brain damage would impair faculty A, while a second or third kind of damage would impair faculties B or C (leaving faculty A intact)? And if intellect were of a piece, how could one explain the child who is prodigious in one area, yet perfectly ordinary in other spheres? Or the occasional savant or autistic child who displays a stunning island of preserved expertise surrounded by a sea of grossly abnormal performances? Without being conscious of it, I was beginning to think about the idea of multiple intelligences. To borrow the imagery of Nicholson Baker: A Geschwindian breakthrough moment—like a tossing of the shoe out the window—was masking a more gradual change in intellectual allegiance—like loss of ardor for a contemplated exotic seating arrangement in an apartment.

All of this raises the issue of forms of thought—in particular, the question: When a mind change occurs, how is that shift expressed in the unique languages of the mind?

THE FORMS OF THOUGHT: MULTIPLE INTELLIGENCES

One position in psychology holds that there is just a single language of the mind—this language even has a name, *mentalese*. Proponents of mentalese believe that all thought, all mental computation, takes place in this singular language, which is somewhat like natural language. Were this characterization correct, all of our thinking would take place in a format that is, roughly speaking, like the language being used here. To put this in the terms of science fiction: if we could somehow spy on how thought occurs in the brain, we'd find neurons chatting with one another in a language like English, French, or Swahili.[3]

The most obvious challenge to the mentalese hypothesis comes from the existence of imagery, particularly visual imagery. Most of us report a generous supply of visual mental imagery, and many of us, including such estimable thinkers as Albert Einstein, report that vital thinking occurs in imagery: in Einstein's phrase, "of the visual, muscular, and body type."[4] I happen to lack visual imagery but compensate by having considerable auditory imagery. To be sure, I am not quite up to the level of the late pianist Arthur Rubinstein, who reportedly could listen to a gramophone record in his imagination and even hear the periodic scratches! But I have little trouble conjuring up a tune or even a rather full orchestral sound in my own mind. If you are capable of mental imagery, you probably spied those neurons in conversation at the end of the preceding paragraph.

Defenders of the mentalese theory do not deny the existence of imagery: indeed, they would sound foolish if they were to deny the evidence of their own introspections, not to say the introspections of the rest of humanity. Their response is to claim that these images exist but are epiphenomenal—they do not *really* entail thinking; at most they are the outer garb that cloaks an underlying singular mentalistic thought process. It may well be that certain problems that appear to be solved through imagery in fact rely on underlying logical operations. But as an individual with a deep involvement in the arts, I cannot take this "imagery as epiphenomenon" position seriously. To claim that Wolfgang Amadeus Mozart with his 626 Koechel-listed compositions, Martha Graham with her dozens of dances, or Pablo Picasso with his thousands of paintings and drawings are carrying out the same set of logical operations as a physicist or mathematician strains credulity. And if a defender of mentalese were to claim that, "well, these artists aren't really thinking," I would rejoin that this philistine had no understanding of the artistic process.

If mentalese is not the answer, then what *are* the forms of thought? One clue is to think in terms of the various sensory modalities. Indeed, we take in information through our eyes, our ears, our hands, our nostrils, our mouths, and speaking loosely, we can speak of visual or tactile or gustatory information. However, I believe that actual thinking takes place in a number of different formats that rely "for delivery" on the sensory organs but that transcend the specific in important ways.

How did this idea come about for me? And how did this—a new set of concepts, and, ultimately, a new theory—affect how I now perceive changes of mind? My extraordinary first encounter with Geschwind, a subsequent three-year postdoctoral fellowship with him and his colleagues, and the ensuing years of research gradually undermined my belief in a *singular* view of the mind, cognition, human intelligence. In a line of analysis carried out chiefly in the late 1970s and early 1980s, I developed a perspective called the theory of multiple intelligences.[5] The theory was in effect a critique of the standard "bell curve" view of intelligence,[6] which asserts the following:

1. Intelligence is a single entity.
2. People are born with a certain amount of intelligence.
3. It is difficult to alter the amount of our intelligence—it's "in our genes" so to speak.
4. Psychologists can tell you how smart you are by administering IQ tests or similar kinds of instruments.

For a number of reasons, this account was no longer convincing to me. I had studied various kinds of individuals, under varying conditions; I had also taught individuals ranging from kindergarten to college, in subjects ranging from anthropology to piano. Spurning an excessive dependence on psychometric instruments, I instead developed a view of intelligence that was deliberately multidisciplinary. I considered evidence from anthropology—which abilities have been valued and fostered in various cultures during various eras; evolution—how traits have evolved over the millennia in different species; and the study of "individual differences"—particularly evidence from unusual populations such as autistic individuals, prodigies, and youngsters with specific learning disabilities. Perhaps most crucially, I collated evidence from brain study: what we know about the development and breakdown of the brain and the ways in which different regions of the cortex effect different mental computations.

As a result of this interdisciplinary investigation, I arrived at a definition of intelligence and a provisional list of intelligences. I define an *intelligence* as a biopsychological potential to process specific forms of information in certain kinds of ways. Human beings have evolved diverse information-processing capacities—I term these "intelligences"—that allow them to solve problems or to fashion products. To be considered "intelligent," these products and solutions must be valued in at least one culture or community.

The last assertion of "being valued" is important. Rather than claiming that intelligence is the same in all times and places, I recognize that human beings value different skills and capacities at various times and under varying circumstances. Indeed inventions like the printing press or the computer can alter, quite radically, the abilities that are deemed of importance (or no longer of importance) in a culture. And so individuals are not equally "smart" or "dumb" under all circumstances; rather they have different intelligences that may be variously cherished or disregarded under different circumstances. In terms of the argument put forth here, each intelligence represents a distinct form of mental representation.

So much for formal definitions. Informally, we can think of each person—or his mind/brain—as a set of computers. When the computer is fed information in a proper format, it does its work, and that work is the exercising of a particular intelligence.

How are multiple intelligences relevant to mind changing? On the most basic level, a change of mind involves a change of mental representation. If I change your idea of intelligence, I am altering the images, concepts, and theories by which you were accustomed to thinking of intelligence. Accordingly, the more of an individual's intelligences you can appeal to when making an argument, the more likely you are to change a person's mind, and the more minds you are likely to change.

Though I wasn't aware of it at the time, by developing the concept of multiple intelligences, I was engaged in the most ambitious form of mind changing that I have ever undertaken. In a word, I was trying to change the mind of my fellow psychologists—and, ultimately, of members of the general public—about the nature of intelligence. I was arguing that (1) intelligence is pluralistic; it includes fashioning products as well as solving problems, and (2) it is defined neither on an *a priori* basis, nor on test performances, but rather on the basis of what happens to be valued at a particular historical time in a particular cultural context. While I am pleased that my theory has had some impact, I can also say that I have assembled a massive amount of data about how difficult it is to change people's minds about what intelligence is (a *concept*), how it operates (a *theory*), and how to assess it (a *skill*). I could even tell you *stories* about the multiple resistances to mind changing!

Having provided some background, I'm now ready to unveil the intelligence. Those who have read my previous works will, of course, already be familiar with the various intelligences and with the various evolutionary, neurological, psychological, and anthropological criteria by which I identified and confirmed candidate intelligences. But for those who are not, I'll list them briefly here along with examples of how each is employed in a particular realm—that of business. I should add that instances can be drawn from the whole gamut of human pursuits.

The Intelligences of the Symbol Analyst

When I tick off the intelligences, I typically begin with two intelligences alluded to above: *linguistic* and *logical-mathematical*. These intelligences are particularly important for learning in the kinds of schools that we have today—ones that feature listening to lectures, reading, writing, and calculating—and they are crucial for success on those tests that purport to assess human intellect and cognitive potential—tests that ask us to complete analogies or pick the right solution to an algebraic problem from a set of four equations.

LINGUISTIC INTELLIGENCE.   Broadly speaking, *linguistic intelligence* entails facility in the use of spoken and written language. As with all of the intelligences, there are several "subtypes," or varieties, of linguistic intelligence: the intelligence of the individual who is good at learning foreign languages, for example, or the intelligence of the skilled writer, who succeeds in conveying complex ideas in appropriately crafted prose. Within the world of business, two facets of linguistic intelligence are at a premium. One is found in the conversationalist who is able to secure useful information by skilled questioning and discussion with others; the other in the rhetorician who is able to convince others of a course of action through the use of stories, speeches, or exhortations. When an amalgam of linguistic abilities is combined in the same individual, one beholds a person who is likely to succeed in several avenues of business—perhaps "without even trying."

LOGICAL–MATHEMATICAL INTELLIGENCE.   Consider now the complementary intelligence, *logical-mathematical*. As the name implies, this form of intelligence breaks down readily into two classes of capacities. Clearly, logical intelligence is crucial for any manager whose responsibility includes determining what has happened, and what may happen, under various scenarios. (When circumstances are nebulous, perhaps one needs to revert to "modal" or "fuzzy logic"—or to 80/20 style estimates!) Related but separable is the capacity to move comfortably in the world of numbers: to calculate financial or monetary considerations, to estimate profits or losses, to decide how best to invest an unexpected windfall, and so on.

Certain businessmen have stood out in terms of their logical or logical-mathematical capacities. Consider two well-known examples from the automobile industry. Alfred P. Sloan took over a sprawling but limp General Motors in the early 1920s and was instrumental in making it the most successful corporation in the world. His "logical" feat? He created an organization with precise lines of authority throughout its extensive operations, coordinated various branches of the operation, and yet allowed each division to retain the operational efficiencies of its earlier incarnation.[7]

A generation later, in the 1950s, Robert McNamara assembled at Ford Motor Company a group of "whiz kids"; this team created a management system and an array of products that allowed Ford to recapture a large share of the U.S. automobile market. McNamara's triumph involved a powerful combination of logical analysis and numerical computation. Consistent with the "general intelligence" perspective critiqued above, it was assumed that McNamara's genius would translate readily into the operation of another huge bureaucracy that needed to be rationalized and mobilized—the U.S. Department of Defense.

As secretary of defense under Presidents Kennedy and Johnson, McNamara did indeed succeed in streamlining and regulating a massive organization. However, his logical-mathematical genius proved ill-matched to the quite different cultural, historical, and strategic issues posed by the emerging war in Indochina. (Journalist David Halberstam characterized this mentality in ironic fashion when he entitled his study of the McNamara crowd "The Best and the Brightest."[8]) To his credit, McNamara gradually changed his mind about this "IQ" approach to foreign policy; he has spent much of his time in recent years attempting to atone for the "logical-mathematical" hubris displayed by him and his colleagues during the early, "buildup" years of the Vietnam War.

I draw the following lesson. Even when one focuses simply on these two intelligences (the "bell curve" amalgam) that have been widely recognized as such, one can identify a plethora of more specialized capacities. No doubt a few individuals stand out as both linguistic and logical-mathematical geniuses—such as J. Robert Oppenheimer, the physicist who led the Manhattan Project during World War II, or John Maynard Keynes, the brilliant economist and essayist. But it is far more common for an individual to be relatively stronger in language (the prototypical poet or orator) or in mathematical (the skilled hedge fund manager) or in logical (the expert planner) skills.[9] The story comes to mind of the woman stationed at the "12 Items or Less" checkout counter at the Star Market in Cambridge, Massachusetts. Noting that a student is trying to slip by with dozens of products, she quips, "So, is it that you go to MIT and you can't read—or that you go to Harvard and you can't count?"

There would have been little point in embarking on a theory of multiple intelligences simply to peer more closely at the already acknowledged intelligences. The challenge—and the fun—of theorizing about multiple intelligences has been the identification of relatively neglected intelligences—in our terms, other forms of mental representation.

"Noncanonical" Intelligences

I believe that human beings possess at least six or seven other identifiable intelligences; that is, a half-dozen or more additional forms of mental representation. Like linguistic and logical-mathematical intelligence, each can also be broken down into subtypes. Not surprisingly, certain of the "noncanonical" intelligences prove more relevant than others in the realms of business. Yet each deserves at least a moment in the cognitive limelight.

MUSICAL INTELLIGENCE. *Musical intelligence*—facility in the perception and production of music—is in many ways analogous to linguistic intelligence. Among the identifiable subtypes are the appreciation of melody and harmony; sensitivity to rhythm; the ability to recognize variations in timbre and tonality; and, speaking more holistically, the capacity to apprehend the structure of works of music (ranging from the loose interplay characteristic of jazz riffs to the highly specified architectonics of the classical sonata form). Of course individuals involved in the worlds of art and entertainment give pride of place to musical (and, so to speak, other artistic) intelligences. It is less frequently appreciated that musical intelligence figures prominently in almost any kind of public presentation, ranging from television commercials to full-length movies to organized conferences, athletic events, and religious services.

Elements of musical craft underlie many productions that ostensibly foreground other symbol systems. I write books, using words and occasional graphic images, but the way in which I assemble these linguistic and graphic forms draws on principles of organization that, at least in my case, have their apparent origin in musical structure. Perhaps that is because music is the least overtly semantic of the major symbol systems: It does not convey discrete meanings. Instead music deals, on the one hand, in the pure architectonics (or syntax) of organization and presents, on the other, the forms and shapes of our feeling life. As the nineteenth-century British essayist Walter Pater memorably put it, "all art constantly aspires to the condition of music."

Recently, in collaboration with Rosamund Stone Zander, conductor Benjamin Zander has pointed out an intriguing affinity between business and music. In his view, the management and motivation of a large organization draws on principles involved in presiding over a symphony orchestra. We should remain alert to the musicality inherent in effective business planning, organization, and communication.[10]

SPATIAL INTELLIGENCE. A fourth form of mental representation is *spatial intelligence:* the capacity to form spatial representations or images in one's mind, and to operate upon them variously. One species of spatial intelligence involves wide spaces—the operations needed by the airplane pilot, the rocket scientist, the sailor. A complementary form involves more circumscribed spaces—the operations deployed by the chess player, the sculptor, the painter, the designer of tools, toys, or television sets. As with musical intelligence, the appreciation of spatial relations may also come into play at a metaphoric level; many individuals who create performances or products conceive of and work on their chosen entities in a spatial format.

Indeed, each form of intelligence can be brought to bear on a variety of materials. One can approach almost any kind of content by "spatializing it." Thus one can think of a play, a song, a sales plan, a management chart as embodied in spatial (or graphic) form; further, one can create a spatialized set of marks to designate the aforementioned play, song, or plan. (I think, for example, of my colleagues in psychology who map out an experiment as if it were a new geological terrain.) Once one has created a spatial representation of an entity—say, an organizational chart that portrays the lines of authority that govern two recently merged companies—it is possible for the creator (as well as others) to work on this new representation, transform it, and confer on it various meanings. One now has a "semantics" captured in spatial format.

With respect to the world of business, we can observe spatial intelligence at work both literally and by extension. To begin with, we can identify those individuals involved in occupations that directly treat the spatial world—for instance, aerospace, architecture, design, perhaps "cyberspace" as well. In addition, we can identify aspects of planning or creation that employ the principles of spatial organization in realms that—strictly (and metaphorically!) speaking—seem remote from the spatial firmament. While some planners "think" in logical analysis or musical forms, the majority may well attempt to express (i.e., make public to themselves and/or to others) the content of their mental representations in tangible spatial forms. The "Mac" (as opposed to the "PC") mind, a mind that focuses on the illustrations (as opposed to the text) in the *Scientific American,* reveals its preference for spatial forms of representation.

BODILY-KINESTHETIC INTELLIGENCE. In some ways analogous to spatial intelligence is *bodily-kinesthetic intelligence:* the capacity to solve problems or to create products using your whole body, or parts of your body, like your hand or your mouth. There is little doubt that this form of intelligence was crucial in human prehistory, where it has sometimes been described as "tool" or "technological" intelligence. To survive as hunters, fishermen, gatherers, or farmers, to be able to make clothing, build shelters, prepare food, and defend themselves against enemies, our predecessors relied on skilled use of body.

One should distinguish two varieties of bodily-kinesthetic intelligence. There are artisans, craftspeople, artists, surgeons, and athletes who still depend directly on their bodies in order to carry out their work. In complementary fashion, there are those who make use of bodily imagery and metaphors in their conceptualization of sundry topics. The ranks of entrepreneurs and salespeople are filled with individuals who were at one time competitive athletes. Noted basketball player and former U.S. Senator Bill Bradley has reportedly said, "If I spend an hour playing basketball with a person, I know all I need to know about him."[11] Corporations analogize themselves to athletic teams; they conceptualize their relations to one another, and to rivals, in terms borrowed from the basketball court or the soccer field. Their innovations—for example, the intuitive uses of a computer "mouse" or the paraphernalia of virtual reality—may draw heavily on bodily imagery. Nor is bodily intelligence absent from frankly intellectual pursuits. As mentioned earlier, no less an authority than Albert Einstein denied that his thinking proceeded in words: instead, he claimed, "the psychical entities which seem to serve as elements in thought are certain signs and more or less clear images which can be 'voluntarily' reproduced and combined . . . the above mentioned elements are, in my case, of visual and some of muscular type."[12]

Strictly speaking, every intelligence entails the development of skills. However, just as we think about language when it comes to stories, and logic when it comes to theories, we properly invoke bodily-kinesthetic intelligence when we conceive of those mental representations called skills. And that is because skills invariably involve the use of the body, even though the body's role in mastering a dance is more overt than the body's role in, say, speaking, writing, or solving equations. Studies of practitioners in many domains have documented the extent to which expertise entails the acquisition of ever greater skills in the use and integration of information. When they retain a tangible physical component (as is the case with athletes or artists), these skills are readily observed; but quite often, they become automated and internalized. Thus, while a novice musician can only learn a piece by playing it on an instrument, skilled musicians can accomplish much by simply reading a score or "playing it" in their minds. Over time bodily-kinesthetic intelligence retreats from view.

NATURALIST INTELLIGENCE.   Only after publishing my original theory did I become cognizant of a sixth form that I have dubbed the "naturalist intelligence."[13] *Naturalist intelligence* entails the capacities to make consequential discriminations in the natural world: between one plant and another; between one animal and another; among varieties of clouds, rock formations, tidal configurations, and the like. As with bodily-kinesthetic intelligence, this form was absolutely pivotal in our hominid past. Our ancestors would not have survived if they could not tell a poisonous from a nutritious plant, an animal that was good to eat from an animal that one had best flee from instantly, inviting from treacherous land, water, or mountain formations. Nowadays, there are still regions of the globe in which one's survival depends on the constant activation of naturalist intelligence. And even in our own postindustrial world, those involved with the preparation of foods, the construction of dwellings, the protection of our environment, or the mining of precious ores, must draw on their naturalist capacities.

What may be less evident, but even more consequential, is the extent to which our consumer society is also built on naturalist intelligence. The ability to distinguish one sneaker or sweater from another, to discriminate among brands of automobiles, airplanes, bicycles, scooters, and the like, draws on pattern-detecting capacities that in earlier eras were used to distinguish varieties of lizards, bushes, or rocks from one another.

Here lurks an important insight about the human intelligences. Each intelligence evolved over long periods of time to allow individuals to survive and reproduce in particular ecological niches—most notably, the savannas of sub-Saharan Africa where hominids developed over the last few million years. A particular intelligence may well remain undeveloped if there is little use for that intelligence in contemporary settings. However, being opportunistic creatures, urban dwellers who have never glimpsed a farm or a forest may well draw on, even exploit, their naturalistic intelligence in their capacities as vendors, purchasers, or "window" or "video" shoppers.

Fixing the boundaries between intelligences is not easy; admittedly, this delineation constitutes to some extent an aesthetic rather than a scientific judgment. Let me share my own thinking. On the one hand, naturalist intelligence may seem to involve simply the exercise of our sensory organs: keen eyes, ears, hands, and the like. This observation is no doubt true, but it is also insufficient; even if one is bereft of one or more sensory organs, like the distinguished blind naturalist Geermat Vermij, one may still be able to make consequential distinctions. In this sense, naturalist intelligence—like the other intelligences—is "supersensory." On the other hand, naturalist intelligence can appear as just an exercise of our logical-mathematical intelligence—the capacity to categorize. But this reductive analysis does not quite work either. The discrimination between two entities is prior to their classification, and, indeed, any biological classification scheme is always secondary to some set of perceived criteria. As a rule of thumb, we might invoke this sequence: first, one perceives objects through one or more sense modalities; next, one makes consequential distinctions through the use of naturalistic intelligence; ultimately one classifies (and perhaps reclassifies) according to specific logical criteria. This sequence may even have been at work as I—making use of my naturalist intelligence—developed the theory of multiple intelligences a few decades ago.

Turning briefly again to the world of business, I suggest that anyone involved with tangible products of any sort is necessarily using naturalist intelligence. Our discriminating capacities are essential if we are not merely to lump together all automobiles or, indeed, all vehicles. The naturalist intelligence is needed whether one purchases the raw materials, extracts them from the earth, mounts a campaign to advertise them, or uses them in one's daily work, household chores, or play. While our world has recently become inundated with "clicks," that does not mean that we can totally avoid "bricks" or "sticks." Shorn of our naturalist intelligence, we become completely dependent on someone else's capacity to discern patterns in the world.

The Personal Intelligences

So far, each of the intelligences that I have described falls, roughly speaking, into one of two categories. Either it is engaged primarily with material objects, as is the case with spatial, bodily, and naturalist intelligence. Or it works primarily with symbols and strings of symbols, as occurs with linguistic, musical, and logical-mathematical intelligence. Both categories involve concepts, stories, theories, and skills. We associate the former, "object-based" category more with skills and the latter, "symbol-based" category more with concepts, stories, and theories.

A third group of intelligences, of much interest lately, involves knowing human beings. One uses one's *interpersonal intelligence* to discriminate among persons, figure out their motivations, work effectively with them, and, if necessary, manipulate them. *Intrapersonal intelligence,* its complement, is directed inward. The intrapersonally intelligent person possesses a good working model of herself; can identify personal feelings, goals, fears, strengths, and weaknesses; and can, in the happiest circumstance, use that model to make judicious decisions in her life.

Writing in the early twenty-first century, I hardly need to insist on the importance of interpersonal intelligence. Nearly all business involves working with other persons, and those individuals who have effective knowledge of people—generically and specifically—are at a singular advantage. Whether one is in marketing, sales, or public relations, leading a team or serving as a member, sensitivity to others emerges as a crucial asset. The enormous popularity of Daniel Goleman's concept of emotional intelligence is a tribute to the newly acknowledged importance of such sensitivity to others.[14]

That sensitivity is not a single holistic capacity, however. Among the separable facets of interpersonal intelligence are sensitivity to temperament or personality, ability to anticipate the reactions of others, the skills of leading or following effectively, and the capacity to mediate. Indeed, the deeper that the personal intelligences are probed, the more facets emerge. One now reads of six varieties of leadership,[15] four approaches to negotiation,[16] and thirty-four personality types that the shrewd practitioner of human resources should discern.[17]

Complementing knowledge of others is knowledge of oneself: We come to know ourselves by making use of the distinctions involved in coming to know others; by the same token, discriminations that we make in the course of self-reflection help us penetrate the psyches of others. Still, the core of intrapersonal intelligence is distinctive from the capacity to understand and interact with other human beings. Central is the capacity to distinguish one's *own* feelings, needs, anxieties, and idiosyncratic profiles of abilities and to assemble them in a way that makes sense and is useful in achieving various personal goals. While the remaining intelligences lend themselves to particular roles and sectors in business, intrapersonal intelligence is a dimension on which one can evaluate individuals "across the board." Some U.S. presidents, for example, such as Abraham Lincoln, seem to have had a great deal of self-knowledge, while others, such as Ronald Reagan, gave few signs of introspective tendencies. One can also distinguish executives, entrepreneurs, or investors in terms of the extent to which "knowledge of self" seems developed, stunted, or atrophied and the extent to which they draw on such knowledge to create compatible working environments for themselves and others.[18]

It is not easy to assess intrapersonal intelligence. Why not? First, people differ from one another (that's the reason we *need* the personal intelligences) and so the metric for one person cannot simply be applied to others. Second, intrapersonal intelligence is a quintessentially subjective matter; we do not broadcast or demonstrate to others how much we know about ourselves, nor how accurate is that self-knowledge.

But in terms of our topic of how minds get changed, it would be a grave mistake to minimize the importance of intrapersonal intelligence. Nowadays, nearly all of us in the industrial and postindustrial worlds make our own decisions about where to live, what jobs to pursue, what to do when one becomes dissatisfied, downsized, or just plain dismissed. Those with keen understanding of their strengths and needs are in much better position than those with limited or faulty self-knowledge. In such circumstances, I would hazard, accurate self-knowledge is worth at least 15 to 25 IQ points—and that's a lot!

Existential Intelligence

Recently, I have pondered whether there may be a ninth, or existential, intelligence. This endeavor began because many contemporaries had speculated that there was a "religious" or "spiritual intelligence" and not a few had stated, erroneously, that "Howard Gardner believes in the existence of such a supernatural intelligence." After examining various accounts of spirituality, I concluded that it did not meet the criteria of a specific intelligence.[19] But a component of spirituality—existential thinking—may well do so. *Existential intelligence* entails the human capacity to pose and ponder the biggest questions: "Who are we? Why are we here? What is going to happen to us? Why do we die? What is it all about, in the end?" All over the world, children and adults pose these questions, and many religious, artistic, philosophical, and mythic "symbol systems" have arisen in an effort to provide satisfying answers to (or at least compelling formulations of) these questions.

Such an intelligence fits the psychological and biological criteria (see note 19) for an intelligence reasonably well. For example, there is a developmental course to existential intelligence; various symbol systems have evolved across the planet to capture salient existential questions and concerns; and certain individuals stand out at an early age in terms of preoccupation with such big questions. My chief hesitation in claiming a full-fledged "ninth intelligence" is that we do not yet have convincing evidence that "existential thinking" draws on special dedicated neural or brain centers or has a distinctive evolutionary history (though commentators have offered intriguing speculations about a "God spot" underneath the temporal lobe of the brain[20]). And so the most recent candidate for "intelligence status" remains in a holding pattern; recalling a classic film of Federico Fellini's, I allude nowadays to "8 1/2" intelligences.

The place of a candidate existential intelligence within business is intriguing. Typically, we think of business as being mundane, practical, everyday; themes of existence, religion, and spirit remain in abeyance until the arrival of the appropriate Sabbath. Yet many business products, either primarily or secondarily, speak to broader issues of existence, identity, faith. I need only allude to the numerous books, compact discs, movies, and television programs that deal with the realms of the spirit—from angels to devils; or to the numerous organizations, institutions, and experiences (including theme parks!) that are devoted to tending the human spirit; or to the realm of religion, be it organized or marginal, traditional or cultish. "Existence" is big business.

However, existence is not just a product. It is also an underacknowledged facet of the workplace; if people do not find meaning in their work lives, they are destined to be dissatisfied and—perhaps even worse—unproductive. Certainly, finding meaning in one's work is not simply a challenge in business; it is a strongly felt need in every profession and craft.[21] By the same token, I believe that one can find evidence for a range of intelligences in nearly every occupation. A musician, for example, may exercise her musical intelligence constantly, but if she is to be able to per-form effectively in public, she must draw as well on bodily intelligence, spatial intelligence, the personal intelligences, and—perhaps especially—the existential intelligence. It is also worth noting that individuals may succeed at the same cultural role using different intelligences. Mathe-matician and physicist Stephen Wolfram comments on the different pos-sible approaches to mathematical thinking:

> *Of the limited set of people exposed to higher mathematics, different ones often seem to think in bizarrely different ways. Some think symbolically, presum-ably applying linguistic capabilities to algebraic or other representations. Some think more visually, using mechanical experience or visual memory. Others seem to think in terms of abstract patterns, perhaps sometimes with implicit analogies to musical harmony. And still others—including some of the purest mathematicians—seem to think distinctly in terms of constraints, perhaps using some kind of abstraction of everyday geometrical reasoning.*[22]

WHY A COGNITIVE APPROACH?

By now, we have become deeply immersed in a cognitive approach to understanding human beings: the *contents* that we think about—concepts, theories, stories, and skills—and the *formats* in which our mind/brain does that thinking—our eight or nine different intelligences. To the ex-tent that you favor psychological explanations, this way of thinking may seem reasonable, even self-evident. But thinkers from other disciplinary backgrounds do not simply move to the sidelines when we psychologists march in with our theories of mental representation clutched in one hand and our list of intelligences in the other.

So now that I've introduced the cognitive approach to psychology, let me spell out its advantages in the context of changing minds. Part of its advantage, to be frank, is "in-house" within psychology. As long as behaviorist view held sway, it was not possible to address in a productive way the most important issues of the human sphere and the human spirit. The cognitive view reopens the windows of the mind, so to speak, to all thoughtful people, even including psychologists! We can concep-tualize what people are thinking, how they are thinking, and how, when necessary, *that thinking can be changed*—important endeavors at a time when "knowledge is king."

Rival Accounts: Sociobiological and Historical-Cultural

Turning to rival accounts, I believe the cognitive approach holds clear advantages over two other discipline-based perspectives that are being applied by savants to human affairs today: the sociobiological approach and the historical-cultural approach. My quarrel with these rival perspectives is that, unlike the cognitive approach, they stipulate that the moves that active human agents can make are severely constrained. Let me introduce both approaches by way of an example drawn from the automobile industry.

Until the 1960s, the automobile industry belonged to the United States. Most cars were manufactured here; there were plants overseas and a market abroad for American cars; and manufacturers around the world looked to the United States for leadership in this sector. Within a decade or two, however, the situation had changed dramatically. Led by the German Volkswagen and the Japanese Toyota companies, foreign producers made cars that were both less expensive and perceived to be safer, more reliable, and longer lasting. These corporations increased market share through new working arrangements on the assembly line, an obsession with quality control, smoother labor-management relations, a savvy appreciation of changing tastes, and other strategies. U.S. companies first ignored the threat to their leadership position (as this self-confident country often does) and then undertook a number of initiatives designed to regain leadership and ensure profitability. By the 1990s, this effort seemed promising, but at the beginning of the twenty-first century, as European and Asian companies once again respond to changes in technology and taste, the prospering of American automobile companies is once more in doubt. How would different disciplines explain this turn of events?

SOCIOBIOLOGICAL PERSPECTIVE. Inspired by the success of Darwinian theory in the area of biology, a sociobiological approach (recently repackaged as an evolutionary psychology approach) attempts to describe such events in terms of human (or primate) characteristics.[23] Like individuals, human groups align themselves in dominance hierarchies. For many years, General Motors and other leading U.S. companies ruled the roost in the manufacture and sale of cars. With entrenched dominance and longevity often comes complacency. The U.S. corporations ignored signs that others situated at lower niches in the dominance hierarchy were preparing an assault on the "alpha" figures of the industry. The attack was quick, stealthy, and surprisingly effective. Since the late 1960s, the once-dominant entities have been trying to reestablish their authority, through both competitive and cooperative strategies, but the challenges to dominance continue.

To its credit, the sociobiological approach points to previously neglected aspects of the human condition—the extent to which our lengthy evolutionary history colors how we (as individuals or groups or even industries) perceive and act. However, for our purposes, a sociobiological tack has two disadvantages. First, by and large, the claims cannot really be tested; we simply cannot determine *which* factors in our remote prehistory influenced the human genome over time or prompt the manifest behaviors of human beings today. For example, is the behavior of various players in the automobile industry better explained in terms of our selfish or our cooperative genes? Second, the sociobiological approach basically documents human limitations. It asserts, for example, that we are destined to be organized in dominance hierarchies and to jostle endlessly for position. If we were to accept these limitations as a given, there would be no reason to attempt to create major transformations at all; we would just follow the script inscribed in our genes. And when sociobiologists say, as almost all eventually do, "Well, we need to know limits in order to transcend them," then they basically have given away the game. Let's just concede that there may be limits to human flexibility but do our best to test and overcome them.

HISTORICAL–CULTURAL PERSPECTIVE. A rival perspective draws on history and the study of different cultures. On this account human beings are more than simply another species.[24] We have a lengthy prehistory and history and a powerful cultural or multicultural background, and both cast lengthy shadows if not powerful shackles on who we are, what we believe we can do, what we actually accomplish, and how.

Let's apply this historical-cultural approach to the car industry. In Germany, pride and economic power were seriously shaken by defeats in two successive world wars. But Germans are industrious and diligent workers, their country possesses crucial natural resources, and aided by the Marshall Plan and various European economic alliances, they were able to build on the success within their country of the inexpensive yet appealing Volkswagen. At mid-century the automotive industry became a leading contributor to the "German Miracle."

Like Germany, Japan had a history of leadership in heavy industry in its corner of the globe and had suffered a decisive and humiliating defeat on the battlefield in World War II. Japanese are also excellent workers, and they function well in the small, closely knit groups that compose their mammoth manufacturing corporations. They are also skilled at mastering the procedures developed by others (e.g., the Total Quality Management approach pioneered at mid-century by American engineer W. Edwards Deming), then adapting them to current circumstances, and continuing to transform them as conditions change. This "culturally torqued" perspective reveals that the hegemony of Germany and Japan in the 1960s and 1970s was predicated on long-standing characteristics of these two highly self-conscious populations as well as on recent historical events. In turn, German and Japanese hegemony can only be challenged by "moves" that draw with equal depth and ingenuity on American cultural and historical traditions.

The historical-cultural approach neatly challenges the univocal assumptions of the sociobiologists: though cut from the same genetic stock, human individuals and groups are fascinatingly varied, owing to our particular histories, experiences, and even genetic accidents. To be Japanese today is not the same as being Japanese in 1850; nor is it the same as being Chinese or Korean, let alone East African or West European. And those of us within the United States appreciate the differences between frenetic Silicon Valley, the Wild West, the Deep South, the solid Midwest, and the stodgy but still enterprising New England that has been my home for over forty years. Yet the problem with invoking culture and history as explanations is that, like sociobiology, their roots extend very deeply. These roots risk becoming nooses that limit our

capacity to change. And once one concedes that it is possible to overcome facets of history or culture (as both the Germans and the Japanese
have done impressively in the last half century), then the power of the
historical-cultural approach is dramatically attenuated. So one can again
concede: Recognize the limits, be sensitive to culture and history, but get
on with it.

Cognitive Accounts

Which, following an elegant dialectic if not a Hegelian synthesis, ushers
the cognitive approach back to center stage. The cognitive approach is
based on emerging scientific understanding of how the mind works,
courtesy of psychology, neuroscience, linguistics, and other neighboring
disciplines. It takes into account our inborn or early representations, and
it acknowledges their debt to both cultural and biological factors. But
most mental representations are neither given at birth nor frozen at the
time of their adoption. In our terms, they are constructed over time
within our mind/brains and they can be reformed, refashioned, recon-
structed, transformed, combined, altered, and undermined. They are, in
short, within our hands and within our minds. Mental representations are
not immutable; analysts or reflective individuals are able to lay them out,
and, while altering representations may not be easy, changes can be effected. Moreover, because we have at our disposal so many mental representations that can be combined in so many ways, the possibilities are
essentially limitless.

   After all, it was possible for American automobile analysts in the
1960s and 1970s to become skilled (though probably unwitting) cognitivists—to sit down and figure out just what had gone wrong during the
period, roughly, from the end of World War II to the Vietnam War. Using
the variety of external marking systems that human beings have created,
they could characterize the options available in the light of possible responses by competitors in other countries and more general trends occurring in engineering, accounting, customer preferences, lifestyle, and
so on. They could come up with plans to regain market share, to bring
about needed changes in the structure and functioning of the corporations, to influence the habits of customers, to renegotiate contracts with

unions, and even to work cooperatively with manufacturers and sales teams in other sectors and in foreign countries. In short, it was within their powers to change their minds, as well as the minds of their employees, their customers, and their rivals. And if these plans did not work out as hoped, they were free to return to the drawing board (or the simulation thereof on the computer screen) and proceed again . . . and again.

Conscious awareness of cognitivism is a boon when it comes to changing minds. One can be quite explicit about the representations of each party in a negotiation or rivalry—where the representations are adequate, where they fall short. One can alter the format in order to ensure that one is being understood; one can challenge the content if it seems inadequate for the situation at hand. One can experiment using new symbol systems that might well raise unanticipated possibilities for action; or one can create new mental representations in one's mind and then devise a set of markings adequate for sharing and implementing these novel ideas. One can use various levers of mind changing—reason, rewards, multiple representations—until a tipping point has been reached. Cognitivism synergistically weds the marks of the hand and the ideas of the mind. In place of the straits of biology and culture, it opens up the sluices of imagination. Neither biology nor culture can explain the events of 1960 to 2003 in the automobile industry; cognitivism at least has a shot.

A cognitive perspective does not guarantee success in business or life, nor does it deny limits in human beings. But whether one is a leader, a manager, a worker on the front line, a therapist, a scholar, a competitor, or a consumer, such a cognitive perspective opens up the possibility of representing constraints and alternatives in various ways, and acting on these representations. It invites precision, testing, revision, progress. The perspective is an optimistic one: It acknowledges that we can envision new scenarios and work to achieve them. Indeed, each of our minds, with its universal and idiosyncratic forms of representation, can be used to understand the minds of others as well as our own minds.

I have now introduced the two major lenses with which cognitivists examine the human mind: One focused on its various contents (concepts, stories, theories, and skills) and the other on the diverse forms (formats, representations, or intelligences) in which these contents can be presented. I have also introduced the handful of factors or levers that, taken together, determine the likelihood of mind change. For some purposes, this tool kit suffices. However, the approach is static because it ignores the fact that we are individuals who need to develop our minds from the start and to keep developing them throughout our lives. To complete our opening survey, we need to take into account the ways in which human cognition develops over the course of childhood. And in turning our attention to the developing mind, we immediately encounter a fascinating paradox that bedevils our fundamental issue of mind changing.

CHAPTER 3

The Power of Early Theories

THE PARADOXES OF CHILDHOOD DEVELOPMENT

Look closely at European paintings from the Middle Ages. You will see numerous portrayals of what, given the creatures' diminutive stature, are clearly young children. Yet to the modern eye, there is something strange about them. As pointed out many years ago by the French social historian Philippe Ariés,[1] the portraits reflect an entirely different set of assumptions about human development. In them, young persons are depicted as miniature adults. Short they are, to be sure; but they dress like adults, they wear adult expressions, and even their physical proportions lack the signs of childhood—no oversized heads, no stubby arms, no bowed legs. Historians like Ariés go on to claim that while they were still young, medieval children were ignored; once they reached the age of reason—usually placed at seven years—they were assumed to think and behave like adults.

Aries' claims have never been completely accepted by historians. Yet, a nuanced appreciation that the psyches of young children are not just miniature versions of the adult mind has only emerged slowly. French Enlightenment thinker Jean-Jacques Rousseau was the first Western writer to dwell on the special status of the child; two hundred years ago the Romantic poets and artists glorified the innocence and beauty of youth; and, in the years following Darwin's discoveries, the first self-described psychologists began to try to decipher the mind of the child.

The study of children's cognitive development offers a window onto the phenomenon of mind change and in particular on two enigmatic phenomena: one having to do with the ease of mind changing, the other with its difficulty. When we are young, our minds change with great ease. We pick up information with facility and retain it readily; we learn foreign languages rapidly and pick up accents accurately; and our understanding of the world alters quickly as well. In many ways, it grows more accurate.

Let me turn first to areas where the mind changes readily. Consider three important mind changes that take place in childhood, as set forth by the Swiss scientist Jean Piaget. Generally considered the most important student of human cognitive development,[2] Piaget provided evidence that the child's mind changes dramatically and qualitatively over the first decade and a half of life. Indeed, Piaget claimed that, in the period from infancy to adolescence, all normal children pass through several qualitatively different stages of thought.

Three classic Piagetian demonstrations illustrate important mind changes that occur reliably around the globe. During the latter part of the first year of life, an infant observes a toy hidden a few times at locus A. Then in front of the infant's eyes, the toy—let's say a rubber duck—gets moved to locus B. Despite the evidence of his senses, an eight- or nine-month-old will continue to search for the toy at point A. At this time of life, the current location of an object seems inextricably tied to its original hiding place. But just a few months later, without any formal training, every normal infant goes directly toward B.

Fast-forward to the age of five. The child is shown two identical beakers (A and A'), each containing an equal amount of water. The child affirms that the two beakers both have "the same amount." Then, in front of the child's eyes, the contents of beaker A are poured into a taller and thinner beaker (B) where, of course, the water reaches a higher level. Asked about which vessel contains more water (A' or B), the child will readily designate the taller beaker (B), even though no water has been added or taken away. Prodded for a reason, the child will respond, "There's more because the water is higher." A year or two later, again without formal instruction in the meantime, the child says, "Of course, the two beakers contain the same amount of water. You just poured it, you didn't change anything else."

Consider, finally, a ten-year-old child. She is shown a balance beam and asked to predict the ultimate position of the arms—left arm down, right arm down, both arms at the same level—should weights of a certain specification be placed on each tray of the beam. Should there be a greater number of weights on the tray on one side of the beam, the child will correctly designate that arm as dropping toward the ground; so long as the weights on the tray on one side of the beam are placed at a greater distance from the fulcrum, the child will again respond correctly. But asked to judge an arrangement where there are more weights on one side, but weights are placed at greater distance from the fulcrum on the other, the child throws up her hands and guesses. She is unable to appreciate the phenomenon of torque—the necessity to take into account *both* specific weights and specific distances and then compute the correct response. Yet by the time of adolescence, whether or not they study physics, adolescents at least come to appreciate the compensatory nature of torque. "Well, there are more weights on the left side of the beam, but the weights are further away on the right, and so the beam probably balances."

These Piagetian demonstrations are striking in two respects. First, they seem counterintuitive; researchers and parents were genuinely surprised to find that children all over the world responded similarly to these conundra. Second, relying essentially on their own wits, children seem able eventually to arrive at the correct responses to these dilemmas.

Here, then, is the first facet of the mind-changing paradox. Children think about the world in ways that are fundamentally different from those exhibited by adults. Unlike those medieval portrayals of children as miniature adults, what we've learned is that, in a sense, youngsters can almost seem—in terms of their mental representations—like members of a different species. And yet, apparently without the need for formal tuition, youngsters come to change their minds in fundamental ways. Moreover, and strikingly, these new ways are accompanied by total conviction. Indeed, most older children will refuse to believe that they had *ever* fallen prey to the earlier misconception—at least until confronted with a video of their earlier response.

But there is a rival phenomenon, chronicled by another great student of human development, the Viennese psychoanalyst Sigmund Freud.[3]

Herewith the second facet of our paradox: though the mind can change quite easily, especially when we're young, it simultaneously proves, in certain respects, surprisingly resistant to change. Let me elaborate.

While Piaget focused on the cognitive, problem-solving aspects of the human mind (which has also been my focus, to this point), Freud probed the complementary realms of emotion, motivation, and the unconscious. Freud argued that young children already had formed strong ties to those around them, and that these interpersonal relations were emotionally loaded. The infant is attached intimately to his mother and will be traumatized by abrupt separations from the maternal figure. The newly arrived second-born will find herself in competition for the mother's affection; thus is born sibling rivalry. And in the most famous (and somewhat notorious) formulation, children around the age of five exhibit direct strong feelings to their parents. The boy in the throes of the Oedipal complex wants to possess his mother and get rid of the rival father; the girl under the sway of the Electra complex forms a loving tie to her father, while rejecting her mother.

Nowadays, even those of us who are sympathetic to Freud's account do not take these portrayals literally. But to many observers, Freud's overall picture has the ring of truth. During the early years of life, children do indeed form very strong emotional ties and exhibit powerful reactions to those around them. And—here lies a principal message of psychodynamic therapy—these strong feelings continue to color our subsequent relations with others. Perhaps one's attachment to one's mother wanes, but its qualities are re-created in love relations decades later. Perhaps sibling rivalry is no longer overt, but comparable tensions are manifest in school or at the workplace when a person resents perceived favoritism toward a peer. And unless the love triangle of the nursery has been satisfactorily "resolved," its reverberations are likely to influence relations in later life—"He will never get married, he is still in love with his mother"; "No one is good enough for her, she is still looking for a clone of her father."

All of which leads us back to the paradox of mind change and how our thoughts develop as children. Simply put, in certain respects per Piaget, children's minds change readily, decisively, without the need for formal teaching. In other respects per Freud, the mind proves remarkably resistant to change, even when such change would be highly desirable—indeed, even when one is willing to pay a lot of money to a psychotherapist. The point for our study seems clear. We need to know as much as we can about how the mind naturally changes, and where the resistances lurk. Otherwise, we are likely to be stymied in trying to bring about voluntary mind changing.

So far, the picture that I have presented is reasonably familiar. Freud (certainly) and Piaget (likely), are among the best-known behavioral scientists. Yet, another feature of mental life is critically important, and yet far less well known. This feature applies the "lifelong" perspective of Freud to the cognitive phenomena investigated by Piaget.

ENTRENCHED THEORIES OF CHILDHOOD

There they stand, clad in their black-and-crimson robes at Harvard graduation. They are about to graduate from a world-renowned university, they must know a lot. A researcher asks each in turn, "Why is the earth warmer during the summer (July) than it is in the winter (December)?" For most of the respondents, the answer is clear. "Why, it's because the earth is closer to the sun during the summer than it is during the winter." Pressed for a reason, the respondents continue "It's always warmer when you get closer to the source of heat, so the earth must be closer." [4]

On one level, the answer seems sensible. You *are* warmer when you are closer to a source of heat. Yet a moment's thought should indicate that the answer cannot be correct. If it were, then the whole globe should be warmer during July than it is during December (or vice versa). But of course individuals in Chile or Australia would have entirely different intuitions from those in Boston or Beijing. The actual answer—seldom given by these self-confident Harvard graduates—has to do with the tilt of the earth on its axis as it travels annually around the sun.

On the surface they look like excellent students. They get high grades in high school or college, and they succeed on standardized tests. Yet, when examined outside of a school context, their understanding is frequently shown to be tenuous. Nor is ignorance limited to the phenomena of astronomy. We now have evidence across the curriculum. Physics students are incapable of predicting the trajectory of a pellet after it has fallen out of a curved tube. Biology students continue to give Lamarckian explanations—citing the inheritance of acquired characteristics—for the ways in which traits evolve across the generations. History students insist on attributing excessive agency to single good or evil individuals, ignoring the role of influential groups, populations, and broad social or economic trends. Arts students adhere to a simple-minded aesthetic: poems must rhyme, paintings must be photo-realistic, and—as for music—the faster you can play it, the better. By and large, students who have had the benefit of secondary education tend to respond in much the same way as individuals who had not studied science, history, or the arts. Behold the power of the "unschooled mind." [5]

To report this phenomenon is one thing; to explain it is another. My research suggests the following explanation—one that draws on the findings of both Piaget and Freud. Early in life, young individuals develop very powerful theories of the world. [6] They do so without the need for formal instruction—we might say that these are natural or "intuitive" theories. Some of these theories are correct; for example, it is prudent to avoid terrains that feature sudden drops in height or organisms that look menacing. Some of these theories are charming; for example, rainbows appear when angels are rejoicing. But many are simply wrong. They reflect common sense or—as my mentor Nelson Goodman used to quip—common nonsense.

Theories, I have claimed, represent our efforts to make sense of the world. Making sense is a deep human motivator, but making sense is not the same as being correct. Human beings did not evolve to be correct on some Ultimate Examination—we (like all other creatures) evolved so that we could survive long enough to reproduce. The effort of humanity over the centuries to achieve accurate explanations is a more gradual enterprise, replete with unexpected traps. Explanations that are robust require careful study, the positing of rival explanations, the accumulation of observations or data that make one point of view more likely, the other less so. We might even say, in our terms, that the search for accuracy is a self-conscious enterprise for changing the minds of the human species.

Back to young people and their powerful theories of the world. I have grouped these theories into four categories and listed representative examples. Each of these theories is prevalent among young people everywhere, and none of them proves easy to change. (You can test that proposition on your children or on yourself!)

Intuitive theories of matter:
- Heavier objects fall to the ground more rapidly than lighter ones.
- When you break a large object into parts, and repeat the process, you have increasingly small parts. When you can't see the parts any more, there is nothing left.

Intuitive theories of life:
- If it is moving, it is alive. If it is still, it is dead. If it is on a computer screen, you can't tell for sure.
- All species, including human beings, were created essentially at one moment and they have not changed materially since.
- If something important happens to an organism, that experience will be passed on to his or her offspring.

Intuitive theories of mind:
- All organisms have minds. The more that they resemble us in outward appearance, the more their minds are like ours.
- We can't have a conversation with a fish, but we can certainly chat with a dog, a cat, or a monkey.
- I have a mind, you have a mind. If you look like me, then your mind is like mine and you are good. If you look different from me, then your mind must differ as well, and we are enemies.

Intuitive theories of human relations:
- Individuals who are big are powerful. It is desirable to be on their side. If you can't seize power yourself, align yourself with those who wield power.
- The goal of life is to secure goods. Whenever a good is scarce, you should try to get as much of it as you can for yourself and for those to whom you feel closest.
- If you can't corner the market on a precious good, it should be divided equally among all parties (so much for the 80/20 principle).
- If someone takes advantage of you, retaliate in kind.

WHY CHILDHOOD THEORIES PROVE
RESISTANT TO CHANGE

These theories are not invented out of whole cloth. They all have a surface plausibility to them. They are based on the evidence of the senses, and they appear to be validated from time to time. Less dense objects do appear to accelerate more slowly because under ordinary circumstances, air resistance is present. Dogs are more attentive to human signals than are fish, even if cocker spaniels have no more idea of what their master is thinking than does a goldfish. Individuals bigger than a child often do get their way in an altercation, even when they do not deserve to prevail on any calculus of fairness.

Moreover, it is possible to assimilate apparently inconsistent information so that it accords with one's theories. When my son Benjamin was five, I asked him about the shape of the earth. He responded immediately, "It is round, Dad." Buoyed by this display of scientific knowledge (or at least cultural literacy), I decided to push him. "Tell me, Benjamin," I prodded, "where are *you* standing?" "That's easy," he responded, "I am on the flat part underneath." More generally, individuals will go to great lengths to square apparently discrepant information with their firmly held beliefs. That is how we cope with "cognitive dissonance"—the apparent inconsistency between what our parents (or our textbooks) tell us and what we believe to be true.

Human beings are not born as blank mental slates, nor are all theories equally likely to emerge. My hypothesis—unveiled earlier—is that human beings are primed to come up with one kind of theory rather than another. To use an example that may seem self-evident, it is natural for humans to theorize that a prior event (lightning) has caused a subsequent event (thunder). Of course, on logical grounds, the co-occurrences happen in both directions; and so, in principle, we could assume that the latter (thunder) causes the former (lightning) or that they are both the result of a third, independent cause (say, the wrath of the gods). However, something in our "wiring" predisposes us to the aforementioned theory, rather than to others that are equally possible on logical grounds.

It helps to think of our early childhood theories as slight dips in the initially smooth terrain of the mind/brain. The more the theory seems to be borne out, the deeper the dips become until a significant valley has formed. Barring mental bulldozing, these valleys are likely to endure. Another suggestive metaphor construes the early theories as engravings in the mind/brain. These engravings are enduring. However, in school, one learns many facts (like "the earth is round") and, when properly prompted, can repeat this sound bite. From a distance, it looks like facts are piling up high and one has learned a great deal. However, all too often, the fundamental engraving has remained unchanged. And so, when one is posed a question for which one has not been properly prepared, not only is one stymied but, more often than not, the respondent reverts to the earlier engraving, or, to shift metaphors, slides back into the valley of ignorance.[7]

So, once again, the second facet of our paradox: theories are difficult to change, and early theories prove especially difficult to alter. Indeed, perhaps it is more surprising that children ever become conservers than that they begin life as nonconservers. We do not know why conservation of quantity is one of those theories that eventually does become virtually universal among children. It may be that the predictions based on non-conservational assumptions are consistently wrong; as the data accumulate, the early engraving becomes dysfunctional. It may be because as a species, we are predisposed to come up with parsimonious explanations, and conservation ("no addition, no subtraction, hence no change") fits that bill (parsimony prevails). What seems clear is that children around the world are not explicitly *taught* to become conservers. They just become conservers at about the time that school begins.

We can point to some factors that help to entrench theories. One factor is emotional resonance—which, not surprisingly, is one of the seven levers that I listed in chapter 1. The more emotional one's commitment to a cause or belief, the more difficult to change. Even after the crimes of Stalin's Soviet Union were evident to the world, those with a strong emotional tie to communism had difficulty recognizing the harm that had been done. Another factor is public commitment. It is potent enough when one has a private commitment to a point of view, but once one has made public pronouncements on that perspective, matters of pride and consistency push one toward hugging the theory, however discredited. Finally, personality factors are at work. The more absolutist one's approach to life, the more certain of one's opinions, the less likely one is to abandon them. Those with "authoritarian personalities" are especially prone to cling to their earlier beliefs. It is far more adaptive to be low key, flexible, curious, or, to use a phrase currently popular among the young, to have a "whatever" attitude toward explanations. Happily, none of these factors seems prominent in young children, and so they do not stand in the way of the appreciation of conservation of matter.

FACTORS THAT IMPEL CHANGES OF MIND

We return now to the more positive facet of mind changing. People do change their minds, and, particularly in the young, the phenomenon occurs frequently. One is helped when there is a natural proclivity to adopt a certain stance—one reason for the popularity of relativistic viewpoints among adolescents. One is also nudged into changing one's mind when a perspective that clashes with one's own is widely shared by a new, powerful, and resource-rich constituency. If one is raised in a family or community that is staunchly conservative, one is likely to experience a shock when one attends a secondary school or college where the prevalent sentiment is middle-of-the-road or liberal. Many studies have documented a shift to the left when youngsters enter college; no doubt this is due at least in part to the influence of a powerful cohort. The reverse trend often commences ten or twenty years later when the same individuals find themselves in a profit-making environment and need resources to pay for a home, tuition for their children, and retirement plans for themselves.

Behaviorists would have us think that the most powerful incentives for alterations in behavior are shifting contingencies of reward and punishment. Clearly, there is something to this argument. I have often quipped as a parent that, when all else fails, I become a behaviorist. If there are clear rewards for mouthing a certain perspective, most of us will learn to say the words and at least some of us may come to believe them. Yet changes brought about chiefly through varying the patterns of reinforcement are superficial ones; they can be reversed as quickly and seamlessly as they have been brought on. In my view that is because the "trainer" is dealing with the overt behavior—what one actually says or does at a given moment—rather than with the underlying belief system.

Here, again, the cognitive perspective flexes its explanatory muscles. The behaviorist looks at a pattern of response and tries to figure out which set of experiences will alter that pattern of responses in a desired direction. The cognitivist tries to ferret out the current mental representation, what it consists of, how deeply it is held. Then, the challenge to the cognitive analyst is to figure out *which* experiences, perspectives, or arguments are most likely to challenge that representation, demonstrate its weaknesses, and cause it to be undermined; the cognitively oriented teacher constructs experiences that will help to bring about the discovery of a more powerful concept, a more compelling story, a more robust theory, a more effective practice, and—in the end—a superior mental representation.

When it comes to the relative complexity of competing theories, an interesting tension obtains. On the one hand, individuals exhibit cognitive laxity. It is easy and comforting to stick with the prevailing line of explanation, particularly when it is neat and simple. The "big guys" have all the resources, and it just makes sense to go along with them. On the other hand, there is a strong desire to understand things better, to have informed control over what happens with respect to those things. And so, when confronted with an explanation that is moderately more sophisticated than their current favorite, children tend to embrace it. Studies of moral development, for example, show that individuals at X stage of sophistication are likely to be persuaded by arguments that are couched at $X+1$ level of complexity. Thus, youngsters at the "might = right" level find convincing an argument that states that a person who is smart or moral might be more worthy of resources than a person with bigger muscles. If the complexity is greater, say +2 or +3 stages, then the youngsters cannot assimilate the argument and simply ignore it (arguments in terms of complex concepts like "distributive justice" or the "categorical imperative" fall on the deaf ears of ten-year-olds). If, however, an argument is at a less complex level than their own, youngsters generally do not take it seriously. For example, on hearing, "That's right because I said so," the more sophisticated youngster will respond, "Oh, that is a dumb argument," or "Only a little kid would say that." [8]

How most effectively to change the minds of children was a particular interest of a third major twentieth-century developmental psychologist, Lev Semyonovich Vygotsky. [9] Vygotsky proposed that in any pedagogical endeavor, the first order of business is to ascertain—through tests or tasks—the child's current level of competence. But he pointed out that two individuals who receive the same "score" on such instruments might differ significantly from one another in the capacity to advance to a more sophisticated level. Suppose, for example, that two five-year-olds fail consistently at the game of tic-tac-toe. Each one is then shown a process whereby one can radically improve performance—say, by varying one's strategy depending on whether one goes first or second. Child *A* catches on immediately and begins to beat his peers regularly; Child *B* makes little or no effort to master the rule and plays no better than before. On Vygotsky's analysis, Child *A* has a much greater "zone of potential (or proximal) development," and educational interventions are far more likely to prove effective. In common parlance, while the task performance at any one moment may not distinguish *A* from *B*, *A* has much greater cognitive potential.

Vygotsky contributed another useful concept to the study of mind changing. When a child is performing poorly at a task, he or she will benefit from a resource called *scaffolding*: the orderly provision of just enough support so that the child can improve his or her performance significantly. Using the tic-tac-toe example, one could scaffold a child by suggesting that she always try to anticipate what her opponent will do if she herself makes a certain move, or by indicating that she needs to adopt a different strategy when her opponent has placed an *X* in a corner than when the same symbol has been placed in the center of the array. One could follow up this advice by pointing out what happens when the child follows this ploy as contrasted to cases when the child ignores it. The resource of scaffolding works when the child takes advantage of such adult support. As in the construction of a building, however, the scaffolding should not remain indefinitely. Indeed, once scaffolding has "taken," it should promptly be removed. According to Vygotskian theory, successful scaffolding is "internalized"; what first must come from outside—usually from an older and better-informed person—should eventually be handled by "conversations" within one's own mind.

Occasional changes of mind—like that of the Jew Saul who was converted to Christianity while on the road to Damascus—can be sudden, dramatic, and permanent; they invade the core of one's being, taking it over. In the same breath, however, we must note that reports of such dramatic mind changes are more frequent than their actual occurrence. Many who tout a new belief that, for example, they've been "born again," have reverted to earlier beliefs within a matter of days or months. And we must also remember, following Nicholson Baker, that significant changes of mind may take place much more gradually and mysteriously, so that a person may become aware of such changes only some time after they have coalesced. Damascene experiences are genuine, but they are but one of the set of circumstances marked by significant changes of mind.

REPRISE

We have now introduced the major aspects of our story about changing minds. To recap, we begin with the human mind, which is stocked with a set of mental representations. These mental representations are characterized by content—they have, or perhaps better, they *are* meaning. But equally they have forms, and the "same" content can be conveyed in diverse formats, in multiple representations. (Recall the different graphic illustrations of the 80/20 principle.) These formats can be variously described: For our purposes, the human intelligences serve as convenient reminder of the varying forms that mental contents can assume.

Mental representations are detectable in various entities. While it is convenient to use the shorthand term *ideas,* I find it more precise to distinguish among concepts, stories, theories, and skills. All of us harbor an ensemble of these kinds of mental entities; and if we knew enough about the mind and brain, we could describe these representations in detail and perhaps even pinpoint how they are encoded in our nervous system.

But how are these entities changed? We cannot do so unless we confront the paradox of mind changing. From one perspective, the mind changes very easily, and particularly so during youth. For certain changes of mind, we can sit back, confident that they will sooner or later happen. At the same time, however, the mind is a surprisingly conservative mechanism. Theories, concepts, stories, and skills are formed early, and many resist change. Indeed, when it comes to the theories that one is expected to master in school, the mind proves remarkably refractory to alteration—persisting in its original unschooled theories even when, on the surface, a person can mouth the appropriate line. Figuring out how to change minds about the fundaments of matter, life, mental phenomena, and real-life human beings turns out to be a formidable educational challenge. Nor does mind changing occur more readily outside of schools: whether the sphere be politics or religion, the workplace or the home, beliefs become entrenched all too readily and thereafter prove difficult to alter.

We've noted a few rules of thumb. It is more difficult to change the mind when perspectives are held strongly, and publicly, and by individuals of rigid temperament. It is easier to change minds when individuals find themselves in a new environment, surrounded by peers of a different persuasion (for example, when one enters college), or when individuals undergo shattering experiences (for example, a severe accident, a divorce, or an unexpected death) or encounter luminous personalities. Even so, however, fans of mind changing must often mute their claims of victory. The opportunities for backsliding are patent among those who make a lot of noise—indeed, they may be especially patent among those who are given to histrionic statements ("it's an entirely new ballgame") and then register disappointment when the rest of the world remains much as it was before. In other words, it's easier to talk about changing minds in general than to effect enduring changes in any particular mind.

A LOOK AHEAD

So far in discussing the mind, I have been an almost pure Cartesian—treating the mind as if it were a disembodied entity. Minds of course are found in bodies—usually human ones, but also those of other animals and, increasingly, in inorganic entities like computers. Sometimes, as in the young, these minds appear to change on their own; at other times, individuals themselves consciously change their minds. For example, I might decide that henceforth I shall be a behaviorist rather than a cognitive psychologist; a libertarian rather than a social democrat; a practicing Christian rather than a secular Jew.

For the most part, however, minds change as the result of efforts by external agents. When we are young, we encounter individuals who are authorized to change our minds: our parents, other older relatives, our teachers, as well as authority figures in the neighborhood and the community. Even during our adult years, we encounter some agents—representing our employer or the legal system—who have sufficient power to change our behaviors and (at times) our minds.

In the next part of the book, I turn my attention to those agents and institutions that have the potential to change minds. I have chosen to do this by examining in a specific order the six different arenas in which mind changing ordinarily takes place. I begin with the mind changes that occur in the largest arena—that of an entire nation—and work steadily toward the most intimate settings, involving two persons and, finally, just one's own mind. Some common features extend across these varied settings, but important factors distinguish each form of mind changing as well.

One can think of these ordered arenas as an inverted pyramid:

Large-scale changes involving the diverse population of a region or an entire nation
Large-scale changes involving a more uniform or homogeneous group
Changes brought about through works of art or science
Changes within formal instructional settings
Intimate forms of mind changing
Changing one's own mind

Perhaps the most recognized agents of mind changing are the leaders in the top row of our inverted pyramid: those who are elected to political office or appointed to positions of authority over large populations. Examples range from British Prime Minister Margaret Thatcher to the world leader Mahatma Gandhi. Operating on a wide stage, these leaders exert influence over the largest number of individuals—individuals who are typically quite disparate from one another. They can even change the course of history—for good or ill.

Presumably, a leader would have an easier time effecting mind change within our second category above: a more homogeneous or uniform group such as a corporation, club, civic organization, or college. In cases involving a corporation head like Lord John Browne of BP or a college president like James Freedman of Dartmouth, the individuals with whom one is dealing share a common knowledge base and a similar degree of expertise. But, as we will see in the next part of the book, changing the minds of such populations has its challenges too—especially when members of the group have developed ideas that differ significantly from those of the designated leaders.

Our third arena of mind changes involves those wrought by the works that an individual creates rather than by any direct words or acts of leadership. For example, the writings of Karl Marx exerted enormous influence on political events in the late nineteenth century and throughout the twentieth century, yet he himself was not a leader in the traditional "direct" sense. Nor are minds changed solely by those in the political or economic sphere. Our understanding of the world has been affected as well by seminal minds like Albert Einstein's in the physical realm and Charles Darwin's in the biological realm. Examples also include the creative works of writers such as James Joyce, musicians such as the Beatles, and dancer/choreographers such as Martha Graham. Even those who do not give speeches or write texts can change our minds. Probably more conceptions of the Spanish civil war were formed or altered by Pablo Picasso's shattering depiction *Guernica* than by a thousand news dispatches.

The fourth arena in our pyramid involves the one institution in the world formally chartered with the changing of minds: the school. Schools stand out because they serve those young individuals whose minds can most readily be changed. They fashion curricula and disciplines that attempt to crystallize the current state of knowledge; and they assume responsibility for monitoring how, and to what extent, the minds of students have in fact been changed. The milieus of formal education vary, from large lectures delivered to many hundreds of students to informal tutorials with one or a handful of students, to the child alone in the library or at the computer screen—and more recently, to lifelong education, including continuing professional development.

A fifth arena in which mind changing takes place involves intimate settings. From time to time, most of us want to change the minds of family members; we want to convince friends—or enemies—of our point of view; we want to be able to work effectively with our boss and with our employees; and we seek to blend our minds with those of our lovers. Surveying the various arenas in which mind changes take place, most of us gain the most when we can bring about such changes in these intimate settings—and it is here that we pay the heaviest prices when our attempts fail. I will look at a range of intimate mind changes: the encounter between a university president and a member of his faculty, the epistolary exchanges between two former U.S. presidents, dream interpretation involving a psychotherapist and his troubled patient.

Finally, we arrive at the fascinating terrain of our *own* minds. Our own minds are changed—either because we want to change them or because something happens in the real world or in our mental life that warrants a major change. The change can occur in any sphere: our political beliefs, our scientific beliefs, our personal credo, our views about ourselves. Relevant exemplars are citizens like Whittaker Chambers, whose radically altered relation to the Communist Party helped bring about a change in American political sensitivity a half-century ago, and scholars like the philosopher Ludwig Wittgenstein and the anthropologist Lucien Lévy-Bruhl, who underwent widely publicized changes of view in their respective areas of research. While sometimes the change of mind can be smooth, it is especially poignant when a change of mind brings about a complete shift in our worldview or lifestyle.

Examined from the broadest perspective, one can identify characteristics of mind changing that cut across these various arenas. Here I make use of the distinctions introduced earlier in the book. As illustrated in the appendix, in each case there is an original ideational *content* and a contrasting perspective, which I term a *countercontent*; the ideational content can be a concept, a story, a theory, or some kind of skill. I also record three other elements: the nature of the *audience* involved in the mind-changing endeavor, the particular *format* (e.g., intelligence, medium) in which the content is presented, and the *factors* (our seven levers of mind change) that lead, or thwart, the change from the original to the new content—that is, that determine whether or not a tipping point has been reached.

Those who think in terms of multidimensional spaces will realize that I have taken into account a dizzying set of dimensions. Were one to fill in every cell in the auditorium of mind changing, there would be hundreds of entries: after all, I have specified six arenas, arranged in a pyramidal form; four kinds of ideational content (ranging from concepts to theories); at least eight representational formats (reflecting the several intelligences); and seven separate levers that bring about or thwart changes (reason, research, resonance, representational redescriptions, resources and rewards, real world events, and resistances).

Fortunately, however, it is possible to survey the terrain of mind changing in a simpler fashion. As it turns out, each arena of mind changing favors certain kinds of content and features certain prevalent levers. It is efficient and effective, rather than misleading, to use illustrations that are representative of mind changing in a particular arena. To cite just a few examples: Leaders addressing large, diverse groups necessarily deal with stories; those who are attempting to bring about mind change in smaller, more uniform groups or in classrooms can introduce theories. Leaders of large groups typically utilize linguistic intelligence and attempt to embody desired changes in their own actions; those who influence minds through their creative efforts employ the whole gamut of intelligences; mind changing in intimate settings places a special premium on interpersonal intelligence.

It also turns out that specific levers of change prove especially germane within specific arenas. Reason and research are most important for those involved in intellectual argumentation; resonance comes to the fore in intimate relations; resistances are particularly notable in formal educational settings when new theories have been introduced; leaders of large groups often rely on the appreciable resources at their disposal but also are buoyed or undercut by real world events. For these reasons, our survey comfortably draws on examples that are particularly associated with a certain form of mind changing.

On an *a priori* basis, one can never predict with certainty whether a candidate mind change will take place. But it seems safe to say that mind changes are likely to occur when all seven factors pull in a "mind-changing" direction—and are most unlikely to occur when all or most of those factors oppose the mind change. The balance or weight across these forces determines whether or not a tipping point in favor of the change is likely to be reached.

I have now introduced the full armamentarium of mind changing: the contents and countercontents of the mind; the various arenas (presented in the form of an inverted pyramid) in which mind changing is most likely to be at issue; the discrete representational forms in which these contents and countercontents can be presented; and the seven factors or levers that, conjointly, determine whether a candidate mind change is likely to coalesce. In what follows, I draw on this framework as appropriate to elucidate examples chosen from the six arenas of principal interest. Those with a desire to use the framework more promiscuously are invited to employ it across the board or to consult the chart at the end of the book, where I have applied it to a gamut of examples. Those who prefer to immerse themselves in the examples may treat the framework as background music—there to be focused on when desired but easily ignored if you'd rather attend to the words.

CHAPTER 4

Leading a Diverse Population

WHETHER THEY ARE heads of a nation or senior officials of the United Nations, leaders of large, disparate populations have enormous potential to change minds. Indeed, they are in the business of changing minds— and in the process they can change the course of history. Of the six kinds of change agents that we examine in this book, leaders of such heterogeneous populations are in a position to influence the largest number of individuals. But how effective those leaders are depends on many factors.

In a democracy, an elected leader has power, but little of it is there for the taking. Rather, she must convince members of her own party to accept her leadership, and she must develop policies that have, or can acquire, reasonable support among both the governmental bureaucracy and the general public. In the absence of such support, she is likely to face a revolt from her own supporters, or to propose laws that are not enacted or not enforced or that result in her defeat in the next election.

To change minds effectively, leaders make particular use of two tools: the stories that they tell and the lives that they lead. In terms of our levers of change, the "resonance" that exists—or doesn't—between those stories and those lives proves of telltale importance. In this chapter I touch on the effectiveness of several world leaders, ranging from Bill Clinton to Mahatma Gandhi. British Prime Minister Margaret Thatcher serves as a vivid example of how one can change the views of a large and diverse population.

MARGARET THATCHER: A STORY AND A LIFE

In 1979, Margaret Thatcher, a fifty-three-year-old member of Britain's House of Commons, made political history. Running as the leader of the Conservative Party, Thatcher embraced a simple slogan: "Britain has lost its way." On Thatcher's analysis, Britain had once been a formidable power, distinguished by its far-flung empire across the globe, its widely admired principles of democracy, and its pioneering business acumen. During the darkest hours of 1940, Britain, under the courageous leadership of Winston Churchill, had stood alone against the Nazi power that had rapidly overrun Western Europe. But paradoxically, with the victory over the Axis powers in 1945, British power and influence had rapidly waned. Churchill was immediately turned out of office. Then a series of unremarkable leaders of both parties forged a postwar synthesis: Britain should be content to be a second-rate power, dismantling its empire, withdrawing to its geographical shores, relinquishing its sovereignty by joining a series of emerging European economic and political entities. In addition, industries and principal societal functions should be nationalized. Unions should be sovereign. Government should operate largely through the forging of consensus among the principal parties, continuity ensured through the civil service. Britain would become a subordinate partner to the United States, an anglicized version of social-democratic Scandinavia.[1]

Were Thatcher to become the prime minister, she promised, all of this would change. British commercial and entrepreneurial genius would be reinvigorated. The stranglehold of the unions would be broken, and industries and other major functions would be privatized. Britain would once again revive its "special partnership" with the United States, and, its sovereignty intact, assume a leadership role in Europe and throughout the world.

A smart, tough, self-made woman, Thatcher was well-suited to bear this message. Her family had been of modest means (she'd grown up in the flat above her parents' grocery store), and yet she had gained entrance to Oxford and secured degrees in both chemistry and law. After taking time off to raise two children, she had advanced in the political ranks and held various "shadow" roles in the no-longer-dominant Conservative

Party. She had been suitably cautious in supporting the party, while at the same time making it clear that she was a woman of strong opinions and strong principles. As she surveyed the scene in the late 1970s, it was clear to her that "no theory of government was ever given a fairer test or a more prolonged experiment in a democratic country than democratic socialism received in Britain. Yet it was a miserable failure in every respect . . . leaving both the country and its industries spiraling downward." [2] If this were true, and Britain had indeed "lost its way," Thatcher seemed the perfect candidate to lead her nation back to the proper course.

From the moment she became prime minister, Thatcher determinedly put her platform into action with the aim of bringing about dramatic change in Britain. She quoted with approval the Earl of Chatham, one of her predecessors: "I know that I can save this country and that no one else can." [3] Indeed, within a few years, Britain seemed a very different country, occupying a position of refreshed importance in its own view and in the view of many other nations. To be sure, Thatcher's policies were not popular with everyone. Indeed, as a scholar in his comfortable perch across the Atlantic, I watched with dismay as she disempowered great universities, broke the hold of local control over the schools, and disparaged eggheads, especially those who dared to question her ends or her means. Many observers felt that in her desire to encourage business interests, Thatcher was willing to run roughshod over those in the society who were disadvantaged. Rejecting this characterization, she once declared defiantly: "There is no such thing as society; there are only individuals." [4] She wanted to level the playing field, give individuals the opportunity to participate in the life of the nation (as she herself had been given such an opportunity some decades before), and then let those with ability and tenacity rise to the top.

Without question, Thatcher succeeded in changing many minds: Due to her influence, Britain today is a very different nation. And she did so more effectively and rapidly than either her supporters or detractors ever expected. Indeed, she continued to dominate political discourse even after she left office in 1990. Both her Conservative successor, John Major, and his Labour successor, Tony Blair, defined issues in the light of considerations brought forth by the Thatcher hegemony. Blair's vaunted "third way," for example, is an effort to mediate between the postwar socialism of the Labourites and the (in his mind) excessive laissez-faire regime of the subsequent Thatcher years. A new story, we might say.

But what of Margaret Thatcher's story? As I argued at the beginning of this chapter, the stories that leaders tell and the lives that they lead can determine their success or failure at changing their constituents' minds. Clearly, Thatcher had a simple and powerful story to tell. Stripped to its essentials, the story claimed that Britain had once been a great nation; it had lost its way in recent decades; but it was possible for Britain to recover its genius. As a teller (and seller) of this story, Thatcher had to be credible. The fact that she herself had risen to a position of power and prominence through cleverness and hard work greatly enhanced her credibility. The life that she had led, and the way that she had led it, *embodied* well the message that she sought to convey in words. And indeed, the courage that Thatcher displayed in office—leading her country in a struggle to retain the embattled Falkland Islands, surviving a bombing at the Brighton party conference and choosing to remain at that locale while under siege—reinforced the national story that she was putting forth and may well have determined her success.

It's important to explain why I speak of a story. Thatcher did not merely put forth a message, a slogan, an image, or a vision—though each of these could be gleaned from what she said. Her message contained the essential elements of any good narrative: a *protagonist*—the British nation (if not British society!); a *goal*—the restoration of stature, the proper international role for Britain; and *obstacles*—the misguided consensual policies of recent years, the willingness to cede leadership to other countries, the power of the unions, the fractiousness of the Commonwealth nations, the absence of a directed National Will. And there was a vehicle for combating these obstacles—the ensemble of policies that Thatcher, as a Conservative leader, was putting forth. Thatcher did not mince words. She continually asked "Is he/she one of us?" In posing this query, Thatcher was deliberately construing the British population as a set of individuals who either bought, or did not buy, into her revised vision, her new story. And since we can assume that her story had not been widely known or believed ten years before, she had to convince many individuals to accept her view of things.

Now it would be relatively easy for a story such as Thatcher's to take hold and become entrenched if there were no prior stories. The mind as a blank slate, a tabula rasa, is an appealing target for any messenger. Yet, even at the time of entry to school, youngsters already know many stories, including stories about the nation in which they live. And certainly by the time they are old enough to vote, individuals have assimilated many dozens of stories about political, economic, social, and cultural matters. Taking an analogy from the writings of biologist Charles Darwin (who himself borrowed the image from the economist Thomas Malthus), we may think of the mind as a vast hall of combat. In that competitive environment, various stories compete, wrestle, vie with one another for survival, for long-time entrenchment in the mind/brain, for the opportunity to stimulate consequential behaviors.

STORYTELLING AND THE DARWINIAN ANTE

It is not easy for a story to gain a hearing. We have all heard a great many stories before, and several of those stories over and over again. Most stories and most jokes are not remembered for long, because they are too similar to what we have already heard and thus lack distinctiveness. Instead they are assimilated to already-accepted or known stories. (That is why we recall relatively few details of most episodes of television shows that we have seen.) On the other hand, stories that are too bizarre or exotic also elude memory. Either they are repressed because they are too alien or too threatening (this is what sometimes happens to me if I view a movie made for domestic consumption in Japan or India); or they are distorted so that they fit comfortably with stories that are already known (this is what happens when one visits a foreign country and mistakenly assumes that events witnessed—say, a political rally or a soccer match— would necessarily have happened in the same way or have the same meaning in one's own land). To take an example with which I am personally familiar, in the 1980s and 1990s the remarkable infant and toddler centers in Reggio Emilia, Italy, were initially (but mistakenly) seen as simple variants of American progressive kindergartens. Over time, careful observers came to appreciate that these Italian schools actually operated in quite different fashion—for example, construing learning as a group rather than an individual phenomenon, basing future activities on a careful documentation of each day's elements and products.

Optimally, a new story has to have enough familiar elements so that it is not instantly rejected yet be distinctive enough that it compels attention and engages the mind. The audience has to be prepared, in one sense, and yet surprised, in another. It is quite possible that Britain would not have been prepared to hear Thatcher a decade before, when the international upheavals of the 1960s were uppermost in everyone's mind. It is equally likely that Thatcher would have been rejected a decade later—as indeed she was. By then her position had become the conventional wisdom and, for that reason, its defects were well known. Though perhaps not conscious of it, Britain had been prepared for a new way, a new story, perhaps a "third way."

I speak of the struggle as a contest between a new "story" and a "counterstory"—more generically, as a battle between "content" and "countercontent." For the Thatcher story of Britain to prevail, it had to gain a hearing and, eventually, ascendancy over the competing counterstories. In the case of England in the late 1970s, the counterstories would have included the following: "Britain was great once, but what is over is over." "The proper status for Britain is as a peaceful, socialistic society, one that no longer seeks to dominate the world." "It would be good to change the direction of Britain, but this has to be achieved through evolution and consensus." "Britain should strengthen its ties to the European continent and emerge as a leader of the European Union." And so on.

Without (I hope) wielding it as a sledgehammer, I have just applied much of the analytic framework to the case of Margaret Thatcher. (To see the framework explicitly at work from now on, you may consult the chart in the appendix.) I have stated the content of her desired mind change and the countercontents with which it had to contend. I have described her audiences—leading members of her own party, the bureaucracy located at London's Whitehall, the broader British public. I have indicated that Thatcher dealt with content by formulating convincing stories and that the stories are represented both in natural language and in her personal embodiment of the key themes.

But what about the factors that bring about, or fail to bring about, change? History does not allow controlled experiments. We can never be certain just which factors tipped the balance in favor of Thatcher's story. At least as a thought experiment, however, it is possible to see at work each of the seven levers of change introduced in chapter 1.

Reason

Thatcher was an excellent arguer and debater. Dating back to her days as a political leader at Oxford, she knew how to analyze an issue and lay out arguments on one side or the other. Influenced by the economist Frederich von Hayek and her close colleague Keith Joseph, she could argue the new Conservative positions effectively to a variety of audiences. In the parliamentary debates and in her weekly "question" session in the House of Commons, she sparkled. In her effort to change the minds of her fellow citizens, she laid out the problems and weaknesses of the past thirty years and showed how her revised line of thinking would solve those problems and lead to a more successful and more powerful nation.

Research

Thatcher was a demon for policy studies. She insisted on the collection of data by the various Cabinet departments and Whitehall offices. She pored over these data, committed them to memory, and peppered her effective arguments with data that supported them. She plotted the increases in unemployment, strikes, and inflation under earlier regimes, and she took pride when these numbers began to turn around in the mid-1980s. And she pointed as well to the favorable attitudinal, behavioral, and performance changes that were taking place in other countries that—perhaps inspired by her success—had rejected socialistic policies.

Resonance

Ultimately, leaders cannot be effective—and cannot call for sacrifice— unless their stories and their persons strike a resonant chord with their audiences. Thatcher synthesized her reasoning and data in an appealing rhetorical manner. As she put it, in reflecting on her rise to power, "Not only had we worked out a full programme for government; we had also taken apprenticeships in advertising and learn how to put a complex and sophisticated case in direct, clear and simple language. We had, finally, been arguing that case for the better part of four years, so our agenda would, with luck, strike people as familiar common sense rather than as a wild radical project."[5]

It would be an exaggeration to say that Britons all liked or responded positively to Thatcher: She had the capacity to alienate both opponents who dared to criticize her policies and supporters when they struck her as "wobbly." But in the main Thatcher directed her message to those constituents who had the potential to be convinced. They found Thatcher to be on their wavelength—in part, no doubt, because of her unremarkable family background and no-nonsense demeanor. In terms of our additional "re-" terms (see chapter 1), they were able to relate to her, to rely on her, and to respect her. Thatcher was quite sensitive to this mutual attraction. She once stated: "I did not feel I needed an interpreter to address people who spoke the same language. And I felt that it was a real advantage that we had lived the same sort of life. I felt that the experiences I had lived through had fitted me curiously well for the coming struggle."[6]

Ultimately, the power of resonance may be most apparent when resonance ceases. Indeed, toward the end of her ten years in office, Thatcher became increasingly imperious in manner and much less willing to listen, to learn, to be corrected. She lost the support not only of much of the public but also—and fatally—of her own party leaders. Her fall from office was swift.

Representational Redescriptions

As a leader addressing a large and diverse citizenry, Thatcher had to depend significantly on the stories—and the Story—that she told. Of course, this was a specific content about the status of Britain, expressed in the ordinary (if not the Queen's) English. Thatcher reinforced her message with clever visuals; for example, her 1979 campaign poster showed a long queue of men and women lined up outside an unemployment office. The poster bore the legend "Labour isn't working."[7] Equally powerful was Thatcher's embodiment of the story of her own life: her modest origins, her self-reliance, and her bravery in open war (the Falklands), terrorism (the Brighton bombings), and in political conflict. Her apparently happy and stable family life and sincere religious conviction reinforced these embodiments. These diverse representations of her central message served Thatcher well, and they help to explain why others with similar messages but less persuasive embodiments—

John Major in Britain, Newt Gingrich in the United States—were not as successful in communicating them.

An important part of Thatcher's embodiment was her confidence that her path was right and that she had to stick to it. "I was utterly convinced of one thing: there was no chance of achieving that fundamental change of attitude which was required to wrench Britain out of decline if people believed that we were prepared to alter course under pressure."[8] Finally this tenacity paid off: "People saw the connection between the resolution we had shown in economic policy and that [we had] demonstrated in the handling of the Falklands crisis."[9]

Resources and Rewards

While politics is partly about ideas, it is also about the accumulation and deployment of resources. Margaret Thatcher knew that she had to have a strong and supportive inner circle. She chose the members with care, conferred on them the requisite power and prestige, and did not hesitate to replace individuals when they did not measure up. Ambitious politicians were unwise to oppose Thatcher; she was quick to retaliate, just as she was certain to reward those who remained loyal.

As for the resources and rewards for the wider nation, Thatcher's key idea was to reduce the size and power of the central governmental apparatus and return resources to individuals, to use as they saw fit. At first this was just a promissory note: Two years into her term, the British public was worse off on most economic indices than when the Tories had returned to office. But when the economy turned up, and unemployment diminished, Thatcher's population began to receive the rewards that they had been promised. In American political terms, they were "better off than they had been" four or five years earlier.

Real World Events

Even those of us who are partial to the "great man" or "great woman" account of events acknowledge the extent to which any leader must work within the framework of his or her era. Factors outside the control of the leader can have huge impact. In Thatcher's case, consider, for example, the negative effects of the oil crises produced by the fall of the Shah of Iran in 1979, or the positive effects of the election of Ronald Reagan the following year. Some of the most memorable events of Thatcher's tenure were not within her power: the seizure of the Falkland Islands by the Argentine military, the terrorist bombings by the Irish Republican Army (IRA), the ascension to power of Mikhail Gorbachev in the Soviet Union. And yet, the mark of the leader lies significantly in the way in which she responds to, and makes her own, these difficult-to-envision-or-control events. Thatcher receives high scores on this dimension.

Resistances

From the first, Thatcher realized that the powerful counterstories (or countercontents) that existed in Britain in the 1970s had to be overcome. She found resisters within her own party and pointedly nicknamed them "the Wets." She attacked them with relish and, after a rocky start, made considerable progress in muting their force. Her personal bravery, her savviness in arraying resources and rewards, and her victory in the Falklands probably tipped the balance.

In an effort to mute resistance, Thatcher sought on occasion to address directly those of a different persuasion, such as members of trade unions: "I understand your fears. You're afraid that producing more goods with fewer people will mean fewer jobs ... but you're wrong.... the right way to attack unemployment is to produce more goods more cheaply, and then more people can afford to buy ... we will create conditions in which the value of the money you earn and the money you save can be protected."[10]

Yet, in reflecting sagely on her tenure, Thatcher admitted that one could never completely overcome such resistances: "Orthodox finance, low levels of regulation and taxation, a minimal bureaucracy, strong defense, willingness to stand up for British interests wherever and whenever threatened—I did not believe that I had to open windows into men's souls on these matters. The arguments for them seemed to have been won. I now know that such arguments are never finally won."[11]

Paradoxically, however, Thatcher's loss of power is related less to the enduring strength of the counterstories and more to her own growing arrogance. In this case, internal pride, rather than external resistances, led to her fall. Had Thatcher moderated some of her more extreme sentiments or political programs when advised to do so by her supporters, she would not have faced a revolt within the ranks of her own party. Nevertheless, Thatcher's case still stands out in my view as perhaps the most successful instance of "mind change" in democratic politics in the last half of the twentieth century. Let us now shift our perspective to the other side of the ocean to consider two leading U.S. politicians of the 1990s: Bill Clinton and Newt Gingrich.

LEADERSHIP, AMERICAN STYLE

Like Margaret Thatcher, U.S. president Bill Clinton provides an example of a political leader who achieved success largely through the effectiveness of the stories he told. In Clinton's case, the stories he related had enormous resonance with his various audiences.

In a manner reminiscent of Franklin Roosevelt and Ronald Reagan, Clinton had a genius for understanding the minds of others. This stunning interpersonal intelligence dated back to his youth. Clinton sought obsessively to learn as much as he could about every individual whom he met and to put this knowledge to use at every opportunity. According to his long-time friend Taylor Branch, the key to Clinton's success lay in his ability to study the personalities of the people with whom he was dealing and to determine what it took to get along with them, where their weak spots were, who was lazy, who was committed. In Branch's words, "he was [Lyndon] Johnsonian in that sense—knowing how to read personalities."[12]

Moreover, Clinton's ability to read and relate to others was versatile. Unlike Lyndon Johnson, who was arresting in intimate settings but offputting in vast auditoriums, Clinton could both charm individuals one-on-one and speak persuasively to large, diverse audiences. As his biographer, Joe Klein, expresses it: "There was a physical, almost carnal quality to his public appearances. He embraced audiences and was aroused by them in turn. His sonar was remarkable in retail political situations. He seemed to sense what audiences needed and deliver to them—trimming his pitch here, emphasizing different priorities there, always aiming to please. This was one of his most effective, and maddening, qualities in private meetings as well: He always grabbed on to some point of agreement, while steering the conversation away from the larger points of disagreement—leaving his seducee with the distinct impression that they were in total harmony on just about everything." [13]

I believe that this impressive talent derived from two capacities that have rarely been so well combined. On the one hand, Clinton carried out *a priori* analyses about what was likely to persuade a particular person or audience—this is an area where Lyndon Johnson and Richard Nixon excelled. But Clinton also combined this analytic capacity with the ability to make small but consequential changes in light of the "real-time" reactions of his audience: a capacity we associate with performers who skillfully adjust their presentation depending on the idiosyncrasies of a particular audience at a particular moment in the day and a particular time in history. He combined the concepts discerned by interpersonal intelligence with the skills of the consummate actor.

And what of embodiment? On some criteria, Clinton lived up to the stories that he told; for example, he came from an unremarkable social and economic background, could identify with ordinary folks, and was comfortable with individuals of different racial and ethnic backgrounds. Yet, unlike Margaret Thatcher and other transformational leaders, Clinton seemed unable to "go to the mat" for issues in which he apparently believed. Indeed, many potentially sympathetic observers became frustrated with Clinton because he often appeared to have squandered his talents. He was a great storyteller, but it was never clear what story he really cared about and embodied. He might have changed the minds of Americans and others on consequential matters, but he too rarely took the risk to do so. Rather than mobilizing people's energies, he sought to win their affection. Defenders of Clinton would claim that his presidency was successful in the terms of the day and that the world was not looking for important "mind changing" during the "go-go" 1990s. More cynically, they might add that Clinton debacles such as the Monica Lewinsky affair demystified the American presidency—a change of mind about authority—and that this shift of view was overdue. [14]

It is instructive to compare Clinton's remarkable ability to change with that of another U.S. leader: Newt Gingrich. [15] Gingrich, who rose to become Speaker of the House after the 1994 election, was a shrewd politician as well as a master of history, current events, and invective. In leading his party to control of the House of Representatives for the first time in forty years, he brought about a political revolution that came to be named after him.

Moreover, these two self-styled politicians, who both arose from obscurity, shared a number of levers of mind changing. Both Clinton and Gingrich excelled at rational argument, coveted and marshaled data on behalf of their positions, were expert at using resources, and sought to take advantage of events in the real world. But Gingrich had three problems. First, while expert at speaking to and exciting the converted, he was not effective in persuading those who did not agree with him. Like Thatcher on her worst days, Gingrich stimulated opposition rather than neutralizing it, much less changing minds. (Democratic fund-raisers could always count on an influx of money after Gingrich uttered an especially offensive remark.) Second, Gingrich had the misfortune of opposing the most skilled politician of his generation, Bill Clinton. While both Clinton and Gingrich were divisive figures, Clinton was a genius at papering over differences of opinions—in our terms, reconciling stories that ordinarily clash. Gingrich, on the other hand, insisted on underscoring these differences and in alienating even some who might have been converted to his causes. In terms of the seven levers for changing minds, the stories he told did not resonate with many of the diverse groups that make up the U.S. political audience.

Finally, and fatally, Gingrich did not embody the story that he told about his own life. He called for term limits—but did not apply this metric to himself. He denounced big government—yet he had been on the government payroll for almost his entire adult life. And perhaps most embarrassingly, he embraced the conservative mantra of family values, yet twice he reportedly walked out on the woman to whom he was then married, both times in a graceless manner. Notoriously, he was found to have been having an affair with an aide during the very time that the Monica Lewinsky affair was roiling the Clinton presidency. Far from reinforcing the contents of his message (and the audience to which it was primarily directed), Gingrich succeeded all too well in undercutting the message because of his own misbehavior. Ultimately, all of these factors tipped the balance against Gingrich and any hope of his being able to change the minds of the American people. Interestingly, his far less vivid successor, George W. Bush, has had considerable success in promoting parts of the Gingrich agenda.

Whether Republicans or Democrats, Conservatives or Labourites, the leaders of nations face a formidable task. They must not only provide leadership and direction within their own camps or parties but also develop and "sell" a message to a decidedly mixed population. The citizens of a country as populous as Great Britain, or as vast as the United States, come from widely diverse backgrounds: rich and poor, of different ethnicities and skin colors, having varied educations and mis-educations, occupying the full gamut of ideological positions at work, at home, and in the community. One cannot assume any universal beliefs or attitudes. Even the presumptive common experiences of times past—say, knowledge of the Bible or Shakespeare, or membership in a common ethnic group—no longer obtain. The melting pot of America is more a memory than a current reality; and today Britain is filled with citizens from African, Eastern European, East and South Asian backgrounds, many of the Islamic faith. It can be said, with little exaggeration, that the major "common experiences" of inhabitants of such countries now are restricted to the television programs and movies that they see, and the athletic competitions that they witness—though their tastes in tubes and teams may well differ.

Short of walking nude through Trafalgar Square or streaking around the Washington Monument (or through Tiananmen Square, or downtown Bogotá, or Jerusalem for that matter), how can one gain and hold the attention of a large, diverse population?

THE CHALLENGE POSED BY DIVERSE POPULATIONS

I have suggested one way to capture the attention of a disparate population: by creating a compelling story, embodying that story in one's own life, and presenting the story in many different formats so that it can eventually topple the counterstories in one's culture. Yet, any old story will not do; it must exhibit certain characteristics.

As a general rule, when one is addressing a diverse or heterogeneous audience, the story must be simple, easy to identify with, emotionally resonant, and evocative of positive experiences. Just think about stories that do *not* exhibit these traits. If a story is too complex, it is likely to be above the heads of some audience members. When contrasted with a simpler story, therefore, complex stories almost always have trouble getting a hearing, let alone carrying the day. Weimar Germany may have been an estimable form of democracy in Western Europe in the late 1920s, but when conditions in Germany deteriorated, the simpler and baser stories of the Nazis prevailed, even in a reasonably legitimate election. On the other hand, if the story is simple but one cannot identify with it, it will also fall flat. For example, at a time when most working individuals are struggling to survive, the story of "trying to aid those who are unemployed"—while certainly simple—may be unable to attract a sympathetic constituency.

In addition to its conscious appeal, a story must also capture an audience at a deeper, more visceral level. Thatcher was able to tap her constituents' sense that their country's greatness had been marginalized; her leadership would help restore the country to the "major power" status of which its citizens could be proud. This kind of resonance works by intimation—rather like those "cool" television figures who are attractive and talk smoothly but who deliberately leave it up to the audience to fill in the details of the story.[16] Politicians who are "cool"—John F. Kennedy and Ronald Reagan being the prototypes in recent times—are more likely to exhibit staying power and persuade others to stay with them. These "cool" personalities encourage audience members to participate, to project onto them the qualities for which the viewers or listeners are looking. Such individuals are more successful than those sharply chiseled personalities, like Johnson, Nixon, and Gingrich, who were "hot": They attempted to say everything and left no role for the imaginative powers of the audience.

In this respect, Clinton constituted an interesting amalgam. By most measures Clinton was a "hot" personality—well-informed, well-defined, "all there," larger-than-life in a Johnsonian sense. (Think of President Lyndon Baines Johnson or Dr. Samuel Johnson.) Yet Clinton was able to present himself as a "cool" person, and his ability to alter his tone and message essentially at will meant that he was not easily pinned down or classified, and could re-create himself when needed. When it comes to political persuasion, then, "coolness" may be positive factor in the Television Age.

Challenging as it may be to lead the nation-state, however, particularly at a time when political parties have lost their coherence and common experiences are scant, it is even more difficult to provide leadership that extends beyond national boundaries and that presents a message of some complexity.

LEADING BEYOND THE NATION-STATE

Although relatively few positions exist for leaders of entities larger than a single nation, the topic is well worth exploring in any effort to understand how minds are changed. Sometimes, such a transnational position has a predetermined constituency; for example, the secretary-general of the United Nations or the head of the World Health Organization. The leader of the Catholic Church, or of other religious bodies, may well have influence that extends beyond a single land. And indeed, Pope John Paul II stands out among the popes of recent times because he has exerted influence not only over the members of his far-flung church but also, in some matters, over non-Catholics as well. Far more than his immediate predecessors, with the exception of John XXIII, John Paul II has been able both to fashion stories about political and personal values and to embody them in the impressive life that he has lived. Pope John XXIII, operating in the 1960s, was an avowedly simple pastor who called for a liberalization of the church and a decentralization of power; in partial reaction two decades later, John Paul II embraced the traditional conservative values of the church and located the reins of power squarely within the Vatican. At the same time, however, John Paul II is the most traveled and international of Popes, one who has forged a special tie with the young of different lands, and one who has been credited with an indispensable role in the collapse of Communism in Eastern Europe.

On rare occasions, individuals with neither vast armies nor vast congregations have succeeded in exerting influence well beyond national boundaries. Like the successful leaders of nations that we've already examined, they have done so because of the persuasiveness of their stories and the steadfastness with which they have reinforced those stories through their manner of living. In the twentieth century, three men stand out as examplars in this category: Mohandas (Mahatma) Gandhi, Nelson Mandela, and Jean Monnet.[17]

Perhaps the most well-known is Gandhi. Growing up in undistinguished surroundings in late-nineteenth-century colonial India, Gandhi spent time in England as a young man and then lived for twenty years in South Africa. There he was horrified by the mistreatment by European colonizers of Indians and other "colored persons"; he read widely in philosophy and religion; and he became involved in various protests. Returning to his native India at the start of the World War I, Gandhi perfected methods of satyagraha—peaceful (nonviolent) protest (or resistance). Alongside his devoted countrymen, Gandhi led a series of strikes and protest marches, destined to throw into sharp relief the differences between the brutal English masters—who sought to hold power at any cost—and the nonbelligerent Indians. These protests were choreographed to underscore the nobility of the native cause and the reasonableness with which Indians were striving to express their goals. Gandhi's overt message was: "We do not seek to make war or shed blood. We only want to be treated as fellow human beings. Once we have achieved the status of equals, we have no further claims."

In one sense, Gandhi's message could not have been simpler: It can be traced back to Christ and to other religious leaders. Yet, it also clashed with an entrenched counterstory: that one can only attain an equal status vis-à-vis one's colonizers if—like the United States in the late eighteenth century or South America in the early nineteenth century—one is willing to go to war. Moreover, Gandhi did not only have a simple linguistic message; he also developed an integrated program of prayer, fasting, and facing one's opponents without weapons, even willing to do so until death. His embodiment of the message could not have been more dramatic; it went well beyond verbal expression, to include a whole range of evocative formats, such as his squatting on the ground and operating a simple machine for spinning cloth.

Gandhi's story reverberated around the world. While annoying some (Churchill memorably disparaged him as that "half-naked fakir"), it inspired many leaders and ordinary citizens—ranging from Martin Luther King Jr. in the American South in the early 1960s, to the students who rallied for greater democracy in Tiananmen Square in Beijing in 1989.

Like Gandhi, Nelson Mandela embodied a message that resonated on a level far beyond the borders of his own South Africa. Indeed, of all the leaders in recent years, Mandela is widely considered one of the most impressive and influential. A lawyer by training, Mandela became actively involved in resistance as part of the African National Congress. At first, he embraced nonviolent resistance, but after a series of frustrating and degrading encounters, he joined a paramilitary group. Narrowly escaping death by combat or judicial sentence, Mandela was imprisoned for twenty-seven years. Although such an experience would likely have demoralized, radicalized, or marginalized most other persons—especially since it occurred at middle age, often considered the apogee of an individual's personal power—imprisonment seemed only to fortify Mandela. On his release, he rejected any effort to engage in armed conflict; instead he worked with his political opponent F. W. de Klerk to set up democratic institutions, and in 1994 he went on to win the presidency of a post-apartheid South Africa.[18]

Rather than seeking revenge against his opponents and jailers, Mandela called for reconciliation. He was convinced—and was able to convince others—that South Africa could not function as a society unless it could put its wrenching history behind it. Under the leadership of Nobel Peace Prize winner Archbishop Desmond Tutu, Mandela convened a Commission of Truth and Reconciliation. The Gandhian idea behind this commission was that it would seek to establish what actually happened during the years of apartheid but would not attempt to sit in ultimate judgment. The truth having been established as well as it could be, citizens of varying persuasions could come to terms with the past and commit their future energies to the buildup of a new and more fully representative society. A master of nonverbal as well as verbal forms, Mandela asked his one-time jailer to sit in the first row during his presidential inaugural ceremony.

Mandela succeeded in changing the minds not only of millions of his otherwise diverse fellow citizens but equally of millions of observers around the world—few of whom would have predicted that South Africa could become a new nation without decades of bloodshed. Ideas like the Commission on Truth and Reconciliation have traveled across national boundaries. The tipping points for Mandela's success entail both his exemplary behavior after his release from jail and the willingness of the entrenched South African leadership to negotiate with him—both examples reflecting Mandela's personal resonance, among other things.

A third figure of global importance worked largely behind the scenes: the French economist and diplomat Jean Monnet, born in 1888. When his comfortable life was shattered by the events of World War I, Monnet—a careful and reflective student of history—pondered why it was necessary for European countries to continue to go to war, as they had intermittently since the time of Charlemagne more than a thousand years before. He began to work toward the creation of institutions that could bring about a united Europe. After the trauma of World War I, the collapse of the League of Nations, the rise of fascism, and the unprecedented warfare of World War II, a lesser person would have concluded that attempts to build a European community were futile. Monnet, however, was a firm believer in his own oft-repeated slogan: "I regard every defeat (or every challenge) as an opportunity."[19] Amid the physical and psychological ruins of war-torn Europe, Monnet envisioned—and proceeded to sow—the seeds of a larger European polity.

Like Gandhi and Mandela, Monnet had been pursuing his mission for half a century and was well into his seventies by the time of his greatest impact. During the post–World War II period, he played a catalytic role in setting up a number of institutions, including the European Coal and Steel Community, the Action Committee of the United States of Europe, and the European common market. He was opposed nearly every step of the way, most notably by General Charles de Gaulle, the charismatic advocate of French autonomy, and by other nationalists of the Thatcher stripe. Yet while de Gaulle may have prevailed with the French electorate in the 1960s, Monnet's vision has ultimately triumphed on the Continent. After Monnet's death in 1979, the European Union was well launched, the euro was adopted in twelve countries, and, as of this writing, the United States of Europe are closer to a reality than at any time since the Napoleonic era.

Unlike a president, a pope, or the leader of an international organization such as the United Nations, neither Gandhi, nor Mandela, nor Monnet had a dedicated, guaranteed audience. They had to create their constituencies from scratch, with neither financial inducements nor coercive political weapons. They had to identify and speak to an opposition that held power: leaders of South Africa and colonial India, in Gandhi's case; the defenders of apartheid in Mandela's case; and the entrenched national interests of Europe in Monnet's case. At the same time they had to address and convince a lay constituency. Neither Gandhi nor Mandela could have led the fight for independence without an "army" of ordinary followers, who, in the extreme, were prepared to die nonviolently for their cause. And while Monnet worked significantly behind the scenes in the manner of what I term an "indirect" leader, (see chapter 6), his vision of Europe ultimately has had to triumph at the ballot box. Indeed, it has still not triumphed in nations such as Switzerland and Norway, which (surprisingly) remain outside of the Union.

As leaders addressing heterogeneous audiences, these men had available only the weapons of persuasion and embodiment. They had to tell their stories over and over again, tell them well, and embody their stories in appropriate life actions and evocative symbolic elements. They had to recognize, acknowledge, and ultimately undermine the regnant counterstories. And it is here that they showed their genius.

Hard as it is to mobilize a heterogeneous audience, the established way of doing so is to fashion and articulate a story that is serene in its simplicity. Indeed, the bitter lesson of the first half of the twentieth century is that the simplest and most awful stories generally triumph: The goal of politics is to attain power and to use it toward selfish ends; Might makes right; The state is all-powerful—one must do what it says or perish. These simple stories led to the triumph of terrifying "isms" of the left and the right: fascism, nazism, bolshevism, communism. One might even say that the hateful policies of Hitler, Mussolini, Tojo, Lenin, Stalin, and Mao Zedong convinced the majority of their countrymen; their popularity only waned when military defeat was imminent or starvation threatened. It appeared that in most of the world's nations, these "isms" were more appealing than democracy. Churchill well described this enigma in his oft-quoted comment that "democracy is the worst form of Government except for all those other forms that have been tried from time to time."[20]

Gandhi, Mandela, and Monnet did not, however, take the easy way out. They did not just tell a simple, familiar story more effectively. Rather, they took on a far more daunting task: to develop a new story, tell it well, embody it in their lives, and help others understand why it deserves to triumph over the simpler counterstory. Moreover, they drew continually and imaginatively on several other levers of mind change: reason, multiple modes of representation, and resonance with the experiences of those whom they sought to influence. At the same time, they attempted to mollify the resistances that they encountered; they took advantage of real world events; and they marshaled whatever resources they had at their disposal. On a personal note, these three men are my own chosen heroic leaders. They took a more complex, less familiar story, a story that was more "inclusive," and succeeded in giving that story life in institutions that continued beyond their own moments in the limelight.

CHAPTER 5

Leading an Institution: How to Deal with a Uniform Population

UNTIL NOW, we have examined mind changing on a grand scale. We have analyzed how extraordinary leaders such as Margaret Thatcher and Mahatma Gandhi attempt to change the minds of individuals—citizens of a nation or community—who differ significantly from one another in background knowledge or attitude. But what of leaders charged with changing the minds of smaller, less diverse groups—such as a university, corporation, or club—whose members have many things in common?

In some respects, the task faced by a corporate executive or a college president is analogous to the challenge faced by a national leader like Tony Blair or George W. Bush. In each case, the leader—together with close advisers—must analyze the current situation, determine what needs to change, and envision an altered state of affairs. Then the leader must create a convincing narrative (such as the story that Margaret Thatcher communicated to the British people) and present it to those whose minds she hopes to change. As we saw in the last chapter, success will depend on various factors, among them the effectiveness of the narrative, the variety of ways in which it is convincingly conveyed, and the extent to which the leader and those around her actually embody the narrative that has been presented.

Yet there are crucial differences in the nature and scope of the task faced by the leader of an organization compared with that of the leader of a polity. One is sheer size. With rare exceptions (such as the Catholic Church, Wal-Mart, or the Chinese army), corporations, universities, foundations, and nongovernmental organizations are relatively small. Their audience consists of dozens or hundreds of people, or perhaps even tens of thousands, but rarely more. The individuals with whom they work are generally employees or members of the organization, and they define themselves that way; their participation is in part voluntary (no one has to attend a university, for example) but it is also temporary (one might choose or be asked to leave the company). Most revealingly, it can be assumed that the members of such an organization have a common knowledge core, a common purpose, perhaps even a common destiny—after all, if a corporation fails, none of its employees has a livelihood.

Although members of such organizations do not necessarily have a particular expertise in common (even where expertise is abundant, it may not be in the same topic), one can reasonably expect that their minds have been schooled in the core philosophy, knowledge, and culture of their particular group. A leader of a relatively uniform group, therefore, can present a story of somewhat greater complexity—perhaps even a "theory" of operations—than can the leader of a nation or one who leads across national boundaries.

Let me be clear about this. It is *never* easy to bring about a change of mind; and it is even more difficult to replace a simple way of thinking about a matter with a more complex way. Gresham's law can be formulated with respect to entities of any size: Simpler mind changes tend to trump more complex ones.[1] But I seek to make a different point. More complex stories and theories have a better chance of success when the entity in which one is working is of limited size and composed of individuals of similar background and with common expertise. Other factors being equal, it is easier to change the minds of the senior management of IBM than the citizenry of Great Britain (or the United States). But in no case is such mind changing a simple matter—as we will see in our first example of a college president who tried to shift the perspective of a group of students, faculty, and alumni and who, in so doing, engaged to one degree or another the gamut of levers for changing minds.

JAMES O. FREEDMAN:
CHANGING THE MIND OF A UNIVERSITY

The trustees of Dartmouth College took a calculated risk when they brought on James O. Freedman as president in 1987.[2] Although his intellectual, professional, and administrative credentials were sterling (a graduate of Harvard College and Yale Law School, Freedman most recently had been the well-respected president of the University of Iowa), Freedman wouldn't be easily accepted by Dartmouth students—and the trustees knew it. Of all the Ivy League institutions, Dartmouth was surrounded by the most social lore—legendary football teams, over-the-top parties, a moneyed elite epitomized by its famous graduate Nelson Rockefeller. In the early 1980s, however, it was not known for its intellectual strengths or its scholarly leadership.

Dartmouth had been in the news of late, chiefly because of its notorious student publication, the *Dartmouth Review*. An unabashedly right-wing publication, the *Review* saw its mission both to advance conservative views and to ensure that Dartmouth remained a bastion of male social and economic values reminiscent of the 1920s, if not the 1820s. Freedman's predecessor, David McLaughlin, had failed to confront the *Review*'s increasingly outrageous behavior, while letting Dartmouth slide in the comparative rankings of universities nationwide. Clearly, had the trustees simply wanted business as usual, they never would have chosen as the new head an intellectual who was also Jewish (an anomaly at Dartmouth). Freedman wasn't afraid to speak on behalf of unflinching academic standards. Moreover, as the *Review* repeatedly pointed out, Freedman was the first president since 1822 who had no prior history with the New Hampshire institution. The question was clear: Could Freedman turn Dartmouth around, or would he be fodder for "Animal House" alumni, for whom a winning football team was the most important consideration—and for their current representatives, the irreverent staff of the *Review*?

Though from the outside, it may seem that the president of a university has significant power and prestige, most individuals familiar with U.S. higher education can readily refute this picture. The cognoscenti are likely to invoke the oft-repeated quip, "The president is a person who lives in a large house and begs for money." To begin with, the ranks of the faculty are loaded with tenured individuals who have scant incentive to change their attitudes or behaviors. Students are on campus for a brief four years, and the intellectual values of the institution are unlikely to be uppermost in their minds. Alumni are mired in the past, and, particularly at a storied place like Dartmouth, their memories are likely to be tinted (or tainted) by nostalgia and anachronistic sentiments. And trustees, although they hold the fate of the university in their hands, are busy individuals with scant time to spend at the university; often they must (or choose to) rely on others for information. Above all, most trustees hope to avoid trouble—for instance, unwanted headlines in the national press—during their term of office.

Yet despite the various resistances Freedman faced from all corners, he is widely credited for having turned the institution around during his eleven-year tenure. I spoke at length with Freedman, a friend of mine, about how he managed to make the changes he did.[3] He told me that when he first came to Dartmouth, he saw his mission as clear: to improve the intellectual quality of the student body, the faculty, and the discourse at the university. He proposed to do this by attempting to attract intellectually powerful students—the kind who would enjoy translating Catullus from the Latin or playing the cello, as he phrased it during his installation ceremony. In another widely quoted remark, he said that while he had nothing against well-roundedness per se, Dartmouth needed students who had "sharp edges" as well.

As for the *Review*, Freedman told me he would have been ecstatic had it mysteriously disappeared. But he believed that this provocateur (heavily underwritten by the conservative Olin Foundation, and supported both financially and intellectually by senior figures from the equally conservative *National Review*) would be dogging him every step of the way and might even try to get him removed from office. In this expectation, he was not disappointed. Indeed, the *Review* even printed out a spoof issue in which the trustees had forced Freedman's resignation, and this spoof was believed by some on campus.

To make the changes he hoped for, Freedman told me, he needed to reach at least two of three main constituencies: faculty, students, and alumni. (He had to deal with one additional constituency—the university trustees—but, happily, they supported him both politically and psychologically from the get-go.) Freedman perceived early on that the faculty was largely on his side. As a group, the faculty liked him, supported his promotion of academic standards, and wanted to improve the quantity of strong students and the quality of all students. Freedman created various awards to recognize outstanding faculty, consulted with them about how to attract intellectually able new faculty, and involved them in decisions ranging from admissions to tenure. He also emphasized the importance of research for faculty both in the college and in the various professional schools. And although Freedman sometimes had strong disagreements with faculty members—and he didn't always prevail—he never came close to an open split with the faculty.

This left the students and the alumni. Here Freedman's task was much more challenging. It was difficult to talk about improving the quality of the student body without, at least implicitly, criticizing current cohorts. And many alumni—rather than caring about higher SAT scores in the incoming class or the quality of offerings in classical music or classical languages—were much more concerned about a football team that was excellent and a campus where they felt at home. Indeed, to the extent that the student body improved in intellectual quality, it suggested to the alumni that they themselves might not gain admission today; and it reduced the probability that their own offspring could attend the Dartmouth that they knew and loved.

In his attempts to win over these various constituencies, Freedman began by talking often and at length about what mattered to him. Indeed, Sean Gorman, longtime associate counsel at Dartmouth, explained that "Jim Freedman changed Dartmouth by his rhetoric."[4] (In our terms, we could cite reason and research that resonated with large segments of the community.) Whenever he had the chance, Freedman would talk about the importance of excellent ideas, the power of intellectual discourse, the contributions to society made by individuals who valued the life of the mind. His opening-year speeches eulogized personal heroes—his own mentor Associate Supreme Court Justice Marshall, social activist Dorothy Day, novelist Eudora Welty. He spoke about these issues on campus, at alumni events, to local and to national audiences, driving home the same points again and again. Moreover, believing (correctly, it turned out) that being seen nationally as an intellectual leader would ultimately impress *all* his constituencies, he cultivated relationships with the press.

But of course rhetoric alone—even the best of stories—cannot bring about change. Fortunately, Freedman recognized the importance of embodying his rhetoric in relevant actions. Taking a cue from Martin Meyerson, another role model of Freedman's who had himself been president of a university (University of Pennsylvania), Freedman introduced a program of presidential scholars—promising students who were given the opportunity to work intensively with faculty and whose names would be listed in the graduation program along with winners of traditional prizes. He chose a faculty member each year to give a presidential lecture, and treated what could have been an academic exercise as a major campus event. To set examples of scholarship and of participation in public debate, Freedman published a book *Idealism and Liberal Education*.[5] He also enlarged the admissions office and made special overtures to promising students at hundreds of high schools nationwide, including many schools that had never before sent students to Dartmouth. And he called attention repeatedly to those members of the Dartmouth community who made intellectual achievements; in fact, he created an office that helped students to compete for prestigious national and international fellowships.

Still, there remained the annoying presence of the *Dartmouth Review.* Indeed, the *Review* was more than annoying; it was outrageous. It attacked Freedman regularly, at one time claiming that he never went to religious services himself, at another time comparing this Jew from New Hampshire to Hitler. In seeming collusion with the editorial page of the *Wall Street Journal,* it portrayed him as an autocratic leader, imposing change in the manner of a totalitarian like Montgomery, Alabama, police chief Bull Connor during the civil rights era. Not content to engage in anti-Semitic palaver, it also brutishly criticized an African American tenured professor, Bill Cole, who taught in the music department. The attacks on Cole eventually forced him to resign. The *Review* also lampooned Freedman's wife, Sheba, a member of the psychology department. And they created absurd rumors, such as the claim that the Freedmans no longer lived in the official mansion because it was "not good enough" for them.

In truth, there was relatively little support for the *Dartmouth Review* among the students, and virtually none among the faculty. Still it was difficult to attack such a student organ without appearing to be a bully, and so the Freedmans and other victims were left to fend for themselves. Freedman said that he was repeatedly advised to ignore the *Review* or to treat it with humor, but he ultimately found it too painful to follow this advice. As he told me, "I was the President of the University of Iowa for five years and never once thought about being a Jew. At Dartmouth I thought every day about being Jewish." In 1988, the *Review*'s scattershot bashing of Jews, women, blacks, liberals, and intellectual life went so far that Freedman felt he had to take action. Following the example of Joseph Welch, the Boston lawyer who had finally challenged Senator Joseph McCarthy directly during the 1954 Senate hearings on the army, Freedman decided to denounce the *Review* at a meeting of the Dartmouth faculty—and he made sure that the press received copies of the speech as well. The affair at Dartmouth—at one time largely a local brouhaha—now became a national issue; the *New York Times*, *Wall Street Journal*, and CBS television's *Sixty Minutes* all reported on the *Review*'s activities and its extensive external support network. And while there was never an apology or an overt retreat by the *Review*, the tide had turned, finally knocking the publication down several pegs. Freedman was now much freer to follow the agenda for which he had been brought to Hanover, New Hampshire.

In the end, it is widely agreed that Freedman accomplished his goals. As the mean SAT scores of incoming students rose, Dartmouth's place in the college rankings of *U.S. News & World Report* went steadily upward. A larger number of students won Rhodes, Marshall, Truman, and Fulbright Fellowships and other vaunted honors. As for faculty, professors reported that they enjoyed their teaching more because the quality of students and class participation had markedly improved. Dartmouth had become a more serious and more impressive university. Alumni were pleased at these changes, the football team continued to win, and everyone connected with the university liked seeing their president and other members of the student and faculty quoted frequently and favorably in the press. And although the *Dartmouth Review* remained, it lost its luster, making the university a more attractive environment for clubs and publications that represented a range of viewpoints.

Words, well embodied in actions, had changed minds. The campus tipped in favor of the president and against the *Review*. Just how the tipping point was reached and what ensued, however, is more speculative. One could take the position that the *Review* engaged in increasingly provocative behavior—such as attacking faculty members Bill Cole and Sheba Freedman—and thus caused its own self-destruction. But it seems more likely to me that it was the president who—with a fine sense of timing—used these events to help tip the balance on campus. Indeed, it is the rare leader who can orchestrate the occurrence or course of real events in the world—but one can certainly take advantage of those events for one's own purposes. Which leads us to the question of which factors can alter the landscape of an institution in favor of change.

STEPS TO CHANGING MINDS

In recounting James Freedman's story, I have already implicitly described several of the seven key levers for changing minds—the seven *Rs* that I outlined in chapter 1. Let us now look at each of these in turn, beginning with the four factors that I believe contributed most to Freedman's success: the way he was able to learn from and emulate other people's examples ("research"); his direct challenge of constituencies that took an anti-intellectual stance ("resistances"); his initiation of new practices at the university to reinforce his call for higher standards ("resources and rewards"); and the way he presented his message in many different forms, thereby reaching the widest range of people ("representational redescription").

Research

Part of Freedman's challenge was to convey to the relatively homogeneous Dartmouth family the importance and desirability of first-rate scholarship. As a first step, then, he took a cue from Martin Meyerson, who had raised standards at the University of Pennsylvania by conferring the prestige of the presidency on scholars and scholarly activity. Freedman launched several initiatives along these lines soon after his arrival. He also observed how his presidential predecessor at Dartmouth had lost favor with the faculty—indeed suffering the obloquy of a vote of "no confidence"—and he determined that he was not going to make the same mistake himself. Learning from others' examples in this way was not unlike what we saw in the case of two successful national leaders in the 1980s—Margaret Thatcher and Ronald Reagan. Across the span of the Atlantic, each observed and emulated the other when it came to policy decisions and the personas they presented as world leaders.

Resistances

A second step to changing minds is to challenge directly the prevailing resistances—the ideas that are stale, erroneous, or harmful. Former U.S. President Bill Clinton took just such measures when he sought not to "end" welfare but to "mend" it. Countering the view on the right that all welfare payments should cease, and the mirror view on the left that any tampering with welfare was immoral and dangerous, Clinton forged a new consensus that recognized the need for welfare under certain circumstances but emphasized a return to work as soon as possible.

Similarly, Freedman faced considerable resistances when he was chosen as Dartmouth's president. In fact, the trustees had picked him specifically because the college needed change: when they had polled leaders in U.S. education, the trustees made the disturbing discovery that many leaders had little or no opinion of Dartmouth. To put it crudely, Dartmouth was off their radar screen. The trustees' supposition that the school was first-rate, in the same category as Brown or Amherst, was shaken; they decided then and there to choose a leader with instant academic credibility: James O. Freedman.

Even so, when Freedman came on board he did not want to make the rest of his school feel inadequate: this too-frequently-employed leadership tactic almost always backfires. So rather than directly challenge the quality of students and faculty, he dealt with resistance by instituting procedures designed to raise the standards of admission and tenure. Regarding his most vocal opposition, the *Dartmouth Review,* his preferred strategy initially was to ignore it, even when it attacked him directly. When the *Review* began to ridicule an African American music professor as well as Freedman's own wife, however, Freedman felt compelled to take on the publication publicly. His chastisement of the *Review* debunked both the conceit that the publication had appreciable support among the students as well as the idea that it was simply an irreverent, innocuous undergraduate broadside.

Resources and Rewards

A third step to changing minds is to use the resources a leader has available, such as an appropriate reward system, to initiate new policies and practices. When inaugurated as president of Dartmouth, Freedman poked gentle fun at the idea of "well-roundedness" and spoke about the desirability of having more students with sharp edges. But to effect this change would not be a simple matter. Alumni and admissions officers had an idealized view of the Dartmouth undergraduate: he (more recently, he or she) was someone who was a reasonably good student, socially adept, with a penchant for athletics. By and large the students were not wonks; they did not have strong passions about a discipline, nor did they excel in the arts or in community service. Freedman encouraged the admission of more students on the basis of their intellectual strengths or their particular talents or passions. He added staff who could reach out to secondary schools that had not sent students to Dartmouth. And he made sure that when a student or a faculty member made an intellectual advance, there was a sufficient reward, including abundant publicity.

Similarly, we saw in the last chapter how, during her election campaign, Margaret Thatcher advanced new national policies such as privatizing major industries and societal functions and reducing the preponderance of unions. These steps, she assured the British people, would result in ample rewards: renewed British entrepreneurship, a country that would once again reign as a major world power, more money in the pockets of the average citizen, and more personal control over how that money would be spent.

Representational Redescription

Any kind of change is likely to initiate some resistance, perhaps justified. In bringing about a shift at Dartmouth, therefore, Freedman took a fourth major step by describing his vision in a variety of ways and providing nonthreatening opportunities for people to "try on" his new vision for the school. Such a strategy takes direct advantage of the notion of multiple intelligences: Individuals learn most effectively when they can receive the same message in a number of different ways, each re-presentation stimulating a different intelligence.

What are some of the options? A leader can create a narrative that tells a compelling story about a new vision for change. Freedman put forth such a narrative in his speeches and news releases: a new intellectually rich and diverse Dartmouth that held students and faculty to higher standards and yielded a school that was widely admired. Leaders can also put forth a logical argument—a reasoned brief in which they present the conditions that existed before, show how each has been undermined by recent developments, and lay out various alternatives. This is what Jean Monnet did with exemplary patience over the decades in order to undermine the view of Europe as a collection of naturally warring nations and to build support for a consolidated union. Such an approach—drawing on logical intelligence—need not always be put forth in language, of course. For some, numbers tell the story; others are more impressed by graphs, tables, or equations.

Another way that leaders can present their case is by appealing to deep questions about life, experience, and possibility. Clearly, this was one way that Freedman changed minds at Dartmouth: He developed intellectually rich standards that reflected the most important thinking of the past and challenged his constituents to meet those standards. In addition, leaders can present their vision through a work of art or otherwise call attention to the aesthetic aspects of the change they propose. Ronald Reagan was a master at invoking imagery from the movies—the heroic roles played by Gary Cooper, John Wayne, and Clint Eastwood, for example—to embody his points. Leaders also can convince people to adopt change by involving them "hands-on" in the new vision. For example, while protesting a salt tax, Gandhi marched toward the sea alongside ordinary Indian citizens, and the ensemble all placed salt in their mouths. Finally, a leader can deal directly with the personal intelligences, encouraging constituents to work together to figure how best to implement the desired changes. Clinton made effective use of town meetings to elicit the views of citizens and make them feel part of the decision-making process.

Let me express this point in cognitive language. New ideas do not travel easily, and it is hard for them to take hold. Because we cannot know in advance which formats will prove effective in communicating a new message, we are well advised to use several alternative formats. Nor can we know for sure how such external formats can end up as internal mental representations. We need to monitor the words and actions of a leader's constituents to glean how ideas have been translated and internalized; and we must be prepared to carry out repeated "surgery" on our and others' mental representations until we "get it right"—or at least until the next change in context challenges current representations and calls for yet another take on the situation at hand.

Whether one is dealing with a diverse audience at a national level or a more uniform one such as that at Dartmouth College, the most important point is obvious yet often underplayed: the amount of time that one is willing to spend in conveying the message, the story, the theory. We all cherish shortcuts to conveying new ideas, having them understood forthwith, changing minds dramatically and decisively; and yet it is not possible, in most cases, to accomplish transmission and acceptance in short order. And although tipping points sometimes occur quickly, in most cases it takes much time, much practice, and considerable backsliding before a genuine tipping point has been negotiated. The clash with the *Dartmouth Review* serves as a convenient emblem, but the actual change of Dartmouth's vision of itself, and the views held by the informed observers, takes many years. Indeed, in the end, it is up to informed observers to judge whether Dartmouth is truly a more intellectual and more diverse community.

In addition to the four main steps I have just outlined, President Freedman also used, to one degree or another, the remaining three of our seven levers when he was changing minds at Dartmouth.

Reason

As a trained lawyer, Freedman's ability to mouth a convincing case— weighing the pros and cons—proved crucial in his efforts to change the minds of alumni and students. Moreover, Freedman did not hesitate to cultivate services in the media to help make the case publicly. There is little question that legal training also helped Margaret Thatcher and Bill Clinton to develop the strongest cases for their preferred courses of action.

Resonance

As we saw in chapter 4, the changes that Margaret Thatcher was proposing to the British people would not have held much sway had her rhetoric not resonated, on the one hand, with the kind of life Thatcher herself had led and the background from which she came and, on the other, with the way that many British citizens saw themselves. Similarly, Freedman made sure that his actions reflected his convictions: He embodied his narrative with concrete plans, such as encouraging intellectual diversity by extending the college's outreach to admit students from schools that had never sent people to Dartmouth before. The particular examples that he used—American icons like Thurgood Marshall and Eudora Welty—stirred the consciences of his audience and catalyzed them to identify with the policies that he sought to implement.

Real World Events

When the *Review* crossed a final line by attacking Freedman's wife, Sheba, as well as Bill Cole, an African American professor, the president used those events as an opportunity to denounce the publication in no uncertain terms. That denunciation, combined with exposure by national media of the *Review*'s escapades and funding sources, led to considerable loss of power and influence for the publication.

As I have said, the overall narrative—the story of change—that Freedman so carefully conveyed at Dartmouth eventually succeeded in bringing about the shift he envisioned for the school. Our popular magazines and books are filled with claims about business leaders who brought about seismic changes in their companies, particularly during the "go-go" 1990s. But what about when a story fails to change minds? Let us now look at what happened, and why, in the case of two leaders of corporate America.

WHEN STORIES FAIL

For most of the 1990s, John Chambers of Cisco Corporation was the golden boy of American business. He seemed to have discovered or perfected a new approach to business. Rather than being content to serve as a leading supplier of routers and switches for the Internet, Chambers was determined that Cisco would participate in the full range of Internet materials and services, becoming a player in the vast amalgam of computing, telecommunications, and news and entertainment that promised to change the landscape of the informational world. Chambers's strategy? To acquire numerous small start-ups, give their owners shares in Cisco, allow the start-ups to develop their products to market scale, and quickly integrate the start-ups' culture into the overall ethos of Cisco.

For a while Cisco's strategy was wildly successful. Between 1993 and 2001, the company acquired and integrated into its fabric seventy-three new companies. Adapting a style that contrasted sharply with that of Microsoft, Cisco resisted hostile and competitive takeovers in favor of friendly and comfortable ones. As a result, in an industry with 20 percent turnover each year, Cisco had an admirable retention rate of well over 90 percent. The story that Chambers and his associates conveyed during the 1990s was clear. As he told a reporter: "The Internet will change our lives in ways that people are just beginning to grasp. We are at the heart of that. . . . We will change the world. And we're going to do it in ways that other people have never thought [of]. We are inventing so many business principles."[6] On another occasion he declared, "This is truly the second industrial revolution and it will change every aspect of people's lives."[7] For a while this story seemed true; indeed at one Camelot-like moment, Cisco was the highest-valued company in the world.

But then came the year 2000 and a rapid reversal of fortune in Silicon Valley, presaging a more general decline in the U.S. economy. The dot-com phenomenon came to an abrupt end, and even larger and more established companies had to retrench. (Johnson & Johnson had been the 114th best-performing company in 2000; in 2001, it was number 1.)[8] Cisco's estimates of continued growth of 30 percent to 50 percent per year were widely off the mark, and, for the first time, Cisco had to lay off a significant number of workers (17 percent of its workforce in the spring of 2001). Cisco's high capitalization abruptly dropped by 80 percent. And it appeared that part of Cisco's high value was due to what the financial publication *Barron's* dubbed its "New Economy Creative Accounting"— for example, using stock options both to pay employees and to purchase other companies.[9]

Chambers could no longer simply be the prophet of endless growth. He had to change his story. As he commented somewhat ruefully, "It is also now clear to us that the peaks in the new economy will be much higher and the valleys much lower, and the movement between peaks and valleys will be much faster. We are now in a valley much deeper than any of us anticipated . . . in fact we are victims of a natural disaster, equivalent [to] once a century floods"[10] He embraced another metaphor: "This is a race being run at a tremendous speed, one that has been modulated by applying more or less pressure to the gas pedal rather than by applying the brakes."[11] And again: "Anybody who has ever raced, you go around that turn at 200 miles per hour and they turn on you, I don't care how good a driver you are, . . . you weren't expecting that."[12]

For the most part, the usually garrulous Chambers remained silent, avoiding public pronouncements. But once it looked like Cisco had weathered the flood (or effected the far turn on the racetrack), he once more embraced an optimistic tone. In 2002, when Cisco still hadn't seen a change in revenue (though it had gained market share), Chambers said: "For the elements we can control, we are doing extremely well."[13] He found a way to put a positive spin on the events of the past two years: "The way to judge whether companies become great companies is how they handle their successes and how they handle the setbacks. In going through the data with my leadership team and reflecting on how we've done versus our peers, the results of the last year really stood out. . . . This is probably the most fundamental breakaway that has ever occurred across any major industry in one year. We're proud of what we've accomplished this year."[14]

While Chambers may well have believed the story that he had told in the 1990s, it seems clear in retrospect that the story was built at least in part on a hyperbolic narrative that could not be sustained. As one unrelenting critic put it at the time: "I think it's a bunch of crap. He goes out and talks in broad terms about how we will all work and play but there aren't a lot of specifics. He does it very convincingly and he gets people to buy into it. But it's totally self-serving. His pitch to corporate America is basically that yesterday's stuff is obsolete.... [Cisco] obsoletes its products fairly rapidly to get whomever he's talking to into this buying cycle. He tells [companies] that your competition will do more than you do and you can't afford to wait. That's a scare tactic. That's his pitch."[15] Chambers knew enough to remain silent during the worst months for his company, when layoffs were the order of the day. But this inveterate storyteller soon found a way to integrate the disappointing events of recent years into a once-more-upbeat narrative.

In terms of the seven levers for changing minds, it could be maintained that Cisco was merely affected by *real world events*—namely, the collapse of the dot-coms. Yet the hyperbole that Chambers relied on rhetorically also contributed to the failure of his "story" of change. He did not pay enough attention to long-term *research* about business cycles (particularly with respect to the speed with which a boom could turn into a bust), and he also ignored the early signs that his customers could not afford the new services that Cisco rolled out. Moreover, Chambers chronically underestimated the *resistances* he faced: He did not appreciate the place and strength of traditional companies and ways of doing business, nor the risks of creative accounting practices, nor the fact that many of the Internet companies on which Cisco depended would not survive the burst of the Silicon Valley bubble.

Another example of a promising story that did not pan out features Robert Shapiro, who became Monsanto's CEO after heading its Nutrasweet division. An enthusiast for genetically modified foods, which he believed could alleviate famine and malnutrition worldwide, he soon became the major international spokesperson for a new biotechnology era in food.[16]

Described as the "Johnny Appleseed" of genetic modification, Shapiro spoke of Monsanto—a life sciences company—as reconfiguring the gap from "dirt to dinner plate," and he described the company as "an institution that's fundamentally based on knowledge and science."[17] Armed with vivid examples and attractive promises, Shapiro crisscrossed the globe with the arresting "mental representation" he'd created—and for a while it took. Shapiro won the backing of many individuals in the company and was hailed by the press as a harbinger of a new age.

But Shapiro was unprepared for the resistance that his "story" would ultimately encounter. He did not fully appreciate the regnant "counterstory": that many individuals both in the United States and abroad felt deeply attached to the "laws of nature" and would permit only very gradual changes in foodstuff. Shapiro relied far too much on the logic of his argument and on the findings of lab science. He did not speak to the concerns of ordinary individuals—and, for that matter, Britain's Prince Charles—who feared possible negative consequences of this unprecedented "experiment with nature" and who believed that genetic modifications needed to be discussed at length in public forums. Increasingly, Shapiro found himself preaching to the converted; and as the espoused leader in this field, Monsanto became the chief target of protesters and other unhappy citizens. The tipping point never happened—perhaps because Shapiro didn't appreciate that it *needed* to happen.

Eventually, the resistance was such that Shapiro had to promise not to make use of the "terminator technology" that produces sterile seeds: at a Greenpeace conference, he apologized for his insensitivity to environmental concerns. He acknowledged that the public wanted to argue about social values and not soybean statistics. As he told his own stockholders: "We have probably irritated and antagonized more people than we have persuaded. . . . Our confidence in technology and our enthusiasm for it has, I think, been widely seen—and understandably so—as condescension or indeed arrogance."[18] Soon after, Monsanto merged with Pharmacia, and Shapiro ultimately left the company. At least in the short run, the counterstory—the competing mental representation—was triumphant.

We might contend that, like Chambers at Cisco, Shapiro was torpedoed by real world events: the rise of anti–genetic modification sentiments in many parts of the world. However, I think that account is simplistic. Both men were guilty of hyperbole—of putting forth a story that was not supported by the current facts. They may have been carried away by their own rhetoric and by the degree to which their story resonated with their own personal aspirations and those of their chosen inner circle. And, like Chambers, Shapiro seriously underestimated the degree of resistance to the stories that he told: He did not appreciate the extent to which ordinary citizens were made nervous by attempts to experiment aggressively with nature. His story may have been buttressed by reason and research, but it failed to resonate with powerful audiences. Perhaps because they had a change of heart, perhaps because they thought it was politic to do so, each man ultimately altered the story that he told. But by that point, it may have been too late.

HALLMARKS OF THE EFFECTIVE LEADER: INTELLIGENCES, INSTINCT, AND INTEGRITY

In this and the previous chapter, I have described a variety of leaders who have attempted—with varying degrees of success—to bring about changes in entities ranging from a single college or corporation to large regions of the world. As I have considered these and other leaders, I have become intrigued with the personal resources on which they draw—intellectual, instinctual, and moral.

Intelligences

Let me begin with intellectual resources. Leaders generally stand out in terms of three intelligences. First, as storytellers, leaders must be gifted linguistically. Even in an age suffused with multimedia presentations, linguistic symbol systems retain special power. Leaders must therefore know how to create a story, how to communicate it effectively, and how to alter it if changes prove warranted. Second, leaders require interpersonal intelligence. They need to understand other people, be able to motivate them, listen to them, and respond to their needs and aspirations. Third, leaders require a considerable measure of what I call existential intelligence: They need to be comfortable with posing fundamental questions. This kind of intelligence is what President George Bush Sr. mistakenly dismissed as "the vision thing." To the contrary, leaders should not be reluctant to share their visions, putting forth their own answers to fundamental questions about life, death, the meaning of the past, the prospects of the future. As we have already seen in examples such as Thatcher's and Freedman's, such "stories" work best when they are embodied, reflecting the authentic conditions and experiences of the storyteller.[19]

Other intelligences will doubtless benefit the leader, in light of the particular kind of mission or organization. Certainly, one should not attempt to lead any kind of large business enterprise without considerable logical-mathematical intelligence. On the other hand, charismatic leadership in the political or entertainment realm does not require much logical-mathematical intelligence. Leaders also benefit from intrapersonal intelligence—a good working knowledge of oneself. And yet, one can certainly be an effective leader—consider Ronald Reagan or Margaret Thatcher—without displaying much interest in or expertise about the rumblings of one's own psyche.

The individual profiles of intelligences will differ across leaders—that is to be expected. Indeed, it is often productive when a new leader displays a spectrum of intelligences that differs from her predecessors: Ruts are likely to be avoided, new paths opened. Leaders often say (and sometimes even *mean*) that they like to hire people who are smarter than they are. They might better say that they like to hire people whose intelligences complement their own. Most important, leaders must be able to think and act "with intelligence." By that I mean that they set forth a clear-cut set of goals and values and can act consistently and transparently in terms of these goals and values.

Individuals who work best with diverse audiences have knowledge of, and can speak to, the "unschooled mind" and thus avoid alienating at least part of the collectivity very quickly. When it comes to dealing with more uniform audiences such as a university or corporation, on the other hand, the individual who knows that audience well is at a distinct advantage. The leader can draw on shared experiences, images, and "institutional culture" in creating a convincing narrative.

Never has it been more desirable to have leaders who can address both heterogeneous and homogeneous groups. On the one hand, most group members have less and less common in their backgrounds, and so heterogeneity is becoming the rule. On the other hand, knowledge of technical matters grows ever more important, and this variety of knowledge entails the sophistication that we associate with homogeneous entities. Even those who could not abide President Clinton—or his wife Hillary—acknowledged the Clintons' genius in addressing both the schooled and the unschooled mind. The Clintons could shift almost effortlessly from a broad television audience to a group of experts in economics or health care and back again. Even more impressively, they could signal to each audience that they were capable of the *other* kind of communication as well: hinting to the unschooled that they were knowledgeable, revealing to the cognoscenti that they were also capable of communicating effectively with a demotic audience. Margaret Thatcher and Tony Blair also possessed this combination of capacities—in contrast to Ronald Reagan and George W. Bush, who are seen as having the popular touch without the sophisticated expertise. Monsanto's Robert Shapiro, on the other hand, fared better with a homogeneous elite than with variegated audiences.

Instinct

The second important personal resource that leaders need is a well-honed instinct. Indeed, it's often said that great leaders operate on the basis of "gut instinct"—a feeling for the right move in a particular situation. There is, alas, no way to program your instincts. Still, my guess is that gut feelings do not arise fully formed, like Athena from the head of Zeus. More likely, they represent a partially conscious but difficult-to-articulate recognition of the resemblance of a present situation to earlier ones, where one course of action proved far superior to its rivals.

How to arouse and jostle one's gut feelings? Leaders find it helpful to put their intuitions into words, to try them out on trusted associates and seek their candid reactions. Taking a cue from former Secretary of the Treasury Robert Rubin, leaders should acknowledge that sometimes a decision, whether based primarily on the head or on the gut, will be wrong. Rather than engaging in extensive Monday-morning quarter-backing (we should have done *A* rather than *Z*), those charged with learning from mistakes should spend more time analyzing the *processes* that went into decision making—where they were appropriate, where they fell short. Nor should one condemn failure in absolute terms: re-calling the powerful concept—or mental representation—of world economist Jean Monnet, crises create opportunities.

Integrity

Finally, in addition to intelligence and instinct, impressive leaders have integrity. They take time for daily analysis and reflection, as well as occasional periods of deeper analysis, when one "goes to the mountaintop."

And they are marked by an openness to changes in the world and in oneself; sensitivity to the valid strains in both stories and counterstories; flexibility in the presentation of one's fundamental themes; and a sense of deep commitment to a mission coupled with humility about one's actual potency.[20] Some would call these features the prerequisites to wisdom.

As anyone who has ever heard a graduation speech can attest, certain themes endure: the importance of hard work, of loyalty, of a sense of responsibility. Other stories will resonate powerfully in a given cultural or historical era; for example, "Engine" Charlie Wilson's statement "What is good for General Motors is good for the country" or General Electric's "Progress is our most important product" (memorably articulated by then television pitchman Ronald Reagan) fit in comfortably with the prevailing ethos of the 1950s.

For a new era, different themes are desired, and leaders need to be able to affect the minds of those who have been reared on the old stories. Decades ago, the successful ad campaign of IBM told us to "Think"; its successor in computing, Apple, asked us to "Think Different" (an imaginative if ungrammatical injunction). AT&T determined it is not in the telephone business, but rather in the information business; General Electric that it makes not kitchen appliances but rather a range of outstanding products and financial and communication services, and that it expects to be first or second in every business in which it participates. Similarly, Dartmouth trustees, alumni, and students have come to see the school not as an increasingly anachronistic preserve of traditional male values but rather as a community that is diverse and intellectually vibrant.

The stories that one tells to one's own employees nowadays are also different. Rather than stressing lifelong service, for which retirement benefits and a gold watch are the reward, companies now stress the development of skills that, if necessary, travel with the individual to the next job.

When downsizing or reengineering are more likely than lifetime employment, and when executives regularly (if irresponsibly) jump ship in search of a more attractive financial package, the messages must also be delicately phrased. If the story is too facile, it will not be believed . . . and properly so. What may be most effective is a constant provision of information about what is happening in the company (and abroad), a frank discussion of difficulties that are being faced, and a commitment to help individuals "land on their feet" should their job be in jeopardy.

Still, sugarcoating cannot (and, in my view, should not) mask the fundamental, often brutal realities about the marketplace today.

I have thought a lot about the existential themes that make sense to the young workers and entrepreneurs of Silicon Valley today and to their close cousins working in the financial institutions of our major cities or at the cyber- and biotechnology companies that form concentric rings around our downtown areas. There is little doubt that the prospect of striking it rich is a compelling theme, one that induces many younger persons to leave college or graduate school and to work "24/7," as some like to boast. Some want the money to buy personal possessions; others want the money to "do good," to retire early, or even just to proclaim that they have accumulated it. Yet, I believe that even the more selfish among them are in many cases propelled as well by a more idealistic, or at least a more exciting vision than the sheer accumulation of personal wealth. They sense that they are living in a special historical moment—a time like the invention of the printing press or the beginning of the Industrial Revolution—and they yearn to be active participants in that revolution. Leaders who can mobilize this sense of excitement—Cicso's John Chambers and Apple Computer's Steve Jobs on their better days—are likely to stimulate those mental representations that have always been needed for dogged involvement in an exciting enterprise.

And yet, in the end, while stories need to be dramatic, motivating, memorable, picturesque, even garlanded with appropriate music and graphics, they also need to be honest. That is where integrity comes in. Stories that do not resonate with reality ultimately prove frustrating and ineffective. Louis Schweitzer, long-time CEO of Renault, learned that the French public considered his company's automobiles to be overpriced. At once, he authorized a public announcement that acknowledged this sentiment and promised to rectify the situation during the following year. To his (and everyone else's) amazement, sales of Renault vehicles increased in the following weeks.[21] When all is said and done, then, the most important ingredient for a story to embody is truth; and the most important trait for a leader to have is integrity.

CHAPTER 6

Changing Minds Indirectly— Through Scientific Discoveries, Scholarly Breakthroughs, and Artistic Creations

UNTIL NOW WE HAVE FOCUSED on individuals—be they political, religious, educational, or corporate leaders—who change the minds of others in the most direct manner possible. They appear in public and address audiences of various sizes, attempting to convince members through their own rhetoric. Their face-to-face interactions involve many other members of the society or, in the case of uniform audiences, of the relevant domain or institution.

But major changes of mind also may be wrought by the works that a person creates rather than by his or her direct words or acts. Karl Marx was not a leader in the ordinary sense, and yet his writings exerted enormous influence on political events in the late nineteenth century and throughout the twentieth century. We might therefore speak of Marx and others like him as "indirect" leaders, as opposed to more "direct" leaders such as Prime Minister Margaret Thatcher or General Electric CEO Jack Welch.

Indirect leaders operate beyond the political sphere. Consider how our understanding of the world has been affected by Albert Einstein in the realm of physics, and by Charles Darwin in the realm of biology. Creative works have changed our minds about what constitutes art—and often our perceptions of the world itself. As the nineteenth-century British writer Percy B. Shelley memorably remarked: "Poets are the unacknowledged legislators of the world." More conceptions of the Spanish civil war were formed and altered by Pablo Picasso's *Guernica* and by the novels of Ernest Hemingway and André Malraux than by a thousand news dispatches.

So far in this book, the major ideas have been captured in leaders' "stories," but major creators go beyond stories. If they are scientists or scholars, they work primarily with theories; if they are artists, they change minds by introducing new ideas, skills, and practices in their works. We examine indirect leaders by looking at the work of scientists, great thinkers, and creative individuals from the world of dance, music, literature, and painting and sculpture. While mind changes in all three of these areas usually hinge, to one degree or another, on all seven levers of mind change, representational redescriptions and awareness of resistances play particularly critical roles in the indirect leader's ability to change minds.

CHANGING MINDS THROUGH SCIENTIFIC DISCOVERY: CHARLES DARWIN

While occasional scientific breakthroughs have been readily accepted by the scientific community and the general public, Charles Darwin's theory of evolution was scarcely granted a welcome reception. How it eventually gained widespread acceptance has much to do with the multiple ways, over many years, that the theory was presented—the "representational redescriptions" of each of the crucial concepts and the relations among them. Indeed, the way that the idea of evolution congealed for Darwin himself is a product of such multiple redescriptions.

Darwin's interest in the origins of diverse species was initially influenced by his grandfather Erasmus, a physician and naturalist who had explored the ideas of evolution. Darwin's own theories originated during his youthful voyage on *The Beagle* (1831–1836), but they didn't crystallize until he read—or, as it turns out, became reacquainted with—economist Thomas Malthus's reflections on the struggle for survival in times of limited resources. According to psychologist Howard Gruber, who carefully studied Darwin's notebooks, the English naturalist had been exposed to Malthusian ideas earlier in his education.[1] He'd therefore played with notions of natural selection for some time before they erupted into his consciousness and he became explicitly aware of their revolutionary implications. In our terms, Darwin may have felt that his change of mind was sudden, but the written record indicates that—as is usually the case with apparent breakthroughs—his change occurred far more gradually than he recalled.

Once aware of where his ideas were leading, Darwin devoted the bulk of his time over the next two decades to culling information pertinent to evolution. So heterodox were his theories, so likely to offend both his scientific peers and the general public (which included his wife, Emma, a devout Christian), that Darwin hesitated to publish them in his lifetime. Only when the young Alfred Wallace arrived at essentially the same insights did Darwin reluctantly agree to a joint presentation at the Royal Society in 1858. The following year, Darwin's epoch-making publication *On the Origin of Species* appeared.[2]

The initial resistance to Darwin's ideas is well known. Most of his scientific contemporaries rejected them outright, including his own venerated teacher, geologist Charles Lyell. Darwin was vilified by the clergy, politicians, and the general public. Fortunately, he also had eloquent defenders, most notably the sharp-tongued biologist Thomas Huxley. As the evidence in favor of evolution continued to accumulate, and both experts and laypersons grew accustomed to the ideas, these once iconoclastic notions began to be accepted. Still, even today, most Americans do not understand the major claims of evolutionary theory: Most do not appreciate the difference between evolution—a scientific theory, which is subject to disconfirmation in the light of newly acquired evidence—and creationism or its variants, basically an article of faith. (The theory of evolution seems less problematic to citizens of other countries.)[3]

There is a footnote here, one especially delicious for prospective mind-changers. According to historian of science Frank Sulloway, willingness to change one's mind about evolution hangs significantly on an unexpected factor: birth order.[4] It turns out that later-borns have been much more willing than firstborns to accept the basic tenets of Darwinian evolution. Indeed, it took a full century (!) for first-borns to accept evolution to the same degree that the theory was originally accepted by later-borns. Apparently, those who from the start have to contend with rival siblings are more sympathetic to the outlines of Darwinian theory than those who, at the beginning, had it all to themselves. Sulloway has shown that the same pattern holds for other revolutionary perspectives, whether they are introduced in science, politics, or religion. In a nutshell, if you want to change minds about consequential ideas, find an audience of later-borns.

To be sure, Darwin's ideas are not intuitive. We know this because, by and large, eight-year-olds are creationists.[5] No matter whether their parents are evolutionary biologists or fundamentalist preachers, young schoolchildren become intrigued by the question of origins, and it seems patent to them that all organisms were created at a certain historical (or prehistorical) moment and did not change significantly thereafter. Moreover, these same children are likely to believe that a significant change that occurs during the life of an organism (e.g., the building up of biceps) will be passed on to the offspring of that organism (suggesting that the earlier ideas of the French biologist Jean-Baptiste Lamarck are more intuitive than those put forth by Darwin). A whole theoretical framework, then— that there was no single moment of creation, but rather a gradual process that took place over millions of years and is still ongoing; that human beings and contemporary apes evolved from the same common ancestor a few million years ago; that (at least until the possibility of germ therapy) the biological heritage that we pass onto future generations cannot be affected by experiences in our own lifetimes; and, above all, that scientific evidence refutes the biblical account of creation at every turn—all of these ideas were (and for many people remain) very difficult to accept.

In addition to the curious finding about birth order, we can make some educated guesses about the factors that disincline individuals to accept the theory of evolution. Clearly those fundamentalists who have the strongest belief in religious accounts of human origins will find the ideas unpalatable. To the extent that they have expressed their own antievolutionary views publicly, this resistance is likely to be strengthened. Thus, for example, despite the evidence that the formidable mid-nineteenth-century Swiss-American scientist Louis Agassiz gathered in favor of evolution, he had already publicly committed to the biblical account and was thus unlikely to change his mind, let alone announce any such change to his illustrious colleagues. Another factor that would prevent someone from changing his or her mind about evolution is the individual's understanding of the scientific method and of the difference between matters of science and matters of faith. Scientists and those who understand the scientific method find it increasingly difficult to overlook the enormous geological, fossil, and laboratory evidence in favor of evolution. Those scientists who wish to maintain a belief in the religious account must somehow be able to perform cognitive surgery, and, so to speak, keep two different sets of mental books. Reason and research favor the evolutionary option.

So how are minds changed when it comes to scientific theories? In his famous work *The Structure of Scientific Revolutions* historian of science Thomas Kuhn offers the most plausible account of how revolutionary theories—or paradigms—come to be accepted.[6] As Kuhn describes it, the leading mature scientists of a generation are least likely to be able to accept a dramatic new line of explanation. This skepticism greeted Copernicus's heliocentric view of the universe, Einstein's theory of relativity, Heisenberg's quantum mechanics, Freud's theory of the unconscious, and Wegener's continental drift, among others. Why? Because senior savants, trained in the old way of thinking, would have to abandon deeply ingrained and dearly held notions. The new paradigm is most likely to be embraced by individuals who are just beginning to work in a particular domain. These "young turks" lack a vested interest in the old perspective, they are more likely to be flexible, and, indeed (particularly if they are later-born), they may gain a certain pleasure in seeing the old dogmas overthrown and in having the opportunity to pursue a freshly opened line of work. (Indeed, I remember well how, as a budding psychologist, I felt much more energized aligning myself with the innovative cognitivists than with the establishment behaviorists or the antiquated psychophysicists.) For a youthful or iconoclastic segment of the population, then, the very resistance to an idea in general can incline members of that segment to accept the idea more readily.

As I have already pointed out, unlike the leaders of large entities, indirect leaders do not change minds through elegant public discourse or convincing face-to-face rhetoric. For much of his adult life, Charles Darwin was essentially a recluse. He lived far enough from London that he did not venture into the metropolis with any regularity. He had undiagnosed illnesses that he seems to have used as a pretext to avoid unwanted encounters; most of his interactions with other scientists, therefore, occurred through the mail. To be sure, Darwin was lucky to have an eloquent and tenacious spokesman, the aforementioned Huxley, who fully earned the nickname "Darwin's bulldog." For Darwin and his ilk, then, direct interpersonal interactions with others are not an important part of their endeavor. Rather, they change minds through the work that they carry out.

Consider another scientist whose ideas changed minds on a massive scale: Albert Einstein. From an early age, Einstein wrestled with questions about the nature of space and time. At age five he wondered why the needle of the compass always pointed in the same direction; as a teenager, he pondered what it would be like to travel on a beam of light; as an adult, he imagined the locations of items in an elevator as the elevator itself moved in free fall through space.[7] Einstein was not intimidated by the extant theories of explanation of the physical universe. In a series of radical reformulations, he put forth both a special and a general theory of relativity.

Initially Einstein's ideas were difficult to follow, and few individuals fully understood their implications. (Whereas Darwin's contemporaries understood the implications of his ideas only too well.) But Einstein worked in a field where the opinion of the leading figures mattered decisively, and fortunately his original papers were accepted for the *Annalen der Physik* by Max Planck, the preeminent physicist of the day. Therefore, among the relatively homogeneous set of experts in physics, Einstein's work was appreciated more quickly than that of Darwin's—and when in 1919 a prediction that he had made about a solar eclipse proved correct, Einstein's scientific immortality was assured. (Still, when Einstein received the Nobel Prize for Physics in 1921, it was for his discovery of the photoelectric effect and not for his theories of relativity—the latter were still considered too speculative.)

While few people would doubt the place of Darwin and Einstein in the pantheon of the greatest scientists of all times—they belong right up there with Galileo and Newton—the scientific status of Sigmund Freud's propositions are more questionable. Scientific evidence hasn't coalesced in favor of psychoanalytic theory; in fact, to the extent that psychoanalytic propositions can be tested, considerable evidence runs counter to them. Rather, it seems more accurate to say that Freud developed—in admirable if not always accurate detail—a perspective on human nature that deserves to be taken into account. In poet W. H. Auden's memorable phrase, Freud created a "climate of opinion." As such, Freud qualifies less as a scientist than as an original and bold thinker—a category of indirect leadership to which we now turn.

THINKERS WHO CHANGE MINDS ABOUT THE HUMAN MIND

A century ago, Sigmund Freud introduced some of the most challenging ideas in psychology.[8] This neurologist-turned-psychologist became intrigued by anomalous human behaviors, such as hysterical symptoms, dreams, slips of the tongue, and various neuroses. Seeking to make sense of these puzzles, Freud developed still-controversial theories about the power of unconscious factors, the sexual nature of dreams, and the determinative influence on adult personality of early social and sexual experiences. Going beyond armchair theorizing, Freud also pioneered therapeutic techniques that are still used today, including free association, dream interpretation, and strategies for handling the "transfer" and "countertransfer" of powerful feelings between the therapist and the patient.

Freud's work can be distinguished in a number of respects from that of Einstein and Darwin. First, Freud was dealing with human beings, who have consciousness and intentions and cannot as readily be studied in a distanced or disinterested way; unlike the planets or long-extinct species, humans can understand scientific claims and attempt to prove them right or wrong. Second, Freud did not just describe the world as he had come to understand it; he developed therapeutic techniques—in our terms, skills or practices—that he then employed with his troubled patients. Third, Freud was also ambitious in an institutional way; he empowered others to become psychoanalysts, ultimately creating a secretive and prestigious priesthood of his closest followers. In this sense, more so than most other aspiring scientists and scholars, Freud was acting as a direct leader.

While the mind-changing effects of Freud's work operated indirectly, they nicely illustrate our levers of change. As a scholar, Freud relied on *reason* and data derived from his own patients. He was also a master rhetorician, who won literary prizes as well as scientific accolades. He se-cured *resources* to set up institutions, deftly *rewarding* those who supported him and in effect excommunicating those analysts who deviated too far from the catechism.

His principal ideas were described not only in theoretical essays but also in vivid case studies and, ultimately, in works of literature, cinema, and art. Freud seized on events in the *real world*—such as the horrors of World War I—to document his assertions about the destructive tenden-cies in human nature. And he was a brilliant detector of *resistances*—often going so far as arguing that resistance to one of his ideas was actually a sign that the idea was probably correct!

It is worth mentioning two women psychologists who have recently challenged orthodox views of human nature. In her groundbreaking book *In a Different Voice,* Harvard psychologist Carol Gilligan pointed out that studies of moral development have historically all been with men—and that perhaps women reason about moral dilemmas differ-ently.[9] Independent scholar Judith Rich Harris also put forth a provoca-tive hypothesis, based on behavioral genetics studies, that parents do not mold their children beyond the parental genetic contribution.[10] The big socializers of children, she argued in *The Nurture Assumption,* are their peers. Working very much in the manner of Freud, these iconoclastic theorists marshaled reason, research, rhetoric, and real world phenomena to bolster their positions. And when the Establishment questioned their provocative ideas, both Gilligan and Harris deftly countered these resis-tances and located powerful allies who would vouch for the tenability of their ideas.

Thus far in this chapter we have looked at scientists such as Einstein and Darwin, who initiate fundamental advances in how we understand the physical and biological world. And we have considered major thinkers —"climate creators" such as psychologist (and aspiring scientist) Freud (other prominent examples would be political thinker Karl Marx and philosopher Friedrich Nietzsche)—who change the way in which we think about ourselves and our society. Whether Gilligan's and Harris's ideas have similar staying power remains to be seen. A third category of individuals also change minds on a massive scale, indirectly: those who create powerful artistic visions.

HOW ARTISTS HAVE CHANGED MINDS

Creators in the arts—be they in dance, music, literature, cinema, or the fine arts of painting and sculpture—change minds primarily by introducing new ideas, skills, and practices. They rarely wield the theories, ideas, and concepts that scientists and thinkers employ, or the stories that leaders of nations or more homogeneous groups use to create large-scale shifts in thinking. Similarly, rather than operating primarily with linguistic intelligence, artists make use of diverse forms of mental representation captured in a variety of traditional and innovative symbolic systems: composers and musical intelligence, painters and spatial intelligence, dancers and bodily-kinesthetic intelligence, and so forth. Tipping points have been achieved when fellow artists alter their practices and when audience members alter their tastes.

The beginning of the twentieth century is generally deemed an artistic watershed that eventually changed a great many minds and sensibilities. The classicism that we associate with the seventeenth and eighteenth century—the plays of William Shakespeare and Jean-Baptiste Molière, the music of Franz Joseph Haydn and Wolfgang Amadeus Mozart, the paintings of Thomas Gainsborough and Nicolas Poussin—had given rise to the romanticism of the nineteenth century—the novels of Victor Hugo and the Brontë sisters, the music of Hector Berlioz and Richard Wagner, the paintings of Eugene Delacroix and J. M. W. Turner. But by the twentieth century, the romantic spirit had gradually been exhausted; scientific and technological breakthroughs, as well as shifts in the political winds, signaled the beginning of a new era.

In each art form, a few individuals stand out as having ushered in a modernist world. In classical music, the Russian Igor Stravinsky and the Austrian Arnold Schoenberg challenged tonality in music and created powerful new idioms that dominated classical composing for decades. In painting, Pablo Picasso (working for a time with Georges Braque) broke down the centuries-long prominence of realism and impressionism and created powerful new cubist works out of fragmentary graphic units. Picasso also laid the groundwork for a completely abstract art associated with the "New York School" of the 1950s. In the literary arts, the powerful influences included poet T. S. Eliot, novelists Marcel Proust, Virginia

Woolf, and James Joyce, and playwrights Bertolt Brecht and Luigi Piran-dello. In dance, the barriers were kicked down (so to speak) by the American pioneer Ruth St. Denis, and then new forms were created by St. Denis's protégé, Martha Graham (and Graham's rival, Doris Humphrey), as well as by Merce Cunningham, George Balanchine, Paul Taylor, Pina Bausch, and other leading dancers and choreographers.

When it comes to such artists, it makes little sense to describe their ideas in words—or, as I've already pointed out, to speak about concepts, stories, theories. Artists work in their respective media or métiers, and are appropriately understood in terms of how they convey their personal visions using light and color, sound and rhythm, metaphor and rhyme, bodily movement and facial expression. The ideas of Darwin or Einstein, Gilligan or Harris, can be paraphrased by others and captured in textbook form. The visions of Picasso, Schoenberg, Woolf, and Graham can be apprehended only by those who understand the nature of the media or symbolic systems—the artistic forms—in which these creative giants worked and who are able to appreciate the breakthroughs that these artists respectively fashioned.

But how do such artistic visionaries change minds? After all, they are not putting forth propositions to which one can assent or claims from which one can dissent—unless one uses that linguistic terminology in a deliberately metaphoric way. Thus reason and research are not particularly relevant. Nor do most artists have available vast resources, and only some of them (like Picasso or Hemingway) react specifically to real world events (like the Spanish civil war).

I propose that artistic masters alter our minds in three ways. First, they expand our notion of what is possible in an artistic medium. Before Picasso, few appreciated that great art could be made out of bits and fragments, in a cubist fashion, let alone in pure shapes and forms. By the same token, even avid music lovers of the nineteenth century would not have been able to assimilate the atonalities and discordant passages of Stravinsky's *Rite of Spring* or Schoenberg's *Pierrot Lunaire* (their most sophisticated predecessor, composer Claude Debussy, could not make sense of these early twentieth-century iconoclastic works). We might say that these kinds of individuals develop new skills in a medium and that they call on members of their audiences to develop a complementary ensemble of perceptual skills. Second, artists change minds by employing themes that rarely if ever had been the subject of art: thus Cunningham and Balanchine play with pure bodily forms, independent of plot line, while Woolf and Joyce explore the stream of human consciousness. Third, artists help us to understand, indeed help us to define, the spirit of an era. It would be hyperbole to suggest that modern times were *made* by paintings like Picasso's *Les Desmoiselles d'Avignon,* novels like Joyce's *Ulysses,* or compositions like Stravinsky's *Les Noces,* but it is certainly arguable that our own understanding of the era in which these artists lived would be impoverished in the absence of the motifs and forms embodied in such epoch-defining works.

I propose that such groundbreaking artists make use primarily of three levers: *representational redescriptions, resonance,* and *resistances.* By the nature of their enterprise, artists are constantly experimenting with a medium, and such experimentation entails a series of redescriptions. Picasso quipped that painting is a science of which the individual paintings are the experiments. It is not difficult to make an innovative work of art, but it is challenging to create a work or a series of works that resonate with informed audience members and, eventually, with a larger public. Indeed, the twentieth century witnessed any number of artists who were a success with the most sophisticated connoisseurs (so-called succès d'estime) but who never resonated with the general audience. In our terms, the resistances to these innovative works proved too great. The artist who would break through to popular acceptance must somehow neutralize the resistances—much as a persuasive storyteller manages to undermine the prevailing counterstories.

All of the breakthroughs that we've examined thus far—in the arts, in scholarly thought, and in science—represent hard-won victories, gleaned from the plethora of creative misfirings. We remember and honor the handful of scientists and artists whose works have endured over time and have shaped our consciousness. We forget the many thousands whose work made little impact, or whose own contributions are as lost to history as the names of the individuals who designed and the more numerous individuals who built the pyramids of ancient Egypt or the cathedrals of medieval Europe. (In an attempt to ingratiate himself with T. S. Eliot, a fellow writer once declared deploringly, "Oh, editors. They are just failed writers." "Indeed," responded Eliot, "and so are most writers.") Moreover, as psychologist Dean Keith Simonton has demonstrated, the most acclaimed creators not only create more works than their peers, they also generate more failures; the notion that every work by a master is equally meritorious is dead wrong.[11] Those of us involved with one or another art form will have developed senses of what is possible in that art form, what we like and don't like, how we think of our era, how we think of human beings. Many new works that are created will be consistent with these shared notions. We may gain pleasure from them but—as with twice-told stories—we are unlikely to be bowled over by them. Rather, they are like the typical television show or movie that we may enjoy at the moment but which soon fades from consciousness and leaves little or no trace in our memory. Works that differ radically from the norm may well alienate an audience or even fail to get a hearing or a viewing. (Admittedly, nowadays, it sometimes seems that only those works that represent radical departures gain attention, but typically such attention is short-lived. Nothing is so boring as endless unalloyed novelty.)

I assume that I am not alone in being able to recall those artistic experiences that were personally shattering and mind-changing. Having become conscious of modernism in my college years, my artistic consciousness was formed by the artists I've mentioned above: Stravinsky, Picasso, Eliot, and Graham in particular. Such major shifts in taste do not occur frequently in one's life—unless one is a professional taste maker or inveterate iconoclast. Still, I can remember other more recent artistic experiences that have also expanded my consciousness; for example, reading the short stories of Raymond Carver and the poetry of Adam Zagajewski, seeing the movies of Ingmar Bergman, viewing the paintings of Mark Rothko, visiting the artistic spaces created by James Turrell. Each of these creators works in a symbolic métier, altering mental representations appropriate to that format. I have little hesitancy in stating that my mind was changed by these artistic experiences, each with its idiosyncratic format of presentation, and I am optimistic enough to hope that my consciousness can again be changed in the event that I encounter works or workers of equivalent power. Again, these creative achievements affect the practices of other artists and the contours of my own taste.

The mind changes that indirect leaders catalyze may draw on various levers of change. But one of those Rs—resistances—plays a particularly powerful role in how a theory or creative work eventually gains acceptance, or does not.

THE USES OF RESISTANCE

One can be excited or left unmoved by innovations, but one can also be repelled by them. While resistance is usually seen as negative—one of the key factors that prevents a change of mind—it can also play a more positive role: It is valuable to wrestle with ideas we initially resist, to show where they are inadequate or wrong. Such struggle can strengthen one's perspective, help one to understand it better, and, at times, stimulate a change of one's own mind.

For example, I have never been taken with the minimalist music of Steve Reich or Philip Glass, the "pop" or "op" art of the 1960s, or the "new novel" of mid-twentieth-century French writers. Yet because I am not an artist or critic, I have not felt the need to declare my distaste publicly (nor would anyone have cared had I done so!). On the other hand, as one who writes about the world of ideas, I have had strong negative reactions to various postmodern notions—and particularly to deconstructionist approaches to texts, the social construction of all knowledge, and the relativism of all positions. My own resistance to those ideas provides a good example of how mind change can work indirectly.

Arising principally in France in the 1960s, deconstruction (or deconstructionism) questions the possibility of developing a coherent explanatory account of any phenomenon, or of arriving at agreement about what a text means. According to the literary critic and philosopher Jacques Derrida, all texts carry within them contradictions that undermine their apparent claims.[12] As a reader or analyst, the most that one can do is to bring out these contradictions. Social constructivism begins with the unexceptional claim that all knowledge must be constructed (what cognitivist could possibly disagree with that assertion?), but it rapidly escalates to the far bolder claim that science is itself a social invention, which reflects no more than a momentary consensus based on considerations of power and authority. On this view, one scientific explanation cannot be shown, on any objective basis, to be superior to others. There are simply rival accounts that are adopted or not, depending on contingencies like conventional wisdom and the influence of the adopters.[13] Thomas Kuhn is sometimes cited as an advocate of the social construction view of science, though I don't believe that he would have embraced these ideas in the form that I have just stated.[14] Relativism embraces the idea that all analyses are equally valid, or at least that there is no independent basis on which to evaluate competing theories of accounts. Taken together, these views do not merely question whether one can ever arrive at a truth: They even question the tenability of truth, of credible explanation, of the validity of any master narrative—except, of course, that narrative which holds there *is* no such thing as a master narrative.[15]

One could simply allow ideas like relativism, deconstruction, or social constructivism to self-construct; I personally believe that in their extreme form these ideas are self-refuting. (Why pay attention to someone who seriously maintains that no ideas or works are intrinsically true or more worthwhile than any other?) But as I've said, there is value in struggling with ideas that one resists. Moreover, I would be disingenuous if I did not concede that I, too, have been influenced by my encounters with these ideas. I feel less prone to make definitive statements about what is right or wrong. I am more likely to acknowledge the importance of stance, power, influence, trendiness. I am more alert to potential contradictions in texts, including (I fear) my own. I can even allow that there will never be a definitive truth, though I totally defend the idea of *striving* for truth, beauty, morality, progress. In the sense just described, we are influenced by those ideas—literary, scientific, artistic—that repel us as well as by those that attract us.

The mention of deconstruction or relativism in the intellectual sphere, and of communism or fascism in the political sphere, serves as an important reminder that not all changes of mind are equally desirable. (Note that a pure relativist would have to defend the opposite proposition—that no change is more or less desirable than any other.) Some individuals—notably the "latest-born" among us—will be attracted to any new ideas, no matter how flaky; others—the most rigid and authoritarian among us—will reject new ideas, even when they merit our attention.

Unless one is committed to religious fundamentalism, one should always remain open to changing one's mind; it is worth attending to ideas that have affected many others, even when one personally finds little of value in them. Our thought processes sharpen when we wrestle with these ideas, and it is even possible that we might eventually find merit in the ideas that we once rejected. In the realm of indirect leadership, awareness of resistance is valuable both to the creator of new vision and to the individual who initially resists a strange and exotic presentation—possibly because it hits too close to home.

Whatever the initial resistance to their ideas, individuals like Albert Einstein or Charles Darwin, Carol Gilligan or Judith Rich Harris, Marcel Proust or Martha Graham, come to exert an influence on a wide audience. Their names become known; their ideas spread, with or without public awareness of the identity of their creators. There may even be schools or institutions that embody their vision. The ownership of the Martha Graham School, for example, had been a subject of controversy even before her death in 1991, and the question of who "owns" her dozens of works (and therefore can perform them) is likely to be disputed for decades. Psychoanalytic associations and training institutes based on the ideas of Freud, are another well-known example of power and controversy.

Still, initially, these creative individuals are directing their efforts to an audience that is limited, domain-restricted, indisputably expert, essentially homogeneous. Darwin had to convince the biologists, Freud the psychologists; Stravinsky had to find an orchestra and a ballet company to perform his works; Picasso needed a gallery to display his workers and people of means to buy them. When it comes to the commercial sphere, however, such limited audiences are neither necessary nor desirable. Individuals who invent a product or develop a new policy seek from the outset to reach the widest possible public, to change the minds of millions. The story of Jay Winsten is a good case in point.[16]

CHANGING THE MINDS OF A WIDE AUDIENCE: JAY WINSTEN

A professor at Harvard's School of Public Health, Jay Winsten is an indirect leader who has marshaled the media to bring about social change on a large scale. Through his creative use of the resources available to him and through representational redescription, Winsten has helped to bring about large-scale changes in public attitudes and behaviors.

His primary resource? The producers of leading television shows and mass-market films. Winsten convinced these media experts that it would be possible to include redeeming social messages in their cinematic or video presentations—representational redescription at its best. But this inclusion would have to satisfy two key criteria: (1) It would not be intrusive and would therefore not disturb the mood, or the entertainment value, of the work; (2) It stood a chance of actually bringing about desirable changes in the wider community.

Winsten's best-known intervention featured the designated driver. In Scandinavian countries, it has long been the norm that those who drink do not drive; when several individuals are involved in a social event where they need to transport themselves, one person will agree beforehand not to drink that night. Winsten reasoned that the designation of a nondrinking driver could fit comfortably into the plot lines of many television shows. And so, working with producers, scriptwriters, and actors from more than 160 primetime television programs, the Winsten team created convincing scenarios in which the concept of a designated driver was featured. The major television networks also created public service announcements that explicitly reinforced the messages that had been built into their programs. And in a happy ending to the story, death and injuries from drunk driving have dropped significantly in the United States, and the practice of assigning a designated driver has become increasingly routine.

Winsten has undertaken other campaigns as well. In an effort to deal with teenage violence, he introduced the campaign of "Squash It." His research team had discovered an interesting phenomenon: in public, teenagers declare that it is cowardly to walk away from a fight, but these same teens privately admit that it shows strength and self-respect to move away from an altercation. Building on this discovery, the Winsten team has created broadcast vignettes in which protagonists demonstrate how to walk away from an encounter rather than resorting to fighting. Such influential models swing their arms down with a swift and decisive motion, accompanied by the phrase "squash it," thereby communicating to their peers that this fight is not worth pursuing. The campaign achieved its greatest success in the African American community: 72 percent of respondents in a 1997 survey reported that they were aware of the campaign, and 60 percent had used the phrase.[17] It has also led to forums in several cities and to an organized "antiviolence" campaign in Kansas City.[18] More recently, in conjunction with philanthropist Ray Chambers, Winsten has sought to increase adult mentoring of disadvantaged youth: His team helped to organize marches for volunteerism, created the organization America's Promise (with Colin Powell as the first chair), incorporated scenes of mentoring into television programs, and sponsored a "national mentoring month."

According to Winsten, there is a definite rhythm to such initiatives, just as there is to a U.S. political campaign or a Gandhian protest. Social marketing uses the disciplined, iterative methods perfected by "high end" advertisers to promote socially desirable ends.[19] The process begins by acknowledging that most individuals do not even recognize when a particular problem exists; their consciousness must accordingly be raised. Only when the problem is recognized as such is there a possibility for change. Next the individual must become aware of the available options and their costs and benefits; individuals need to be motivated even to consider a new approach. The more convinced the individual becomes about the seriousness of the problem and the chances that some course of action will be able to deal effectively with it, the more likely the individual will consider changing that behavior. The decisive step is taken when one attempts the alternative behavior for the first time. However, unless there is continuing strong support, the new behavior is not likely to be maintained. We see at work here the themes that we've touched on so far in this book: the newly emerging story, the entrenched counterstories, the use of imaginative formats in powerful media, and the possibility of a tipping point.[20]

As an accomplished changer of minds, Winsten provides another compelling instance of the various levers for change. He makes use of *reason* both in coming up with the various campaigns and in sharing with his audience the reasons for the recommended behaviors. As a social scientist, he collects data on the effects of his intervention and informs his audiences about the consequences of their behavior. The availability of significant resources from the telecommunications industry makes a possible a large-scale intervention, even as the formats of these media permit compelling and dramatic *representations* of the desired (and the risky) behaviors. Because the characters in the media presentations are lifelike and appealing, they are likely to *resonate* with the audience. Examples from the Scandinavian countries and statistics from our own country are real-life events that can be invoked. Finally, Winsten takes great care to identify the various *resistances* to behavioral change so that they can be acknowledged and directly countered. Even with all of these levers at his disposal, Winsten faces many challenges; but without them, the chances of affecting human drinking behavior or methods of conflict resolution would be meager indeed.

THE TWO AXES OF MIND CHANGING

Surveying our examples thus far in this book, we can distinguish two axes of mind changing, which in turn yield four distinct forms. Let us look at each of these in turn.

One axis of mind changing that we've explored consists of the *directness* of the effort. Political leaders seek to change minds directly through face-to-face encounters. Artists, thinkers, inventors, policy makers, and scientists are also keen on changing mental representations: representations about specific content, as well as representations of how one goes about executing work in a particular domain or medium. But they go about these efforts *indirectly*, through the works or products that they create in various media or symbol systems.

The second axis of mind changing has to do with the *composition* of an audience: its uniformity or diversity. Political leaders and those who seek to institute policy changes work with diverse or *heterogeneous* populations. Their messages do not presuppose any kind of specialized knowledge or membership. Indeed, the most effective messages for a diverse audience are directed at the "unschooled mind." In contrast, it is also possible (and perhaps easier) to work with groups that in one respect or another are alike: members belong to the same religion or organization, have a degree of expertise in a content area, or have mastered some kind of skill or medium. In these latter instances, the "mind changers" are addressing a relatively uniform *homogeneous* audience, or at least an audience that is homogeneous with respect to the issue or taste in question. In the latter case, one can assume that the audience shares important mental representations and one can initiate efforts to affect that shared mental representation.

Two axes, then, yielding four forms: direct and heterogeneous (see chapter 4); direct and relatively uniform (see chapter 5); indirect and homogeneous (the innovative scientists and artists, described in this chapter); indirect and diverse (public outreach of the sort choreographed by Jay Winsten).

When considering these four varieties of change, however, we need not distinguish the opposite ends of these poles with excessive sharpness. Many effective leaders combine the strengths of direct and indirect leadership. For example, Winston Churchill and Charles de Gaulle were not only expert speakers; they were also outstanding writers, who advanced their causes through books, pamphlets, and articles. Similarly, many domains address both homogeneous and heterogeneous audiences. And domains themselves can shift perspective over time. When television and movies were first created, they addressed somewhat elite and relatively homogenous audiences; over time, as the media became more widely available, and audiences were drawn from all over the world, the audiences necessarily became more heterogeneous. As one addresses the unschooled mind, the stories inevitably become simpler. Commenting on the classic movie of the 1950s *On the Waterfront,* director Barry Levinson said, "We have moved away from this kind of sophisticated storytelling to a place where everything is stories about someone who has a gun and is coming to kill you. If we did this movie today, we would feel compelled to kick it up, to really exploit the violent aspects in the story."[21]

In my writings about creativity, I have found it useful to distinguish between big C and little c creativity. The Einsteins, Picassos, and Freuds of the world are intent on big C creativity: They bring about (or at least seek to bring about) major changes in the domain in which they are working. They want ultimately to affect beliefs and practices across a domain; it matters less *which* specific individuals are affected, so long as a sufficient number are affected and those who are affected have sufficient influence. Darwin did not have to convince skeptics Louis Agassiz and Bishop

Wilberforce (with whom Huxley debated); he just had to influence enough members of the Royal Society or, more crucially, their successors.

Most of us cannot hope to effect big *C* creativity, though my colleague Mihaly Csikszentmihaly quips that we might at least aspire to be "middle *C*" creators.[22] Yet, while the extent of the mind change will vary, there is no reason to think that fundamentally different factors are at work. Both the leader bent on "Mind Change" and the teacher, parents, or storekeeper who is satisfied with lowercase "mind change" aim to change the mental representations of those for whom they have responsibility. The enterprise differs in terms of the number of individuals affected, the size of the impact, and the likelihood that the impact will be long-lasting and far-reaching. There are false positives as well as false negatives: yesterday's "cold fusion" can be a flash in the pan; the inconspicuous artist or scientist or thinker of one generation may impact succeeding generations—the examples of painter Vincent van Gogh and plant geneticist Gregor Mendel come to mind. Crucial for our purposes is the realization that, irrespective of the ultimate significance of the mind change in the eyes of eternity, it matters profoundly to those affected at the time—for, as economist John Maynard Keynes was fond of remarking, "In the long run, we are all dead."

With that chilling thought in mind, we can now turn to an examination of how minds are changed through more formal and direct means: in schools and other educational settings.

CHAPTER 7

Mind Changing in
a Formal Setting

THUS FAR we have been looking at how people—or the works that people produce—change minds. But what of formal institutions that are designed with mind changing as their goal? Schools stand out because they serve those young individuals whose minds can most readily be changed; they fashion curricula to convey disciplines that crystallize the current state of knowledge; and they have responsibility for monitoring how, and to what extent, the minds of students have in fact been changed. The milieus of change in formal education vary, from large lectures delivered to hundreds of students to informal tutorials, to the child alone in the library or at the computer screen. More recently, new forms of lifelong education, including continuing professional development and corporate universities, have come to the fore. But for a long time, the educational heartland has been the classroom, where somewhere between a dozen and fifty students grouped together attempt to acquire basic literacies, master particular disciplines, or prepare for specific vocations. Let us turn our attention, then, to the mind-changing aspects of schools.

SCHOOL: THE INSTITUTION
DESIGNED TO CHANGE MINDS

From an amazingly early age, youngsters catch on to the teaching-and-learning enterprise.[1] Children as young as two or three years already recognize teaching situations.[2] They ask to be shown how to do something; they attend carefully; as they gain proficiency, they can show others how to do it; and they adjust the pace and detail of their modeling to fit the presumed knowledge base of their own "students." Not only do young children change their own minds easily; they are also predisposed to change the minds of others. As with so many of children's capacities—ranging from learning of languages to picking up tunes—it is difficult to see how these youngsters could ever acquire the knack of teaching and learning if they were not "wired" to do so. Just try to get a dog or cat to transmit some newly acquired knowledge to a fellow member of its species: neither cognitive science nor behaviorism can save the day.

In prehistoric times, most learning appears to have taken place in the natural surroundings of everyday existence. Youngsters watched adults engaged in hunting, gathering, making clothing, constructing shelters, and preparing food; the youngsters were slowly (or not so slowly) inducted into these activities and given the opportunity to carry out comparable actions on their own as soon as they were ready to do so. Sometimes, the assumption of an adult role was marked by a rite of passage. Children also heard the stories of tribal origins, triumphs, and calamities and were expected to master this lore and, eventually, to pass it on to their own offspring. Such were the educational regimens of cultures of yore, and such are the regimens of the few surviving Stone Age or Stone Age–like cultures.

Around five thousand years ago, however, knowledge had accumulated to such an extent that these spontaneous forms of induction no longer sufficed. Increasingly technical knowledge about navigation, tool making, and healing, as well as a growing amount of commercial information, needed to be mastered. Most saliently, various means of written communication began to be used for consequential purposes, ranging from record keeping, to the promulgation of laws, to the spreading of crucial information about war, genealogy, and rituals.

We do not know the specifics of how schools came into being in most cultures. But we do know that, over time, certain individuals were designated as masters or teachers and given authority over young charges; specific written and oral materials were deemed as important and these became the "subjects" that were taught; buildings, parts of building, or other sites were set aside for student instruction. Early schools covered only a few years of instruction, were restricted to males, and were charged principally with conferring literacy on select groups: those who would enter the clergy, those who would serve the rulers, and those with sufficient means and motivation to become literate.

Fast-forward to the present. All over the world, education is considered one of the most important functions of a society. Universal basic education is the goal everywhere, and in many developed societies, it has virtually been achieved. The means and ends of education may differ across societies, but it is widely appreciated that, in the absence of education, individuals will not be able to function adequately in the contemporary world, let alone the world of the future. Schools are key to my investigation because they are the institutions that have been explicitly charged with the changing of minds. I see schools in our contemporary world as engaged, in rough sequence, in helping students to acquire three new mental skills: (1) learning to learn in non-natural settings; (2) learning to make sense of squiggles on a piece of paper or computer screen; and (3) learning to think in the manner of several key disciplines.

Schools as the Context for Out-of-Context Learning

Children are natural learners. But the kind of learning that takes place in school proves far less natural than that which occurs in the fields, on the savanna, or on the street. In school, a collection of youngsters comes together for stated hours each day; the students are expected to be civil to one another, to heed the dominant adult figure(s), and to sit still for relatively long periods of time so that they can master materials whose application to their daily lives seems obscure.

A first challenge to educators is to socialize youngsters into the school setting. This is mind changing at the most basic level: helping children to progress from learning through observation to learning through formal tuition. This opening gambit can be treated as a moment of wonder—in traditional Hebrew schools, for example, the young schoolchild is served edible letters of the alphabet that have been coated with honey—or as an introduction to more punitive means, such as being caned if one does not obey promptly. Increasingly, in developed countries, preschools or kindergartens help to familiarize youngsters with the specific kinds of interactions that occur in a classroom. The mind change brought about by such attendance at school is significant. In the first years of life, youngsters learn chiefly by observing older persons carry out daily activities; but once a child has gotten the "school idea," she can learn about objects and events in a setting remote from their actual location and time of occurrence.

Schools as a Means for Becoming Literate

The world on paper differs profoundly from the oral-aural world. In ordinary conversation, meaning is carried by many indices, including tone of voice, eye contact, and gesture. The young child who does not know a language can still pick up much from a conversation because he inhabits the same space as the conversant; indeed, this "bootstrapping" is the only way in which children come initially to master the language(s) of their surroundings (and the chief way adults can communicate when they don't speak the same language). But when it comes to written language, the entire meaning must be picked up from the squiggles on a piece of paper. Irrespective of one's intuitions on the subject, written language is not merely a transcription of oral language (as anyone who has read a verbatim transcript of an interview or impromptu talk can confirm). Rather, written language represents an attempt to capture *in precisely chosen words* everything that might have been gleaned from context.[3]

Since, until recently, we have lived in a world in which the printed word was paramount, the chief burden of schools has been to enable children to understand and produce with facility the written language of their society. Yet other forms of literacy have become increasingly important in the twenty-first century. Much communication in our world takes place through graphic means—both static and dynamic. Web sites incorporate print, but they also feature cartoons, films, music, and the like. Representational redescriptions abound. Moreover, the print on computer screens is often far less linear in form and argument than the print in a book like this. Texts blend into hypertexts; links are numerous, idiosyncratic, and sometimes remote; information need not be presented or followed in a prescribed order.

This relative decline of the primacy of print literacy is a phenomenon of our time. This trend helps those individuals for whom traditional reading remains difficult, and it stimulates even the most skilled readers to broaden their arsenal. For our purposes, it is important to stress that minds differ from one another significantly depending on whether they have been reared in a preliterate culture, steeped in a classical or modern culture where text is primary, or thrust into a postmodern culture, where a whole gaggle of literacies is now available and work in tandem, sometimes synergistically, sometimes chaotically. All of this is to say that today, the task of changing minds is changing as well. If one wants to infiltrate the minds of individuals today, one needs to know *which* sort of mind is at issue: that fact will determine the optimal forms of information, the optimal modes of informing, the optimal means of transforming, and the factors that are likely to yield a tipping point.

Schools as a Means for Acquiring Disciplinary Modes of Thinking

At the start of the new millennium I was asked by a pundit to name the most important invention of the past 2000 years. In part because I wanted to be quoted, I quipped "classical music." A more thoughtful answer to that question would have been "the scholarly disciplines." Those of us who live in or around the academy take the disciplines for granted. To so great an extent are we surrounded by the scholarly disciplines, like mathematics, science, history, social sciences, and the arts, that, like the proverbial fish, we are the last to discover that we are in water. And those outside the academy probably also think of these "subjects" as a given part of the human condition.

But as important as disciplinary modes of thinking are to effecting mind changes, those modes were not given to us by God or nature. They were developed gradually, often painstakingly, over many years by individual scholars and groups of scholars. Neither history nor physics just happened: in the West their origins date back to efforts by Thucydides and Herodotus, in the case of history, and Aristotle and Archimedes, in the case of physics. And the history that we study today is dependent on important figures like the Frenchman Jules Michelet and the German Leopold von Ranke, just as contemporary physics is unthinkable without the discoveries of Galileo, Newton, and Einstein. Much mind changing throughout large swaths of a culture can be attributed to such brilliant thinkers, some known by name, many others simply part of the powerful Zeitgeist.

Thus we face the following situation. The disciplines represent the most advanced and best ways to think about issues consequential to human beings. Yet from a disciplinary point of view, the ways in which most of us think about these issues are fundamentally flawed. How do we change minds to bring them into closer accord with sophisticated disciplinary thinking?

The sort of discipline involved in scholarly modes of thinking, then is far from intuitive. In fact, studies have shown that most youngsters' intuitive concepts are deeply flawed. Disciplinary understanding is difficult to attain. We *Homo sapiens* may have evolved to climb mountains, swim across channels, absorb with ease (at least through childhood) the spoken languages that we hear around us. But we have not evolved to carry out historical studies, compute trigonometric functions, compose a fugue, pursue a set of experimental investigations in biology, chemistry, or physics, let alone to create testable theories in these spheres. Evolution may be scientifically true, but all eight-year-olds and many adults remain creationists. As developmental psychologist David Henry Feldman has pointed out, initially the aforementioned higher cognitive feats were carried out only by a few persons in society—they are "idiosyncratic" human functions.[4] Over time, due to the greater familiarity of ideas and to our enhanced capacities to teach and learn, such competences become more widely dispersed in society.

Here we enter the heartland of mind changing, school style: getting accustomed to the atmosphere of the classroom may not be fun, but it is not that difficult for most of us to accomplish. Mastering the literacies is time consuming for many of us and extremely difficult for 5 percent to 10 percent of us. Yet the literacies themselves are not counterintuitive (they are better thought of as new sets of representational tools, requiring the flexing of a new set of cognitive muscles). In contrast, studies in cognitive science document that both disciplinary content and disciplinary habits of mind may be *deeply* counterintuitive.[5]

Consider a few examples. Galileo tells us that all objects accelerate at the same rate; Newton tells us that the same laws of motion govern a falling apple and a planet in orbit; Darwin tells us that we and contemporary chimpanzees have evolved from a common primate ancestor; Einstein challenges the evidence of our senses that time and space can be absolutely determined. None of these understandings of the physical world is in the least bit intuitive. Equally significant, the ways in which disciplinarians go about their business are arcane. Historians don't look out the window and report what they see: They sit in libraries, read dusty books, pore over ancient records, and try to make sense, to "triangulate" what they have gleaned from disparate written (and more recently, photographic, video, audio, or digital) records. Physicists may begin with curiosity about the natural world, but they spend their time tinkering with equipment in a laboratory, building supersonic devices, juggling equations on a computer screen, and creating models that may entail an unfathomable number of dimensions.

So if we want to change the minds of learners, if we want them to make use of the discoveries made by disciplinary scholars over the centuries, we need to devote years to educating students in the arcana of the disciplines. From my perspective, this is the chief reason for remaining in school. It has been estimated that it takes ten years to become an expert in a domain (and perhaps another ten years to make truly original contributions to that domain). Even if this estimate is rough at best, it is evident that most individuals will not pick up the tools of the disciplines without guided application over a significant period of time.

But how best to acquire disciplinary modes of thinking? My studies indicate that disciplinary understanding is most likely to come about if three conditions are met. First, it is necessary to confront directly the many misconceptions (literally, wrong concepts) that youngsters hold: both the misconceptions of *content* (e.g., humans are a species unrelated to the rest of the animal—and for that matter, plant—kingdom) and the misconceptions of *method* (e.g., experiments need only be carried out once and their interpretation is straightforward). Resistances must be clearly recognized and confronted. Youngsters need to see that—however strongly held—their conceptions are not necessarily correct. This realization can only emerge by virtue of regular and systematic confrontation of their "natural" but typically inadequate modes and conclusions of thought.

Second, individuals must absorb themselves deeply in examples: specific scientific theories, historical examples, works of art. In *The Disciplined Mind,* I suggest that one could build an entire curriculum around a small set of rich examples.[6] From science, I selected the theory of evolution and, for greater focus, the problem of the distribution of finches around the several Galapagos islands. From the arts, I selected Mozart's *The Marriage of Figaro* and, for greater focus, a vocal trio of a few minutes in the first act thereof. From recent history, I selected as my focus the Holocaust of World War II, with the pivotal Wannsee Conference of January 20, 1942 (where the "Final Solution" was put into motion). By careful study, using research or reason, one comes to a detailed understanding of these three examples, and, of consequence for future study, one has a privileged opportunity to appreciate the ways in which disciplinarians conceive of and interpret such seminal cases.

Once one decides to focus in detail on an example, the third opportunity arises: the chance to approach a topic in a number of different ways.

CHANGING MINDS THROUGH
REPRESENTATIONAL REDESCRIPTION

Of all seven levers for mind change, representational redescription, as I've called it, is probably the most important way of changing the minds of students. Here, the concept of multiple intelligences is key. All the topics that I mentioned—and innumerable additional ones could be cited—are susceptible to entry via a number of different routes, and these routes correspond, roughly speaking, to our different intelligences. These entry points include the following:

1. *Narrative:* telling stories about the topic and the people involved with it (e.g., the story of Charles Darwin for evolution or of Anne Frank for the Holocaust)
2. *Quantitative:* using examples connected to the topic (e.g., the puzzle of different numbers and varieties of finches spread across a dozen islands in the Galapagos)
3. *Logic:* identifying the key elements or units and exploring their logical connections (e.g., how Malthus's argument about human

survival in the face of insufficient resources can be applied to competition among biological species)

4. *Existential:* addressing big questions, such as the nature of truth or beauty, life and death

5. *Aesthetic:* examining instances in terms of their artistic properties or capturing the examples themselves in works of art (e.g., observing the diverse shapes of the beaks of finches; analyzing the expressive elements in the trio)

6. *Hands-on:* working directly with tangible examples (e.g., performing the Figaro trio, breeding fruit flies to observe how traits change over the generations)

7. *Cooperative or social:* engaging in projects with others where each makes a distinctive contribution to successful execution

It would be foolish, and in any case unnecessary, to claim that every topic should be approached in six, eight, or a dozen ways. Yet it is equally misguided to approach each topic in only one way. Any topic of significance can be represented mentally in a number of different ways; and the more deeply one understands the topic, the more ways in which one can readily and appropriately conceptualize it. Moreover, if one can present a topic in several ways, two important outcomes ensue. First, one reaches more students; after all, some students learn better from narrative entry points and others from social or artistic entries. Second, one conveys to students the idea that disciplinary experts readily conceive of topics in more than one way.

There is no royal road to disciplinary understanding. One can say, equally, there are several royal roads to disciplinary learning, with the most versatile teachers serving as the most reliable guides. The main points are these: Education in the disciplines is a formidable challenge. The mind changes involved in disciplinary learning are profound ones; given the strength and ubiquity of resistances, they are difficult to effect even under favorable circumstances; and those educators who can help to bring them about constitute a precious human resource. The critical point here is that there are many effective formats, and the sought-after tipping point is most likely to be reached if a teacher uses several formats flexibly and imaginatively.

The surest route to mind changing in the disciplines, then, is the effective exploitation of multiple intelligences. Much the same could also be said of changing the minds of adults who have long been out of school. In the remainder of this chapter, we will examine how, among the several levers for effecting mind change, representational redescription emerges as an especially powerful tool. Let us begin with an example set in a corporation that urgently needed a change of mind.

BEYOND SCHOOL: CHANGING ADULT MINDS THROUGH REPRESENTATIONAL REDESCRIPTION

No question about it, BP, the British oil company, has had a glorious past. Founded as British Petroleum in Persia (now Iran) a century ago, this well-regarded company was a leading producer of oil throughout most of the twentieth century. But in the 1970s and 1980s, the industrial giant had fallen on hard times. Part of this decline in fortune was due to outside forces: In the years following the oil embargo of 1973–1974, the petroleum industry was subjected to a roller coaster of unpredictable political and economic events.[7]

Yet some of BP's decline can be blamed on ill-adapted conditions within the company. BP had a huge and poorly disciplined employment force scattered all over the world. Nor was the company sufficiently strategic; for example, much effort was spent digging for oil in the Netherlands, though mega-rival Shell was much more likely to succeed on its home soil. Neither highly positioned managers nor ordinary workers were held accountable for their achievements and lapses, let alone their specific contributions to profitability. In crude behaviorist terms, there were few rewards (or positive reinforcements) for outstanding performance and few penalties (or negative reinforcements) for failure. Far too much of the company's business was focused on oil, though the extent of world reserves was unknown and the possibility of seizure by nationalistic leaders (or followers) was ever present. Perhaps most disturbingly, there were no plans for dealing with such destabilizing situations. BP stood at considerable risk of becoming an industrial dinosaur, going the way of once-dominant companies like Westinghouse, American Motors, and Montgomery Ward.

In the early 1990s, however, BP began to change. First under the leadership of David Simon (CEO from 1992 to 1995), and more recently under John Browne (Lord Browne, as of 2001), BP revamped its profile within the petroleum industry and among corporate giants more generally. It cut down its core workforce by over half, from 120,000 to 53,000, in the 1990s;[8] at the same time, it acquired major natural resource companies. At the start of the twenty-first century, BP had climbed from being the fifth largest and least profitable of leading petroleum companies to the second largest and most profitable; in the first quarter of 2001, a bleak period for most corporations worldwide, BP reported a record-breaking $4.13 billion profit.[9] Its main activities include the exploration and production of crude oil and natural gas, manufacturing and marketing, and solar generation—activities that have earned it the nickname "Beyond Petroleum." Having long been viewed as one of the principal contributors to pollution, BP now aims to become an environmentally friendly, self-styled "green company." It regularly reports on its performances vis-à-vis health, safety, environmental care, social investment, and responsiveness to local conditions.[10]

But perhaps most astounding are the shifts that have occurred within BP itself, introduced by CEO Browne and his top executives. Once a conventionally hierarchical firm, BP is now organized in a flat way. Once an organization where responsibility was diffuse or altogether absent, it is now a company where each individual is expected to contribute directly to profits or to engage in creating or distributing knowledge that will ultimately increase profits. Those who cannot justify their contributions are rapidly and, some would say, ruthlessly dismissed from the company.

How did this dramatic turnaround occur? BP became a "learning company," trafficking (self-consciously or not) in the creation and alteration of mental representations. For example, BP executives now spend a great deal of time in strategy sessions—reflecting on the current state of the petroleum industry as well as the opportunities available, the possible pitfalls, and alternative courses of action. Moreover, the company is now characterized by considerable experimentation and virtually instantaneous communication of all knowledge within the company.

But let's step back for a moment. It is one thing to instigate such changes; it is quite another to weave them into the well-worn corporate

fabric and the DNA of its workforce. Indeed, few goals are more challenging to achieve than significant, lasting change in adult human beings.
So, even when everyone agrees in broad terms on what needs to change,
someone still needs to work out a plan to implement change in a lasting
way. To put this in terms of a cognitive perspective, a leader must proceed
from her own internal representations of both the present and of the
desired (new) state of affairs to some kind of a public presentation that
captures this vision. Moreover, each member of the leadership team will
likely have his own mental representation, and each will likewise utilize
modes of expression that are comfortable. The team must hammer out an
acceptable consensual representation. The leadership team then needs to
communicate this representation widely—preferably in a number of discrete yet compatible forms—and test whether it can gain support. In our
terms, a leader must first define the content of the message she wishes to
convey and then find the formats that convey that message well enough
to create meaningful and lasting changes of mind—first in the leadership
team, eventually throughout the company.

Let's say that most members of the company still believe in the traditional hierarchical authority structure. How should the leader attempt to
change this mind-set? A simple announcement that this is no longer true
is unlikely to prove effective. A graphic presentation or film of new kinds
of decision-making entities will at most capture the attention of some
employees. Say, however, that each month a pressing new problem in
search of a solution is posed to various groups of frontline managers.
The managers are given time each week to meet on this problem as well
as resources to hire consultants and carry out experiments. After some
months of such problem solving, a diverse set of managers is constituted
as a special review group. These managers examine each of the candidate
solutions, review the newly conducted research, and choose the most
promising one. The designated leaders of the company then pledge to institute this new procedure, evaluate it, and, if it proves successful, announce that it has become company policy.

No one of these moves is likely to change the minds of most employees. But if the company leadership approaches the problem in a
number of different ways, and if these methods work well together, then
mind change becomes a distinct possibility. Consider such a BP-style
agenda in terms of our mind-changing levers. Foremost, there needs to

be a clear and *reasoned statement* of the proposed mind change (which includes *research* into why traditional authority structures no longer work); substantial *resources* need to be devoted to the change (which would involve several teams working over many months); powerful *resistances* must be recognized (e.g., most employees are used to a top-down structure); *resonance* must be cultivated (e.g., reinforcing the idea that it is pleasurable to work together on consequential problems with individuals whom one likes and respects); and *real world events* (for BP, the threat that oil supplies will be seized or that this old, venerated company will collapse altogether) must be recognized and exploited. Perhaps most important, the leaders who seek to bring about changes of mind must attempt to capture and convey the desired shift in a multiplicity of formats (*representational redescription*). If the new way of thinking is embodied in multiple forms over a significant period of time—if it is well stated and well embodied in spoken policy, in modeled behaviors, in groups that actually do what they are empowered to do—then and only then is a major change of mind likely to occur throughout the company.

Let me add one important note about resistances. One can—and must—go through an exercise of deep and pervasive mental surgery with respect to every entrenched view: Define it, understand the reasons for its provenance, point out its weaknesses, and then develop multiple ways of undermining that view and bolstering a more constructive one. In other words, *search for the resonance* and *stamp out the resistance*. Consider three such entrenched views—each familiar to anyone who has worked in any organization—and the ways in which these views might profitably be reformulated:

- *Early representation:* Bigger is always better.
- *Better representation:* It all depends. Sometimes small is beautiful. Assets of scale are often at odds with flexibility, comfort, innovation. The behemoths of one era may well become the dinosaurs of the next.

- *Early representation:* It you don't like your situation, scream, quit, or do both.
- *Better representation:* All niches have pros and cons. If you act shrewdly, you may be able to improve your situation, not only benefiting yourself but also improving the atmosphere for others. It is

also important to listen to what others are saying because you might not grasp the whole picture.

- *Early representation:* I've done it this way so long that I know it is right.
- *Better representation:* There is merit in tried-and-true practices, but sometimes—and particularly at a time of rapid change—such practices can become dysfunctional. Items of inferior quality that are less expensively made sometimes dislodge quality products. Keep an open mind, be willing to experiment, blend the best of the old and the new.

There are usually good reasons why such entrenched views persist and defy ready abandonment. Yet there are times when the entrenched view is counterproductive, the need for a "counterstory" acute. Having identified this challenge, it is the task of the authorized leaders to determine the best ways in which to challenge the "earlier representation," demonstrate its limitations, suggest reasons for another perspective, and embody the alternative stories in as many impressive and diverse formats as possible. Only if an individual truly becomes convinced that bigger is not always better, that all niches have their advantages, that experimentation can be empowering is she likely to begin to think and to behave on that new basis.

TAKING CHARGE OF YOUR OWN EDUCATION

We can draw many lessons from the example of BP. But perhaps the main point is that as adults, we need to remain open to changing our minds and to having them changed by outside influences. We need to cultivate the habit of continuous learning; to make it something we do, as educator Theodore Sizer has put it, "when no one is looking."

Indeed, such lifelong learning is more important today than ever. Once upon a time one could complete one's years of formal study in childhood or adolescence and then remain up to speed for the rest of life. Jobs changed gradually enough, companies and employees were loyal enough, so that little or no additional study was necessary. Few would doubt that we have today crossed the Rubicon that separates a guaranteed lifetime job from a turbulent occupational marketplace. Hardly a vocation can be named where lifelong learning is not becoming the norm. Conditions of work across the globe change at unparalleled speed. Most anything that can be automated will be. Those who can stay ahead of the curve are likely to be well positioned; those who rest on the laurels of a mind stocked long ago are likely to become anachronistic and—I might add—unemployable.

To be in charge of changing one's own mind is a heady undertaking (pun intended). It means that the individual himself has internalized the supportive roles that used to be played by parents, teachers, and other designated conveyers of knowledge and skill (shades of the developmental scholar Lev Vygotsky introduced in chapter 3). The lifelong learner needs to know how to monitor changes in relevant domains. Such monitoring can be done in part by talking to others, in part by observing them, but it typically involves as well more targeted searches through the printed literature, the relevant Web sites, the offerings of adult "continuing education" institutions. Whatever one's business, one needs to be in touch with what else is going on and what else is being thought around the globe. That is how the content of one's mind becomes updated.

It is equally timely to understand how your own mind works: The most effective mind-changers build up accurate mental models of their own minds. Some aspects of mind are true for everyone; for example, we all learn better when we use new knowledge frequently and in varying contexts. But other aspects of mind may be idiosyncratic. I learn the best when I confront written text and can review it a number of times. Others like to learn from oral briefings, from lectures, from heated conversations or arguments with others. When I look at an article in the *Scientific American* I always begin with the text, and even while examining a diagram, I generally read the legend first. But many others approach scientific publications in the opposite manner: examining photos, diagrams, and drawings first and only resorting to the text when all else fails. I avoid Web sites as much as possible and, when surfing them, treat them as written texts and print them out as quickly as possible. (Conversely, I turn to my new *Webster's* or my old *Oxford English Dictionary* at the drop of a word.) Many others wallow in the visuals, rarely encounter a link to another site that they fail to explore, and avoid the "print" command.

A person who knows her own mind—how it learns best—is most likely to be able to change her mind effectively. Where once adults had few options for continuing education—the university being the main one—today think-tanks, adult education institutions, weekend and summertime "cognitive camps," and training divisions (or even self-styled corporate universities) at large organizations are all arrayed to assist in the mind-changing process. Corporate training, for example, currently amounts to at least a $100-billion-a-year effort.

Educational institutions have until recently engaged in mind change en masse; that is, they have treated individuals as if they were members of a group and sought the most effective generic strategies for mind changing. The creation of powerful new technologies has altered the situation permanently: though mass production is still the rule, we are now free to personalize both instruction and assessment as much as we would like. (I predict that multiple pathways to instruction and assessment will become the norm in the coming decades.) In contrast, when one is in a more circumscribed institution—dealing with experts or with a homogeneous audience—there is once again reduced incentive to personalize instruction. One looks for the formula that is most effective for a group or, if one includes a number of different strategies (as in the use of multiple entry points), one presents these options to the entire group.

Once one has entered the terrain of working on one's own mind, however, there is little point in searching for generic solutions. One is in the position now of the rich person who can hire a tutor for a child: The tutor's challenge is to ensure that the child in question learns what he should, and the tutor has every incentive to be as opportunistic and personalized as possible. So, too, in serving as one's own tutor, it is important to know as much as one can about one's own mind, one's own learning proclivities and quirks, and to seize on these in finding the optimal "pedagogy" and "curriculum" for one's own idiosyncratic array of intelligences and stupidities.

I call this change of perspective Intimate Mind Changing. In the next two chapters, I examine the most intimate forms of mind changing: those that occur with individuals with whom one has an intimate relation (chapter 8) and those that feature the most intimate relation of all—to one's own mind (chapter 9).

CHAPTER 8

Mind Changing Up Close

WE ALL HAVE A KEEN INTEREST in mind changing in intimate settings—situations in which our persuasive energies are directed at just one or two people. In fact, most of us probably spend the bulk of our time thinking about how to change the minds of those to whom we are closest. We want to change the minds of family members, including parents, siblings, and children; to convince friends or defang enemies; to be able to work effectively with our boss and with our employees; to fuse our minds with those of our lovers. In such personal settings, we gain the most when we successfully change minds and pay the heaviest prices when our attempts fail.

Few encounters are more personal than that between patient and therapist. I often think about the interaction between a famous psychotherapist (who happened to be my undergraduate tutor in college) and one of his most troubled patients.

ERIK ERIKSON AND THE SEMINARIAN

While working with severely disturbed adolescents at the Austen Riggs Clinic in Stockbridge, Massachusetts, in the 1950s, Erik Erikson treated a young seminarian who had become so unhappy and confused that he was scarcely able to function. At one point in the treatment, the patient presented a dream—one so threatening that it tested his sense of reality. In the seminarian's words: "There was a big face sitting in a buggy of the horse-and-buggy days. The face was completely empty and there was horrible, slimy, snaky, hair all around. I am not sure it wasn't my mother."[1]

Erikson felt that the seemingly sketchy dream was important: a synopsis that captured in a vivid image the most important themes that had been swirling about in the young man's psyche. After listening to the patient free-associate to the dream for almost an hour, Erikson decided to take a risk—since the patient had been in fragile shape—and to offer an interpretation in hopes of instigating in his patient a healing change of mind.

Erikson suggested that the patient had become distraught because of the mixed messages conveyed to him by the most important individuals in his life. The dream image evoked in the patient nostalgic thoughts of a more comfortable and restful past, a time when his grandfather had been a rural clergyman. The absence of facial features suggested that the figure might be the patient's mother, a person who was difficult to define; his mother had also romanticized the past but had been remote and inaccessible to the patient during periods of his childhood. Erikson also saw the featureless face as reminiscent of other important figures in the man's life. One was Erikson himself, a man with unruly white hair. The therapist attributed his own presence in the dream to the fact that the patient had been upset at him for having been sick and abandoning him temporarily. Other relevant figures had a religious connotation: the patient was torn between his love of God and his feelings of sexual inadequacy, as captured by a threatening Medusa image. And, finally, the absence of facial features was, in Erikson's view, a reminder that the patient remained uncertain about his own identity.

Simply sharing this dream interpretation with the patient, of course, was not enough to bring about a change of mind. (It might also overwhelm him.) Unless the seminarian was somehow able to come to terms with the dream's messages where possible, and to cut his losses where necessary, he would continue to feel unproductive and immobilized. But before describing the change that actually occurred for the seminarian, let me describe how such therapist-patient interactions may change minds.

The Therapeutic Encounter

In centuries past, the role of "confessor" or "wise person" was generally allocated to a senior religious figure, like a priest, rabbi, or mullah. In times of turmoil, one went to this individual, spilled one's guts (with the promise of confidentiality), felt a load lifted from one's shoulders, secured advice and/or absolution, and went back—emboldened or subdued—to face the world anew. In the last century, a new relationship developed—that between a designated professional called the therapist and the patient (or client). The patient sees the therapist more or less regularly and pays the therapist an agreed-on fee for serving as a sounding board and dispersing interpretation or advice when such feedback is deemed appropriate.

At the most general level, the patient comes to the therapist because of problems with which he cannot cope adequately.[2] The purpose of the therapy sessions is to change the patient's mind and/or behavior in ways that make his life ultimately less problematic and more fulfilling. The therapist has a wide store of knowledge of human troubles and a set of strategies that help to tease out problems and to reflect on how they may be alleviated. The patient is expected to be honest about his situation, to engage in reflection about what might be done, to report on what happens between sessions, and to problem-solve with the therapist as indicated. At a minimum, the patient hopes to acquire a better understanding of his plight and some strategies for dealing with it. If all goes well, the patient also anticipates that he will emerge from the therapy as a happier, healthier individual, better able to deal with inevitable conflicts and to lead a fulfilling life.

Both the therapist and the patient, then, can see their joint endeavor as an extended exercise in mind changing. A major task of therapy is to open up the contents of the mind—the mental representations lurking in both the conscious and unconscious mind. Therapy is a somewhat painful process that includes identifying the major ideas—concepts, stories, scripts, theories, models, practices—that the patient currently embraces, and pinpointing the ways in which these are productive and worth retaining, or insidious and worth abandoning. Of course, the success of a therapeutic encounter depends on many factors, including whether the patient has a realistic or unrealistic picture of her situation in the world, and whether she is able to confront events in her past that left a powerful (and perhaps too powerful) mark on her personality. Good luck also helps.

As he attempts to figure out the optimal intervention, the patient's particular stories, themes, or scripts, as well as their formats, are also crucial. Here, as for any skilled professional, knowledge of previous similar (and informatively contrasting) cases is at a premium. The therapist must try to understand the given situation as clearly and coolly as possible and help the patient to share this understanding as well—and this calls for skills far beyond the sympathy that the untrained friend or stranger can supply.

While the mind of the patient appropriately assumes center stage, the mind of the therapist must be open to change as well. The therapist has to come to know the patient well; that involves empathy, but also the capacity to change his own mind—should, for example, the patient reveal new information or differ in unanticipated ways from previous clients. In nearly every therapeutic encounter, there is not only transfer of strong feelings on the part of the patient, but also *countertransference* on the part of the therapist; and that countertransference can be quite potent. Both patient and therapist need to be aware of these strong feelings, but it is especially important for the therapist to be sensitive to how her own mind is being invaded and affected by encounters with the patient.

The crux of therapy consists of examining events that have happened (or that one imagines have happened) and the meanings that the patient attaches to them. As a reflexively interpretive entity, the mind will naturally come up with explanations and rationalizations. Individuals often end up in therapy—and some never terminate!—because the meanings that they attach to events are distorted, their perceptions are faulty, their feelings are inappropriate, and their behaviors are counterproductive. Accordingly the core of the therapeutic encounter is the construction of interpretations that undo destructive habits and help patients realize their stated goals. A multitude of techniques—ranging from the telling of powerful stories by persons in authority to the processes of identification that powerful individuals exploit—are relevant. The task of the therapist is to figure out which of these techniques, singly and in combination, is most likely to be effective in the long run for this particular patient with his presenting symptoms. Rarely is this a job of straightforward persuasion; it is better described as an effort to create conditions for change and to keep hope alive.[3] To as great an extent as teaching algebra to a child with learning problems, or convincing a strong-willed faculty member to change his course of behavior, this task is an individually nuanced craft-like undertaking.

Changing the Mind of a Patient

With that background in mind, consider the synthesis of ideas that Erik-son arrived at and eventually offered the young seminarian:

> *Tracing one main theme of the dream retrospectively, we have recognized it in four periods of the patient's life—all four premature graduations which left him with anger and fear over what he was to abandon rather than with the anticipation of greater freedom and more genuine identity: the present treat-ment—and the patient's fear that by some act of horrible anger (on his part or on mine or both) he might lose me and thus his chance to regain his iden-tity through trust in me; his immediately preceding religious education—and his abortive attempt at finding through prayer that "presence" which would cure his inner void; his earlier youth—and his hope to gain strength, peace, and identity by identifying himself with his grandfather; and, finally, early childhood—and his desperate wish to keep alive in himself the charitable face of his mother in order to overcome fear, guilt, and anger over her emotions. Such redundancy points to a certain theme which, once found, gives added meaning to all the associated material. The theme is: "Whenever I begin to have faith in somebody's strength and love, some angry and sickly emotions pervade the relationship, and I end up mistrusting, empty, and a victim of anger and despair."* [4]

From one perspective, this venture into interpretation seems over-wrought. After all, the patient has said only a few words, it was only a brief report of a single dream, and some of the points in the interpreta-tion were hardly hinted at. And yet, in this instance Erikson's gamble paid off. A breakthrough happened in the course of the therapeutic hour. This reorienting mental representation was possible not because of the con-tents of the particular dream per se, but rather because the dream served to crystallize a congeries of themes that had been swirling around in the patient's unconscious and that had emerged in the course of extended free association. Indeed, rather than spurning this interpretation, the seminarian discerned that it made sense and that it insightfully wove together the various themes with which he had been struggling. Erikson recalls, "It so happened that this interpretation proved convincing to us both and, in the long run, strategic for the whole treatment. . . . The patient left the hour—to which he had come with a sense of dire disaster—with a broad smile and obvious encouragement."[5]

Erikson would have been the first to admit that such success does not always come easily, nor can a mind change ordinarily be crystallized by a single interpretation. Even if the therapy session represented a tipping point, it certainly did not come about without much preparation and considerable subsequent reworking. Like Darwin's Malthusian insight about natural selection, the apparent breakthrough is actually an overt manifestation of a far more gradual process. Erikson's decision to share his bold synthesis may well have reflected his own, perhaps unconscious or preconscious, realization that the patient was ready to hear a new "story of his life" and to take a new step.

In this example of mind changing, we can see at work the unproductive old stories, a more promising new story, a powerful format in the guise of a dream, and a range of intelligences and emotions being brought to bear in order to draw a sensitive young person to a new place and a new understanding. Note, however, that "putting it into words" is but one means for therapeutic progress: Formats and processes may vary. Therapist Leston Havens points out, "[E]very account of what we do distorts the organic nature of all these interactions as well as the curious mixture of letting alone and occasional nudging which is the task. As time passes, that task seems to me more and more a matter of growing things, of movements and feelings, and less a matter of words and ideas."[6]

Accordingly, we can identify in this example at least four of the seven Rs of mind change: the use of *reason* in the form of analysis is important, of course, as are the *resources* of time and energy invested by both therapist and patient. The dream was important though clearly fragmentary data, to be added to other scattered data about the thoughts and feelings of the patient. The capturing of important themes in a vivid though

sketchy dream is a textbook example of *representational redescription*. Ultimately, however, *resonance* is key: Does Erikson's dream interpretation
make sense to the seminarian on a visceral level? Clearly it did, as evi-
denced by the patient's welcome lightness of heart at the end of the therapeutic hour. Conversely, a lack of resonance can cripple an attempt to
change a person's mind. Let us consider an encounter between a university president and a professor—a compelling example of what happens
when one strong-willed person seeks to change the mind and the behavior of another equally strong-willed person.

THE PRESIDENT AND THE PROFESSOR

In 2001, economist Lawrence Summers, former U.S. Secretary of the
Treasury, had just commenced his term as the twenty-seventh president
of Harvard University. An energetic man in his late forties, Summers had
many plans for the school: to improve undergraduate education, stem
grade inflation, nurture young faculty members to tenure, and trim the
plethora of new and variably successful programs that had burgeoned on
campus during the terms of his immediate predecessors, among other
things.

It was in this spirit of crafting change that he called for a meeting, in
October 2001, with Cornel West. Along with novelist Toni Morrison and
literary critic Henry Louis "Skip" Gates, West was one of the best-known
African American intellectuals in the nation. The author of many books
in philosophy, politics, and current events, West had been brought to Harvard from Princeton with considerable fanfare in the early 1990s. There
he had established a reputation as a charismatic lecturer and an individual who was integrally involved with American political and social issues
beyond the campus. Before long he had received the highest scholarly ac-
colade at the university: He was named as one of the approximately fifteen University Professors, who are allowed to teach in any department
at Harvard. In the months before this fall meeting West had been ill and
had taken off time from his teaching.

As far as I have been able to ascertain, West and Summers were not personally acquainted before their meeting. But one thing is certain: by the
end of the encounter, West had become so upset by Summers's reception

that he considered resigning from the university on the spot. (Because he was scheduled for surgery, he decided to postpone his decision until the following spring—at which time he did indeed resign his post to return to Princeton University.)

Word of the meeting leaked out shortly thereafter, becoming front-page and cover story news in national publications.[7] The story circled the globe: In January 2002, I traveled to Hong Kong and Denmark and was questioned in both places about "what actually happened" on that October day in Cambridge. The "word" was that Summers had been very confrontational with West, criticizing him for, among other things, his failure in recent years to carry out serious scholarship and for his far-reaching activities off campus, which included involvement in two presidential campaigns. West's issuing of a "rap" CD was also brought up, according to reports.

The initial reaction from the African American intellectual community, and from many others as well, was critical of Summers. While no one on the Harvard campus is treated as sacrosanct, West came as close to being an "untouchable" figure as anyone. A leading African American public intellectual, West was wounded by what he saw as an attack on his life commitments and on his scholarly integrity. He and others began to talk about a mass exodus by the African American department—a department that (with support from the previous university president) had been built up energetically by West's close colleague, Henry Louis Gates. Indeed, within two months, another respected professor in the African American department, philosopher Anthony Appiah, announced that he was going to Princeton University—Harvard's chief rival in the recruitment of distinguished faculty of color.

For his part, Summers issued both a private apology to West and his colleagues for a "misunderstanding" and a public announcement that he was committed to a strong African American department and, more broadly, to the strengthening of diversity on campus. (Making good on this promise, Summers approved several new appointments the following year.) Nonetheless, after complaining that Summers had not reached out when West had undergone a second operation for prostate cancer (both the president and provost of Princeton had reportedly called him regularly during his convalescence), West decided to leave Harvard.

The synopsis I've just given is part of the public record, and not in contention so far as I have been able to determine. We will probably never know the full story, from the perspective of the two participants; consistent with university policy, the office of the president never issued a description of the meeting. For this very reason, however, the Summers-West encounter provides an opportunity to speculate on the various ways in which an effort to change minds can have gone wrong. I will first put words into the mouths of the two participants and then talk about how the communication might have been more successfully effected. While this example comes from the world of academe, similar miscommunications no doubt occur across multiple realms, from conversations within the family to encounters in the boardroom.

The West Account

I hardly know this man, and he is new to the campus. In fact, he has not been in the academy for ten years, but busy in Washington dealing with domestic and international financial issues. He seems uninformed and uninterested in questions of race and diversity, and distinctly unsympathetic to affirmative action. With no warning, without having read any of my writings, he laces into me. He accuses me of having abandoned scholarship, even though I have written serious books in the last few years, and I am one of the most cited intellectuals in the world. He suggests that I have been lax on campus even though my course had over 600 students, I never miss a class, and I even drove from New York to Cambridge so I could meet my class on September 12, 2001! He criticizes my political involvement, but a high percentage of American public intellectuals are involved in supporting candidates; would he have said a word if I had supported Vice President Al Gore (as he did) or Senator John Kerry? He questions my medical leave, but I have prostate cancer and an uncertain life expectancy. Who the hell does he think he is? Who needs this? At the very least I would have expected him to be cordial and to save any so-called issues for another day. After all, we are both major figures in America and we need to get acquainted first. I would like to leave Harvard—which is not a very happy place anyway—and nothing would please me more than if Skip Gates, Anthony Appiah, and other valued colleagues would join in a mass exodus to Princeton, where the new president and provost both "get it."

The Summers Account

I am newly returned to the campus and it is important for me to meet the major figures here. After all, I'm the leader of this flagship institution and what we do here is widely watched. West is one of the elite University Professors, and, as such, he is under my supervision (the other, less-exalted 1,200 professors answer to their respective deans). I don't know the guy, and I certainly have no prejudices against his or any group. But I believe in being direct, expressing my views, and letting the chips fall where they may. I have heard some disturbing things about West, and I want to bring them out into the open and hear what he has to say in response. I understand that his books are reviewed in the popular press but no longer have scholarly standing. Is this true? I understand that he had a medical leave but that instead of convalescing, he was touring around the country, giving political talks, issuing a rap CD, etc. If this is true, it sounds dubious to me; if not, let's hear the facts. Here's a guy who is in a position to be an enormously positive influence not only on younger African Americans but also on the broader scholarly community. I want to see whether I can motivate him to do a better job; everyone will thank us for this. The last thing I want to do is to "diss" him or to drive him and his colleagues to a rival institution.

MEETINGS CAN GO WRONG, seriously wrong. Unless one adopts a cynical view—that is, that Summers wanted to squeeze West (or perhaps even the entire department) off campus or that West was simply looking for a pretext to justify an already-made decision to return to Princeton—such a derailment is what actually happened. Instead of having a friendly conversation with a new colleague, West found himself in the midst of a national media maelstrom—one that he had hardly sought. Instead of prompting a colleague to consider engaging in a new pattern of behavior, Summers had to backtrack feverishly.

One could speculate that while Summers called the meeting to change West's mind, the end result of the meeting was to bring about changes in Summers's mind. He may have thought that he was the boss, but he now had to realize (in a visceral way!) that members of the Harvard Senior Faculty—all tenured, often self-satisfied, sometimes arrogant—were (at least in some ways) in as powerful a position as he was. He thought that he could pressure West, and perhaps others among the University Professors or the African American department, to pursue a new line of behavior; but his capacity to bring about change, at least in this manner, was far less than he had thought.

In the final analysis, Summers and West had come to the meeting with entirely different mental models of their roles and their aspirations. There was no resonance, and the resulting clash was counterproductive. My goal is not to pass judgment on the respective merits of either party's position, nor on the ultimate denouement of the Summers-West brouhaha. But I will say that West showed himself to have a thin skin. And I will add that, with this encounter, Summers used up some of his most precious resource—the goodwill that attends the assumption of a leadership position at a major institution. Throughout the media coverage of this event, I was reminded of a job requirement for a college president that I had once heard: the president needs to be able to "listen charismatically." Individuals who have a reservoir of goodwill, who can make colleagues (and potential donors and potential adversaries) feel that they matter, are most likely to bring about the changes that they desire. In fact, as illustrated by the case of James O. Freedman of Dartmouth, even those with abundant listening skills may have to tolerate a fair amount of carnage (not to say personal vilification) when they are trying to bring about difficult changes.

CREATING RESONANCE IN INTIMATE SETTINGS

When one is dealing with a large audience, especially one that is heterogeneous, it is not possible to customize one's approach. When, however, one is attempting to craft a change of mind in a small group or in a single "target" individual, one can adopt a much more nuanced tack. The key is the creation of resonance.

If a social psychologist[8] had been summoned to advise President Summers on how to proceed, what insights could she have offered—either for the initial meeting or for possible follow-ups? To begin with, it is important to establish common links between the protagonists. In addition to their both being professors and intellectuals, Summers might have emphasized that he and West were about the same age, had commuted back and forth between the academy and the wider society, had strong commitments to public service, jointly admired certain individuals (e.g., department chair Henry Louis Gates), and shared common aims for the university (e.g., to have an excellent and diverse student body, to train future leaders). Neither had avoided controversy in their public lives— another potential bond!

A second piece of advice would be to engage West in a common enterprise. The more that West felt that he was able to pursue what he most wanted to, in the way that he wanted to, the more likely that he would embrace an initiative proposed by Summers. Suppose that Summers wanted West to adopt a tougher stance in grading: He might have asked West how he thought that students ought to be evaluated for their classroom performance. Summers might have then presented some contrasting scenarios about classroom performance, and asked West how he would have handled them. If West seemed interested in this set of issues, Summers might ask him to come to an additional meeting or join (or even head) a task force on the evaluation of student work. If, however, West showed little interest in this topic or seemed to be on a wavelength very different from Summers, the president would have been well-advised to drop the issue, at least for a time.

From a social-psychological perspective, another important consideration is that the two participants be engaged in give-and-take. From what we can gather, at the October meeting, Summers was pointing out a lot of things and asking West to react. It might have been more prudent for Summers to begin by finding out what West wanted to achieve at Harvard and in his broader enterprises off campus. At an initial meeting Summers could show interest in these issues or politely ask about them even if his actual interest was modest. In seeking to connect with someone, asking questions, listening carefully to the answers, and following up appropriately are almost always wise tactics. Then, when the conversation shifted to Summers's concerns, it would be equally important to make sure that the conversation not be one-sided. And if Summers put forth his own views about what should be done, these should be accompanied by a willingness to consider other approaches, to compromise, to rethink his position. In any event, both participants should feel that they have some control over events—that they are not being coerced into a position or mode of behavior.

Finally it would be important for Summers to monitor the overall tone of the conversation and to keep the atmosphere open, upbeat, optimistic. Should the tone have turned silent or hostile, it would be up to Summers to make repairs. It is bad form to let a conversation deteriorate in tone—even worse to allow the conversation to end on a downer.

Here we enter the arena of interpersonal sensitivity. It is crucial for any interlocutor—and especially for one in as powerful a position as Summers—to be attuned to signs that he is alienating a constituent. Indeed, Summers would have been well-advised to stop more than once during the conversation, ask West how he was feeling, and be prepared to backtrack or alter course if things were not going well. Particularly in view of West's recent illness, Summers might have tempered his remarks. I doubt that such "temperature taking" ever took place. Nor is there any reason to think that West attempted to put himself in Summers's place, that he tried to understand the president's motivations in bringing up the particular issues that he did in the way that he did or the mandate that the new president may have received from Harvard's governing corporation. But then, so far as I am aware, Cornel West had no agenda for changing the mind of Lawrence Summers.

Individual differences, of course, can be crucial in such intimate encounters. If one hopes to be effective with a particular person, it is vital to find out as much as one can about that person's traits, dispositions, scripts, and favored mental representations. Part of this individualized portrait can be gleaned from due diligence beforehand; part must be picked up "on the fly" in the course of a meeting or series of meetings. (It is the latter facet of interpersonal intelligence that distinguished Bill Clinton.)

Let's move away from our example. In evaluating a high-stakes encounter, here are some of the general considerations that I would monitor. Note that in most cases there is an implied continuum—for example, ranging from reliance on reason to reliance on emotional reactions. People can be placed along the continuum, and the aspiring mind-changer needs to alter his approach accordingly if resonance is to be achieved.

- *Argument, facts, rhetoric:* Is this person moved chiefly by argument, with its logical components? What role do facts, information, and data play in this person's hierarchy of considerations? Are rhetorical flourishes or logically ordered propositions more likely to capture attention and bring about changes?

- *Central versus peripheral routes:* Is this person more likely to be engaged by a direct discussion of the issue? Or would it be best to bring up one's concerns indirectly—through questions, examples, tone of voice, gestures, pregnant pauses, and well-timed silences?

- *Consistency:* How concerned is this person with consistency? Does this person care about whether stated beliefs, attitudes, and actions are consistent with one another? If so, how can one help this person deal with any inconsistencies?

- *Stance on conflict:* How much is this person bothered by the give-and-take of argument? Does this person like to match wits, or is it preferable to avoid sharp exchanges? If one has gone too far, how does one restore calm or equilibrium?

- *Emotionally charged territory:* What are the issues and ideas about which this person feels strongly? Should one engage these or avoid them? Can one mobilize this person around an area of strong feeling? How does one avoid the minefields that stand in the way of the desired change? Is this person motivated more by attraction to what she likes, or by fear of what she dislikes?

- *Current scripts—content:* On any topic, the conversants will have certain scripts or mental representations that are more or less well consolidated. If possible, it is important to determine beforehand what those scripts are, and how strongly they are held. Such information can be gleaned from a person's writings, conversation, or discussions with others who know the person well. Any negotiation will necessarily begin from those deeply held scripts—whether the ultimate goal is to build on these scripts or to call them into question.

- *Current scripts—form:* Individuals differ in the symbol systems, formats, or intelligences in which they habitually encode their mental representations. To the extent possible, it is desirable to determine which "forms of representation" are favored by an individual and to embed new concerns in those familiar forms. So, for example, if a person favors graphic demonstrations, these means should be employed when feasible. If, on the other hand, the person is influenced by the human embodiment of a desired perspective, the mind changer should try to model or embody the desired changes.

The most important consideration for those engaged in mind change, however, is probably the following: Avoid egocentrism—becoming ensnared in one's own construal of events. The purpose of a mind-changing encounter is not to articulate your own point of view but rather to engage the psyche of the other person. In general, the more that one knows about the *scripts* and the *strengths* of the other person, the resistances and resonances, and the more that one can engage these fully, the more likely one will be successful in bringing about the desired change—or at least holding open the possibility of such changes.

I don't know enough about either Lawrence Summers or Cornel West to have "prepped" them for the meeting. But I know enough about mind changing to say this: One must handle an encounter with an "other" who cares about logic, consistency, directness, and verbal argument very differently from an encounter with an "other" who is concerned about emotion, respect, subtlety, and nonverbal forms of communication. Encounters where these concerns are in synch are far more likely to go well than encounters where the mismatch is pronounced.

Finally, we must confront the possibility that some efforts to change minds are destined to fail. Perhaps, for example, Summers and West have mental representations that so differ from one another that no meeting of the minds would have been possible. In such situations, it might have been preferable to work through intermediaries, rather than risk the likelihood of a clash.

A PRESIDENTIAL ENCOUNTER ON PAPER

John Adams and Thomas Jefferson first came to know one another in the heat of the American Revolution—members of the Continental Congress, contributors to the Declaration of Independence (drafted initially, of course, by Jefferson), fierce partisans in the historic years that followed.[9] Hailing from a politically engaged family in Massachusetts, Adams was the senior figure: an early convert to the Colonial cause, direct, pugnacious, self-assured. The Virginian Jefferson, seven years his junior, was the more diplomatic person—a polymathic thinker and brilliant writer who, while equally ambitious, disliked direct confrontations and preferred to work behind the scenes. Having begun in the 1770s as close colleagues—indeed, by their own testimony, friends—they had by the close of the century been drawn sharply apart by personal and political events. And yet, miraculously overcoming decades of estrangement, they ended life once again as friends—each having an apparent change of mind about the other and, perhaps, about himself as well.

Once the Revolution had been improbably won, both Adams and Jefferson found themselves in the diplomatic service in Europe—Adams in London, Jefferson in Paris. This was the period of their lives when they were closest. They wrote many letters to one another, traveled together, gardened together, gossiped, and considered themselves intimates. According to Abigail Adams, no one worked as well with her husband as Jefferson.[10] Yet even at this time of relative calm, there were signs of strain in the relationship. Their different personal styles and political philosophies were emerging: Jefferson, the pure democrat, with distinct anarchic leanings, having more faith in the general population; Adams, distrustful of the mob yet, paradoxically, with greater need for human affection. Writing to a friend, Jefferson described Adams as a "poisonous weed";[11] he spoke of his vanity and his blindness and called him "irritable and a bad calculator of the probable effect of the motives which govern man."[12]

By the end of the decade, the Constitution and Bill of Rights had become law, George Washington had been chosen as first president by acclamation, and the future political trajectories of Adams, the vice president, and Jefferson, the secretary of state, were nebulous. Neither officially revealed his presidential ambitions and yet the rest of the nation assumed that one or another—or, eventually both—would succeed the elder Washington. While it was theoretically possible that the one-time friends could make common cause, they grew apart. Each increasingly vilified the other. In an unfortunate set of incidents, Jefferson referred publicly to "private heresies that have sprung up among us" but conceded privately that he was referring to John Adams. Having got wind of this attack, Adams's son John Quincy called Jefferson to account. Jefferson sent a mild apology to the senior Adams, in which he said, "That you and I differ in our idea of the best form of government is well known to both of us, but we have differed as friends should do." Adams was mollified to some extent but did not miss the opportunity to chide Jefferson: "You and I have never had a serious conversation together that I can recollect concerning the nature of government."[13] And in a private letter to his son on January 3, 1794, Adams charged that Jefferson was "the subtlest beast of the intellectual and moral field . . . he is as ambitious as Oliver Cromwell . . . his soul is poisoned with ambition."[14]

A final opportunity for renewing a friendship, or at least a quiet détente, occurred in 1796 when Adams, the Federalist, narrowly became President, and Jefferson, as Republican runner-up, was the designated vice president. Jefferson wrote a heartfelt congratulatory letter to Adams, making common cause and pledging his support. But Jefferson's brilliant friend and adviser, his fellow Virginian James Madison, prevailed upon Jefferson not to send the letter. He explained that if Jefferson wanted ultimately to pursue his own anti-Federalist policies and forge his own presidential campaign, he could not afford to go on record as supporting Adams.[15]

Tensions were exacerbated during Adams's ill-fated one-term presidency. For over a year the two men did not speak to one another, and Jefferson took advantage of every opportunity to heighten the difference in views and temperament between the two men. Nor was Adams above the fray: hearing of some Jeffersonian criticism, he characterized Jefferson's mind as "eaten to a honeycomb with ambition, yet weak, confused, uninformed, and ignorant."[16]

By 1801, when Jefferson succeeded Adams as the third president of the United States, the two men were literally not on speaking terms. In the period from 1801 to 1812—more than eleven long and fateful years— the two men did not exchange a single spoken word or letter. (Interestingly, Jefferson did have an exchange of letters with Adams's spirited wife Abigail, but this highly charged correspondence only increased the alienation between these two American titans.)

Certainly at the start of the second decade of the nineteenth century, no one expected Thomas Jefferson, then close to seventy, and John Adams, then in his mid-seventies, to reconcile. Contact between the two, now elder statesmen, would probably not have resumed had it not been for the shrewd intervention of Benjamin Rush, noted physician and friend to both men. In 1809 Rush reported to Adams a dream in which the two ex-presidents had become intimates ("rival friends" in his words) again and this unexpected catalyst ultimately stimulated Adams, on the first day of 1812, to write a brief but conciliatory note to Jefferson. As it happens, Jefferson misinterpreted the letter—uncharacteristically taking literally a phrase about homespun clothing that was meant metaphorically. Happily, his misinterpretation did not interrupt the correspondence—and it may have humanized it.[17]

The rest, as they say, is epistolary history. In the fifteen years remaining until their deaths—providentially, on the same day, July 4, 1826, the fiftieth anniversary of the signing of the Declaration of Independence!—the two men exchanged 158 letters. Beginning with modest discussion of their diverse avocational interests, over the course of their correspondence they ultimately engaged in a serious exchange of views on topics where they disagreed (the nature of aristocracy, the relative risks of monarchism versus mob rule) as well as on topics on which they found themselves in agreement. As Adams remarked in an early letter, "You and I ought not to die before We have explained ourselves to each other."[18] Of course, both men realized that they were also writing for history. But only a cynic could ignore the human and personal dimensions of this exchange.

I believe that the friendship was genuinely restored, and the minds of the two men were genuinely changed thereby. And I believe that this change occurred because both men became able to accept and even to value their differences, as well as their common bonds. Adams remained Adams—pugnacious, chatty, scattershot; Jefferson remained Jeffersonian—artful, subtle, less prone to shoot off at the mouth. Neither man shrunk from what he believed, even when he knew that the other did not share a particular belief. At the same time, however, each man allowed room for the other to moderate or modulate his position, without converting the exchange into a battleground. And no doubt, the mellowing with age and the realization that they had both now become historic figures allowed some of the most virulent tensions to be buried or at least subdued. Both found it prudent to blame the worst of their earlier remarks on external conditions or on other malicious individuals and to foreground the strength of their earlier friendship, forged at the start of the Revolutionary war and strengthened by their joint efforts in foreign diplomacy and the founding of a nation in the years immediately after the war.

Yet the friendship could not have been reactivated had the two men not been able to clear the air. During the first year of his presidency, Jefferson had written nastily about Adams, calling him a retrograde thinker who was opposed to all forms of progress.[19] When this letter came to light, Adams demanded the proof. Realizing that he had been wrong, Jefferson indicated that he had really been speaking not of Adams himself, but rather of men who had feigned support of Adams but turned out to be Adams's enemies. The ever-proud Adams went on to point out some other mischaracterizations of his presidency. According to historian Joseph Ellis, "This was the defining moment in the correspondence . . . the dialogue ceased being a still life picture of posed patriarchs and became an argument between competing versions of the revolutionary legacy."[20] Ultimately, Jefferson succeeded in placing the long-standing different perspectives into a larger context:

> *The same political parties which now agitate the U.S. have exist thro' all time . . . we broke into two parties . . . Here you and I separated for the first time and as we had been longer than most in the public theatre, and our names were more familiar to our countrymen, the party which considered you as thinking with them placed your name at the head: the other for the same reason selected mine . . . we suffered ourselves, as you so well expressed it, to be the passive subjects of public discussion . . . and on the same question which now divides our country: that everyone takes his side in favor of the many, or the few, according to his constitution, and the circumstances in which he is placed.[21]*

Even though this historical exchange occurred almost two centuries ago, long before any modern technology could record it, the ability of both men to put their thoughts on paper allows us to chart the course of friendship, alienation, and rekindling of friendship. And we can see in this record how the multiple exchanges of the final decade and a half involved a modification of stance on the part of both former presidents —a modification that was essential if the friendship was to be reforged. In comparison to the Summers-West confrontation, as I've conceived it, each man was searching for common ground: between rational and affective considerations; between direct confrontation and debate by in-direction; between the personal and the political. Each man deliberately pointed to events in the past when they were on the same side and to interpretation of current events where they were in agreement, and they did not perseverate on issues (like the fate of slavery) where they had to agree to disagree. Jefferson admitted that he had been wrong on some issues (such as the French Revolution) and apologized for some of the more vicious attacks on Adams by his political henchmen; it takes a big man to admit such errors. Adams appreciated the apologies, calling one letter "one of the most consolatory I have ever received" and in turn defended Jefferson against charges that he had lifted some of the text of the Declaration from an earlier document.[22] There was genuine give-and-take—no effort on the part of either person to dominate the ex-change. They were able to joke with one another about language, literary classics, which of them had been more vilified; they could com-miserate with one another about their accumulating aches and pains. Happily, they both enjoyed writing and were good at it, and so the for-mat of the exchange was comfortable, indeed invigorating and reward-ing for both men. Each man engaged the psyche of the other, and both psyches moved closer toward one another—a mutual changing of minds. In the end, beyond the reason, beyond the real world events, it was the mutual reestablishment of resonance that melded the friendship. As Adams explained to Josiah Quincy, his cousin by marriage:

> *I do not believe that Mr. Jefferson ever hated me. On the contrary I believe he always liked* me . . . *then he wished to be President of the United States and I stood in his way. So he did everything that he could to pull me down. But if I should quarrel with him for that, I might quarrel with every man I have had anything to do with in my life. This is human nature.* . . . *Mr. Jefferson and I have grown old and retired from public life. So we are upon our ancient terms of goodwill.*[23]

THE MOST INTIMATE MIND CHANGES

Many other efforts at mind changing can be observed in intimate set-tings, ranging from a colleague at work who wants to change the daily routine of the person in the next office to a neighbor who disapproves of the nocturnal habits of the person across the street. I'll focus here on two common varieties of intimate mind changing: within a family and between lovers.

All in the Family

For most of us the principal—as well as the primordial—form of mind changing consists of exchanges that take place within the family. At the beginning, this relationship is asymmetrical. The parent (or guardian) has a premium on knowledge and power and seeks to influence what the child believes and how he acts. Absent the direct use of brute force, adults are aided by a process that psychologists term *identification*.[24] The child perceives similarities between himself and a salient adult, wishes to become like this desirable older person, and so models his behavior accordingly. Should the adult express a strong point of view on a topic, the identifier is likely to espouse that perspective as well. We might say that the words and actions of the model provide multiple representations that resonate with the child. Skilled or manipulative adults are able to exploit the phenomenon of identification in order to bring about changes of mind and behavior that they deem important.

But by about the age of ten, peers rather than parents begin to assume primary importance when it comes to mind changing, especially in the United States.[25] Young children are keenly attuned to what their peers say and do and are inclined to imitate them. This is particularly true when the peers represent a desired status in terms of power, strength, popularity, and/or resources to which they have access. The locus of resonance has begun to shift.

By the years of preadolescence and adolescence, then, youths already have evolved their own strong perspectives and these do not necessarily align with those of their parents or other adults in the community. Moreover, these youths are quite prepared to state their opinions strongly and to stand their ground—rhetorically and physically—in confrontations with adults. Once-young minds are directly challenging other, older minds.

At this point—so long as the participants resist the urge to explode—both participants must be prepared to negotiate a gradual shift from a relationship of authority/submission to a relationship of rough equality. In modern society, by the time the offspring reach the age of twenty-five or thirty, parents hold little if any suasion. The challenge in the interim years is to find ways in which the authority and superior knowledge of parents can be drawn on as appropriate, while the legitimate interests, knowledge, and goals of the growing adolescent are acknowledged. Reason, research, and real events typically gain in power as the levers of resources and representational redescription may be less salient.

In the end, a rough justice prevails. The child grows up, leaves home, sets up his own life, with his own values. For a while, the generations can go their own way. Still, difficult situations—a.k.a. crises—arise, and the mettle of both generations is tested. Many readers will know firsthand the challenging role of the sandwich generation—caught between the conflicting demands of one's growing children and one's aging parents. And toward the end of life, children (now themselves middle-aged) find themselves in a position where they must act as the mental agents of their parents, whose own powers no longer suffice for the demands of the day. When it is no longer possible to change minds voluntarily, then a wholesale "takeover" may be in order.

Lovers

Love is the strongest human emotion—indeed, hatred (its opposite) is its only rival. The love of a parent for her child, the love of a martyr for his cause, the love of two adolescents for one another—these are the stuff of inspiring lyric poetry, arresting drama, powerful graphic and filmic depiction. Experiencing the heights of love, individuals are most prone to extreme changes of mind and heart. There is no greater motivator. The most admired acts in human life have been inspired by love.

Take, for example, the story of Andrei Sakharov, the lauded Soviet physicist, and Elena Bonner.[26] Although Sakharov had invented the hydrogen bomb, by the 1970s he had changed his mind about the use of nuclear weapons—largely because of his guilt over the devastating health problems experienced by people living near sites where the bomb had been tested. It was Sakharov's new lover (and eventual wife) Elena who urged him to go public with his new viewpoint. Sakharov began to publish critical manuscripts, attend protest meetings, and directly challenge authorities in the scientific and political hierarchy. In his candor, he was first vilified, then ostracized, and finally placed under house arrest for seven years in the remote city of Gorky. Elena Bonner's love and support essentially changed her husband's mind about what he was willing to do publicly and how much flagellation and persecution he could bear. But love can also be a trap. A seductive spy can convince her lover to betray his country; the charismatic head of a terrorist organization can convince members to commit dastardly acts; a caring parent may engage in a foolishly destructive act because his offspring has been humiliated. Anyone in the enterprise of mind changing must be alert to the effects of love—for they can either bring about the desired changes in breathtakingly quick fashion or undermine a commitment with devastating speed.

The passions of youth, and of young love, give way to the less incandescent but more deeply rooted bonds of lifelong love—such as that between wife and husband. Often, two individuals with quite different kinds of minds fall in love—indeed, sometimes those scintillating opposites spark the attraction. With time, these contrasting views become known to one another. If the differences persist, they may cause problems for the relationship—especially when the lovers are each strongly committed to their position and engage in public activities that emphasize these differences. (In this respect, the apparently happy marriage between Democratic strategist James Carville and Republican pundit Mary Matalin is intriguing.) Probably in such cases, it is advisable to declare certain territories off limits or to restrict discussions (or arguments) to stated circumstances and shared ground rules. More frequently, however, love succeeds in building bridges between these contrasting perspectives. Both participants moderate their positions, end up compromising about some of their convictions, and find themselves increasingly in agreement—be it about political, religious, social, artistic, cultural, or culinary matters. The same tensions arise with respect to modes of childrearing, and, once again, love often solders or mutes contrasting approaches.

Leo Tolstoy captured well the converging mentalities of two lovers in *Anna Karenina*. When communicating with one another, Kitty and Levin did not need to speak whole sentences. Instead, they were able to use opening letters of words. Thus when Levin wrote, "W Y A: I C N B, D Y M T O N," Kitty correctly understood him to mean, "When you answered, it can not be, did you mean then or never?" They continue to converse by means of this shorthand. Tolstoy explicates: "Levin was used to expressing his thought fully without troubling to put it into exact word: He knew that his wife in such moments filled with love, as this one, would understand what he wanted to say from a mere hint, and she did." [27]

It is often said that as they get older, couples come to look more alike. Be that as it may (or may not) be, it seems clear that over time, couples often come to see the world in similar ways—essentially to change each other's minds to nearly equal degrees. No doubt these lovers ultimately use all the levers that they can grasp. While initially it may be the physical appearance and spiritual vitality that attracts one lover to another, in the end it is their commonly changed minds that may help their relationship to endure.

CHAPTER 9

Changing One's Own Mind

AT THE BEGINNING of this book I described how the author Nicholson Baker came to change his mind about the preferred furnishing of his apartment. Where once he was convinced that he desired exotic furnishings consisting of—of all things—backhoes, one day he awoke to realize that he had rejected that idea. What's more, he could not put his finger on the exact moment or way that he'd come to change his mind; it had occurred gradually, over time, presumably as a result of any number of small shifts in his perceptions and mental representations.

Indeed, of all the explorations of mind change that we've covered so far in this book, from leaders addressing their nations to a therapist interpreting the dreams of a fragile patient, the terrain of how shifts happen in our *own* minds is perhaps the most intriguing. Our minds are changed either because we ourselves want to change them or because something happens in our mental life that warrants a change. As Baker also reminds us, the change can occur in any sphere: our political beliefs, our scientific beliefs, our personal credo, our views about ourselves. Sometimes, the change of mind can be smooth and congenial, but it is especially poignant when a change of mind alters our life space in a fundamental way.

All seven levers of mind change can play a role in changing our own minds. But for simplicity's sake, let us begin with an example of a dramatic

shift that resulted principally from one of our *R*s—a real world event—
and how a fifty-five-year-old leader's mind was changed fundamentally
after September 11, 2001.

PRESIDENT GEORGE W. BUSH:
A CHANGE OF MIND IN WASHINGTON

A playboy without discernible direction or ambition in his earlier years,
George W. Bush nevertheless rose steadily in the business and political
ranks throughout the 1990s and soon set his sights on the presidency.
After his father's defeat at the hands of Bill Clinton in his bid for reelec-
tion in 1992, the younger Bush was determined not to make the same
mistakes—not in the quest for election nor, if he were elected, during his
presidency. After an election that was extraordinarily close, and whose
tense aftermath left many scars in the nation, Bush took the oath of office in January 2001.

Even his closest admirers would concede that Bush was better prepared for the trappings of the presidency than for the difficult decisions—and particularly international ones—that he would soon have to
face. Interviews and news conferences had revealed that Bush was poorly
informed about many issues. Reflecting on a meeting with Bush in June
2001, Representative Peter King of New York said, "He was going
through the motions. He had two or three talking points in his head and
that was it." Echoed Senator Bob Graham of Florida, "He had not been
particularly engaged. It was a tendency and ability to focus on things he
had identified as priorities and to exclude matters that did not meet that
test. To some that might appear as a lack of curiosity."[1] And a Republican
stalwart, Senator Chuck Nagel of Nebraska, remarked that "Bush came
to office with one of the thinnest résumés in foreign policy . . . and immediately drove himself into cul-de-sacs."[2]

Asked about his domestic goals, Bush had little to say that was distinctive; mostly he spoke about the need for lower taxes and reduced
government expenditures on the domestic front. He was best known as
someone who had improved educational opportunities for disadvantaged
youth in Texas and was intent on achieving the same advances on a national scale. On the foreign side, he surrounded himself with advisers

who had served in his father's administration. Critical of the perceived inconsistencies in the Clinton foreign policy, the Bush team called for a lower profile in foreign affairs: a strong military, an avoidance of imbroglios in lands that were not crucial to U.S. security, a disdain for "nation building," and a Realpolitik that downplayed human rights and instead sought relations with China, Russia, Japan, and Europe that were anchored in economic self-interest. Representing the biggest chasm from recent administrations of both parties, the Bush foreign policy was determinedly unilateral: Bush showed little desire to work with other countries and pointedly disdained the Kyoto accords on the use of energy and the antiballistic treaty with the Soviet Union. During the spring and summer of 2001, most analysts—whether supportive or critical—would agree with the description that I have just given, though they might employ verbs and adjectives with different valences.

This panorama changed decisively in the period following September 11, 2001, the infamous day when terrorists from the Al Qaeda network flew jumbo jets into the twin towers of the World Trade Center in downtown Manhattan and the Pentagon outside Washington. In general, we think of young persons as changing their minds readily, of old persons as being set in their ways. In September 2001, Bush was fifty-five years old—by many calculations (though no longer mine!) old rather than young. While he had shown considerable growth in personal maturity since his twenties and thirties, Bush had exhibited little inclination to master the details or think through the broad trends of the international scene. Nor had he displayed much potential for changing his mind about major policy issues—one had the feeling that he was content to follow the advice of his inner circle and, when in doubt, to consult his well-informed and inherently moderate father.

Yet, in the months following the morning of September 11, it was evident to observers that Bush had changed. Once Bush had returned to the White House later that day, he had a new and authentic mission: He was now the President of the United States who was going to do whatever it took to extirpate the terrorist networks and to keep such acts from recurring. As he said to his associates that day, "We are at war. That's what we're paid for, boys."[3] He was focused. He was resolute. He became much better informed about foreign policy. He developed personal relationships with leaders whose names he had not hitherto mastered. His critics reversed their earlier assessments. In Senator Graham's words, "I was impressed with how much he knew the details"; in Representative King's words: "[I]f he knows what he's talking about, takes the time, shows he cares about it and is willing to fight for it, it's easier to stand with him"; and Senator Hagel said that Bush "began to find his way."[4] The unilateralist became the multilateralist, the isolationist became an internationalist. The leader who had not wanted to get embroiled in other countries was willing to become involved in Afghanistan, in India and Pakistan, in the Middle East, to retain troops in the Balkans, and, most notably, to undertake a full-scale war in Iraq. Bush also changed his views on other issues where he had a track record: the need for corporate reform, for example, and the advisability of setting up a cabinet-level post devoted to homeland security.

Bush devoted his energies to building up the same kind of international coalition as had his father for the Gulf War ten years before; prosecuted a successful war to remove the Taliban from power in Afghanistan; continued to pursue Al Qaeda with all available financial, military, and investigative means; and led a multinational war against Iraq—though ultimately one in which he was opposed by several major nations and much of the world's population; and then turned to the United Nations during the perilous months after the war. No longer bent on being unilateralist, Bush worked assiduously to maintain ties with the leaders of all nations who were willing to join in the attack on terrorism and to isolate what he called the "axis of evil"—countries like Iran, Iraq, Syria, and North Korea, which were seen as gearing up for biological or nuclear warfare and as supporting or harboring itinerant terrorists. From all reports, Bush had a newly wrought sense of purpose, a base of knowledge that had not been manifest before; rather than simply strategizing how to win elections, he now sought to use the levers of governing to achieve specific policy goals. As one observer put it: "Events trump intentions but not ideology. Just as Bill Clinton came into office determined to keep his focus domestic, Mr. Bush promised less involvement and more humility in relations abroad. Yet the most dramatic effect of the year has been the tremendous extension in America's foreign engagement. We have sent troops and covert forces into new countries, embraced new allies, put military bases in new regions, become engaged in new conflicts."[5] Said another: "It's now clear that President Bush, once feared to be an isolationist, has an agenda for remaking the world that rivals that of Harry Truman and Woodrow Wilson in its ambitions, scope, and idealism."[6]

Some people change their minds because they want to, others because they have to. It is no disrespect to President Bush to say that his change of mind was not of his own initiative. To paraphrase an old Shakespearean saw, "George Bush was not born as a Mind Changer; he had Mind Changing thrust upon him." What could not have been anticipated was that Bush was up to the occasion.

Of course, we cannot know in any detail what went on in Bush's mind. He is not by nature an introspective person, and, at any rate, he was unlikely to share this introspection with casual journalists, not to mention psychologists who do not live in the neighborhood. Yet I feel on firm ground in declaring that Bush must have had many conversations not only with others but also with himself. The President of the United States, the most powerful nation in human memory, is in a different spot from any other individual. He is free to consult with whomever he likes. But in the end, and especially when a difference of opinion endures, the proverbial "buck" stops at his desk.

Now, a person might appear to others to have changed his mind, while he himself may feel that he is being constant. The belief in consistency, and the need to believe that one has been consistent, can be a powerful motive for perceived steadfastness, and particularly so when one is in public life. Politicians in the United States are loathe to proclaim changes of mind, lest they be seen as weak or inconsistent. As David Brooks comments, "Bush will do whatever it takes to prevail, and senior members of his administration are capable of looking honestly at their mistakes. You will just never be able to get any of them to admit publicly that they've made any."[7] Still, at a minimum, I suggest that Bush changed his mind about the purpose of his presidency. I also speculate that he changed his mind about his own mission in life; the relationship of the United States to other countries; the need to become involved in trouble spots around the world, including ones about which he had known little and where his chances of success were slim; the importance of communicating the national mission both to his own people and to those abroad; the dangers

posed by terrorism; the need for bipartisan consensus on certain key issues; and the importance of powerful, well-run, and intelligently integrated governmental institutions ranging from new homeland security to
the old intelligence and immigration agencies. Indeed, as reported in
Business Week, "Over the last twelve months, America has seen the largest
one-year increase of government spending on national defense as a percentage of GDP since 1982. It has seen more regulation, more legislative
oversight, and more government intervention than at any time since the
late 1970s."[8] It is hard to imagine how these trends could have happened
had not Bush changed his mind on key issues.

Whatever his limitations, George W. Bush seems to have been skilled
at an early age in what I call *interpersonal intelligence*—the part of our intellectual equipment that is engaged in understanding and motivating
other people. He likes other people, and he prides himself in getting to
know them. In school, he may have been an indifferent student, but he
stood out as a skilled maker of friends and student of others. (Indeed, I
would speculate that genuine learning difficulties in reading and other
linguistic endeavors probably pushed the young and gregarious Bush to
sharpen his personal skills.) He continued to hone these skills during college, business school, his playboy years, and over the course of his involvement in business enterprises that achieved varying degrees of
success. Even those who found him unimpressive intellectually liked
Bush personally and were impressed by his skill in getting along with
others and making people feel comfortable. Like other interpersonally
skilled persons (a group that would include most U.S. presidents), Bush
also had confidence in his ability to get along with foreign leaders and to
convince them to work together. As he has phrased it, "Many of these
leaders are coming here to sit down and visit. I think it's important for
them to look me in the eye. Many of these leaders have the same kind of
inherent ability that I've got, I think, and that is they can read people."[9]

All of this is to say that Bush's interpersonal intelligence served him
well for many years in a variety of settings. But I suggest that after September 11, he began to deepen his *intrapersonal* intelligence as well—a
mind shift that was necessary as he proceeded in uncharted political and
military terrain. Intrapersonal intelligence is difficult to understand and

to write about. At its core, intrapersonal intelligence entails the following elements: a good working knowledge of oneself, who one is, what are one's strengths and weaknesses, what are one's goals and how best to achieve them; how to build on one's successes; and how to learn from one's reactions to events, whatever their outcome—in short, having a reasonably accurate mental representation of oneself as a human being, alone and with others, and being able to monitor and, if necessary, to bring about changes in that mental representation. While observing from the outside and disagreeing with many of his policies, I would say that Bush has exhibited an impressive growth in intrapersonal intelligence during his years in high office.

In the last chapter, I focused on changes that occur at the behest of someone to whom one is close—an associate at work, a friend, a parent, a peer, a therapist, a lover. We can change the minds of those to whom we are close, and they can change our minds as well. However, whatever the cause or prompt, we must ultimately be in charge of our own mind changing. At times of such powerful mind changes, the ability of a person to be aware of what is going on in his or her own mind is crucial.

I submit that Bush—not, by nature, an introspective person—came to know his own mind, and its capacity for change, in ways that neither he nor anyone else could have anticipated before the all-too-real-world events of September 11, 2001. He changed much of the contents of the mind—his beliefs about the world system—as well as some of the forms —the way in which he took in information, put it together, and made his own decisions. Bush stands as an intriguing example of how a powerful event can prompt a process of "tipping." As I write in the closing months of 2003, I suspect that ensuing events in his presidency will continue to influence his frames and forms of mind.

Changes of mind are probably most dramatic in realms that mean the most to people—the value-laden realms of politics, scholarship, and religion. In noting what changes and what remains constant in these "charged" domains, we receive insight into the ways in which individual minds can be altered. Let's turn to another example from politics, one in which three of our *R*s—reason, resonance, and real world events—played a large part in one man's dramatic change of mind.

A CHANGE OF IDEOLOGY:
THE CASE OF WHITTAKER CHAMBERS

Ever since Karl Marx began to write about the failings of capitalism and the allure of a utopia devoid of private property and, ultimately, the heavy hand of the state, many individuals—and especially the young—have been attracted to the idealistic visions of socialism and communism. No one was more so seduced than Whittaker Chambers. Born in Long Island in 1901 and raised in a dysfunctional household, Chambers became attracted to the moral vision of communism while studying at Columbia University in the early 1920s and during a subsequent trip to Europe. The first genuinely successful Communist political revolution had occurred in Russia and a Leninist Bolshevik state was being firmly established. To add fuel to the fire for Chambers, around the time of his European visit his beloved brother committed suicide. In Chambers's words, "I felt that any society which could result in the death of a boy like my brother was wrong, and I was at war with it. This was the beginning of my fanaticism." [10] In particular, Chambers was drawn to the communist ideals of helping underprivileged people, alleviating economic crises, and averting war.

A gifted journalist, Chambers began to write for left-wing newspapers and eventually joined the Communist Party. At first his involvement with the Party was limited, but he was gradually drawn into underground spying activities. He spent several years writing publicly from a communist perspective while also attempting surreptitiously to elicit secret American political plans and share them with Party leaders in the U.S. and Moscow. During this time, the "Communist ideal" underwent various changes. Following Lenin's untimely death, Josef Stalin came to power determined to build the first Communist state. He introduced economic plans designed to get rid of the vestiges of capitalism and to set up a society that was exemplary in agricultural, industrial, and military affairs. He presided over the emergence of collective farms, nationalized industries, large public works projects like the Moscow subway; he initially encouraged or at least tolerated avant-garde artists, such as the writer Maxim Gorky and the composer Dmitri Shostakovich. But these apparently laudable aspirations did not last long. An extremely paranoid personality, Stalin was determined to liquidate all potential rivals, arranging to eliminate them through a series of "show trials" in the latter 1930s. In the ultimate act of cynicism, Stalin joined his political archrival, Adolf Hitler, in creating a nonaggression pact in August 1939, just before the outbreak of World War II.

Eventually, the increasingly unjustifiable actions of the Soviet Union became too much for Chambers to swallow. (In retrospect, Stalin's Communist regime was one of the bloodiest in history; it is conservatively estimated that Stalin's policies resulted in the deaths of millions of Russians.) So in 1937, at some risk to his own and his family's safety, Chambers left the Communist Party. In the ensuing decade, he joined the staff of *Time* magazine and became one of its most esteemed writers and editorialists—with an (obviously) unique slant on the role of communism in World War II and its aftermath.

Were it only for these biographical details, few would know the name of Whittaker Chambers today. But Chambers became part of U.S. history because in his 1952 best-seller *Witness* he described—with unparalleled piquancy and precision—the ways in which his mind changed during the period from 1920 to 1950.[11]

Chambers chronicles four successive states of mind: (1) his attraction to communism and his decision to join the Communist Party in the mid-1920s; (2) his heart-wrenching decision, in the late 1930s, to leave the Party; (3) his initial ambivalence about revealing to investigative agencies the nature of his and others' spying activities; (4) his final decision to go public, to bring renown and opprobrium to his family, in order to reveal everything that he knew about the awful story of communism in the United States.

As Chambers saw it, the world in the first part of the twentieth century was witness to a life-and-death struggle between two rival interpretations of human nature. At first, Chambers had become persuaded of the evils of capitalism and looked to communism as the only humane course for the world. In embracing this point of view, he voluntarily decided to avoid harsh judgments about communism—in a sense, he took on the mind-set of the fundamentalist, the true believer. But one shoddy episode after another—personal as well as public, local as well as international—chipped away at these defenses. Chambers saw many killed abroad, and a few hounded or killed at home. He read of mind control abroad and saw it at work firsthand in his own Communist political cell. As a person with a mind that he liked to exercise, Chambers finally decided that he could no longer live with himself if he remained a dedicated Communist. With literal fear and trembling, he began to read works that were critical of Communism and to voice his doubts to a few close associates. Having reached a tipping point, he made the fateful decision. As he put it: "In 1937 I began, like Lazarus, the impossible return. I began to break away from communism and to climb from deep within its underground, where for six years I had been buried, back into the world of the free man."[12]

Chambers gradually became persuaded that his initial dichotomization of the world into good and evil forces had been correct, but the values he had attached to democratic capitalism and communism had been exactly wrong. The genuine tension was between those who believed in God, in a higher order, in human love and sacredness, and those who believed only in man and in a world that was ruled by considerations of power. At first, Chambers felt that he should alert U.S. security authorities to what he knew, but when early attempts to do this failed to be heeded, he was content to close that chapter of his life and to become a well-paid journalist and the father of a growing family.

As is well known, Chambers became a celebrity in August 1948. He revealed that Alger Hiss, known previously as a dedicated public servant in the State Department and the foundation world, had been a member of the Communist Party at the same time as Chambers; shortly thereafter, Chambers revealed that Hiss had engaged in espionage. (In making these statements without qualification, I do so with the knowledge that many people deplored Chambers's actions and some still believe in Hiss's innocence; but in my view both the legal and the historical record validate Chambers's basic charges.) Chambers had no doubt that this exposure of Hiss was the right thing to do. And he did so despite a number of unsettling considerations (what we might term "resistances"): He would be viewed as a tattler and, by some, as a traitor; he would place his wife and children under a permanent shadow; he was giving up a lot of resources that he commanded as a senior writer on a prestigious national magazine; and he believed that communism, and not democracy, would ultimately prevail. Yet in the end Chambers concluded that it was right to make personal sacrifices for a broader good. As he put it, "I know I am leaving the winning side for the losing side. . . . Better to die on the losing side than to live under communism. . . . I am a man who is very reluctantly and grudgingly, step by step, destroying myself so that this nation and the faith by which it lives may continue to exist." [13]

One can criticize Chambers for many things, though not for a lack of courage. He also stands out in recent U.S. history as one who sincerely changed his mind on issues of the greatest personal and public moment and sought to describe those changes of mind as accurately as possible. And while certain facts of the case are no doubt idiosyncratic to the troubled young man from Long Island, the broad story that he relates resembles that of others who reflected on the failures of communism.

Intellectuals such as Arthur Koestler, André Malraux, Ignazio Silone, and Richard Wright also have written about their initial attraction to communism and their slow disenchantment. [14] In articulating their own often painful trajectories, these writers indicate what it takes for a thoughtful (and often opinionated) person to be converted to a point of view; to defend it strongly and publicly; to come to the reluctant conclusion that one has been wrong; and to declare publicly the errors of one's previous thoughts. It may not be easy for nonintellectuals to appreciate how much stock members of this group place in being right, in being able to defend their positions articulately, and in remaining consistent; ideas are the central axis for any intellectual. Intellectuals are particularly susceptible to the tensions of cognitive dissonance. When an occurrence runs counter to their theory, they are highly motivated to reinterpret events so as to eliminate the inconsistency.

An example. When Stalin shocked the world by agreeing to a nonaggression pact with Hitler, his apologists argued variously that Stalin was doing this to gain time, or to have more influence on Hitler, or that Stalin *had* to sign the pact because he was dealing with counterrevolutionary forces within his own country that had gotten out of control. The intellectuals went to great lengths to deny what seemed obvious to many "ordinary" people: that Stalin was simply operating on the basis of power considerations, that he was an old-fashioned murderous tyrant (no different in that respect from Hitler or Genghis Khan), and that his ideological commitment to socialistic ideals was a sham. What is striking to observers like me, in hindsight, is how much counterevidence was needed to convince these individuals that the communist story or theory was wrong, and how hesitant they were to admit publicly that they had been committed to a fatally flawed cause. It is rare to encounter a straight declaration of error: One hungers for a statement like that made by the American Communist Junius Scales: "Stalin—my revered symbol of the infallibility of Communism, the builder of socialism in one country, the rock of Stalingrad, the wise, kindly man with the keen sense of humor at whose death I had wept just three years before—Stalin had been a murderous, power-hungry monster!"[15]

In fairness, the Communist Party did not make it easy to entertain doubts. Italian novelist Ignazio Silone recalls his own painful divorce from its ranks:

> *The truth is that you don't free yourself from the Communist Party the way you resign from the Liberal party, chiefly because your ties with party are in proportion to the sacrifices they exact . . . it is a totalitarian institution in the fullest sense of the word and requires the total allegiance of those who submit to it . . . the sincere Communist who by some miracle retains his inborn faculty . . . before he is able to take a final step in the direction either of total submission to the party or total freedom in renunciation of the party, he must suffer the torments of hell in his innermost being . . . one is cured of Communism as one is cured of a neurosis.*[16]

Recent commentators have suggested another reason for the intellectual's intoxication with communism.[17] In this more cynical view, intellectuals have always been in love with power. They overestimate their own abilities to see the "real forces" at work in society and are unduly flattered when they receive attention from those who wield power. Some also have a fascination with terror and violence and ignore the terrible human consequences of these. This tendency was recently embodied by the contemporary German composer Karlheinz Stockhausen. Ignoring the human misery caused by the bombing of the twin towers, Stockhausen proclaimed the assault "the greatest work of art in the history of the world."[18] Stockhausen was able to overlook the nature and consequences of the act and to call attention to it as if it had been simply a creation of the imagination.

There is an old joke about changing minds. Initially, the critic rejects the new idea as absurd. Some time later, he treats it as if it were the conventional wisdom. Ultimately he declares it was his idea all along. Intellectuals who did change their mind about communism rarely did so gracefully. Rather than declaring that they have been foolish, naïve, or opportunistic, intellectuals are more likely to locate the blame elsewhere or to deny that their change of mind was as dramatic as it appears to the outsider. If at all possible, they try to characterize the change of mind as reflecting a deeper underlying consistency. For example, by saying that their critique of capitalism had been correct all along and that Stalin was initially a wonderful person, but that he had been overtaken by the rise of fascism; the next time a Communist leader has an opportunity, he will learn from Stalin's errors and reformulate the state accordingly. Of course, after the discrediting of a whole raft of Communist regimes, ranging from Cuba to North Korea to Eastern Europe, it is more difficult to hold this position. But at least some Marxists in Europe continue to do so.

This tendency among intellectuals is what makes Chambers's public confession remarkable. In terms of our seven levers of mind change, it could be said that his dramatic shift was due to his own powers of *reason* in the face of *real world events* (i.e., Stalin's Soviet Union) and the lack of *resonance* that those events had with the ideals that Chambers held dear. For others who eventually saw the light, it is possible that the accumulating data, the opportunity for securing additional *resources*, or the encountering of counterevidence in many different *representational forms* —from works of fiction to personal suffering—also played a role in their rejection of communism.

In the political realm, most changes of mind are more gradual and less epochal. Those who were mildly in sympathy with communism become less so; those who had faith in the democratization of new nations gradually lose their faith; those who were skeptical about the benign aspects of market forces look on them more benevolently (or vice versa). Winston Churchill famously declared, "In youth, anyone who is not a socialist is a dullard; in middle age, anyone who is still a socialist is a fool." When such expected changes of mind occur gradually, they are less likely to be noticed by the person himself or by those around her and thus there is less need for a direct confrontation of the change that has been wrought.

Changes in the opposite direction—a conservative who announces that he or she is now becoming more liberal—are more likely to attract notoriety. And indeed, sometimes such changes are not believed. In 2002, the American journalist David Brock,[19] once a rabid right-winger, admitted that he had distorted facts in his earlier journalism (about icons of the left like law professor Anita Hill and Bill Clinton), announced his sympathy with more liberal causes, and sought to atone for the error of his ways. His public announcement attracted attention but remarkably little sympathy either from his erstwhile friends on the right or from his putative new associates on the left. Still, human beings are loathe to admit mistakes in any realm, least of all the political. We search in vain for replicas of Fiorella La Guardia, the New York mayor who disarmingly proclaimed, "When I make a mistake, it's a beaut!"

As if responding to his predecessor, former mayor Rudolph Giuliani, distinguished between two kinds of mind changes reported by politicians: "The notion that changing your minds about an issue is 'waffling' is false. Through trial and error you come to realize that an idea you had was mistaken. . . . It is one thing to change your mind as you evolve intellectually. It is quite another to change your mind because political obedience or a bad press suggest a more popular course."[20]

DAMASCUS, LUTHER, AND THE FUNDAMENTALIST CHANGES IN FAITH

Perhaps the most famous change of mind of all times was that undergone by Rabbi Saul of Tarsus during the first century A.D. Having been a persecutor of Christianity and, indeed, having embarked on a journey to Damascus to suppress this new and troublesome sect, Saul was temporarily blinded. He heard a voice that thundered, "Why persecutist thou me?" On his arrival in Damascus, Saul (now Paul) regained his sight and became a convert to Christianity. He studied the life of Christ and became a leader—an apostle—of Christianity: central in missionary work, setting up churches, formulating doctrine, and writing epistles that explained the faith. Paul had seen the errors of his ways, undergone a dramatic conversion, and was able to use his personal experiences as a basis on which to communicate to others who might be persuaded to change their religious allegiance. In our terms, we could say that a *real event* in Paul's world triggered this dramatic change in his own mind—a change that resonated with him and would eventually resonate with millions of others.

Changes in faith are intensely personal experiences. In general one assumes the creed of one's parents, and the extent of one's religiosity is a joint product of the religiosity of one's family and one's own predisposition to be, in Eric Hoffer's phrase, a "true believer."[21] There is little incentive to change one's religion when all around belong to the same religion, when matters of faith play a comparable role with one's peers, and when events are going reasonably smoothly in one's life.

Changes of mind in the religious sphere, such as that undergone at the start of the modern era by Martin Luther, are therefore of enormous moment. Luther was a dedicated German monk, who, in the manner of idealistic youth, sought to live up to the precepts of the established Catholic faith. But all around him Luther detected signs that the Church itself was deeply flawed. Priests were interested in aggrandizing themselves, not in helping the poor and the faithful. Rome was a center of power and intrigue, not a reservoir of spirituality. Ordinary Catholics felt alienated from the remote language, the degraded practices of the faith, the laxity of the clergy, and the wanton sale of privilege and expiation. Luther found personal salvation in a return to the scriptures and to Christ's messages of faith and love. He was not the first heretic to put his displeasure into words and, within a few years, into deeds. But he stood out in terms of the openness with which he broke with the Church, attacked the papacy, and sought to establish a new reformed church in Germany. His protest was unprecedentedly successful, and, within a few decades, millions of Christians had embraced his rival church. As with Saul, real world events provoked Luther, and he was able to describe his revelation—note the telltale "re"—in a way that resonated with ordinary Christians in the sixteenth and succeeding centuries.

Of all the religious changes of mind, the most dramatic ones today involve fundamentalism. There are fundamentalist strands in every religion, of course, but the ones gaining the most attention in contemporary

America are the fundamentalist branches of Protestantism. Christian fundamentalists adhere to a literal version of scripture. Through perpetual study of biblical texts, these adherents hold, it is possible to understand what has happened in the past, to lead a proper life today, and to predict future events. Fundamentalists live in closely knit communities where they support one another's interpretations of events, develop arguments against nonbelievers, and attempt as much as possible to avoid the mores and temptations of the modern, secularized world.

From social-scientific studies, we know much about the persons attracted to fundamentalism as well as the conditions under which such individuals leave a fundamentalist sect.[22] Many if not most converts come from families that are unhappy: common factors include broken homes, backgrounds of substance abuse and violence, and uncertainty about the identity of one's parents. As described by sociologist Chana Ullman, "the two-year period preceding the conversion was, for the majority of converts, dominated by despair, doubts in their own self-worth, fears of rejection, unsuccessful attempts to handle rage, an emptiness, and an estrangement from others."[23] Would-be converts experience fewer rewards, are depressed by events in the real world, and find themselves resisting the views and ideals of their neighbors. In the midst of despair, such individuals happen upon a community that is warm, welcome, and supportive. Without being asked a lot of questions, the lost soul is absorbed into the community and made to feel an integral part of it. In return, he must eventually do one thing: uncritically accept the central teachings of the sect. Consider the testimony of former fundamentalist David Coffin:

> The important thing to remember is that fundamentalist Christian members will go down into any gutter, barroom of filth, or hellish nightmare of shattered family life and offer a viable alternative with strict rules, "black-and-white" categories of looking at life, and supply a ready-made community of support, friendliness, and interaction. Where else could a total stranger come off the street to share in homemade goods at potluck dinners, uplifting singing, and people shaking hands and embracing each other? Contrasted with a life of drinking to excess and receiving total wages in a job the breadwinner hates,

Fundamentalist Christianity offers an opportunity for that person to have dignity, honor, and blessings.[24]

I would describe the mind-set of the fundamentalist as follows: An adherent voluntarily decides that he will no longer change his mind in any significant way. All of the efforts within the fundamentalist community are directed toward shoring up the current belief system and rejecting notions that are alien to the doctrine. I might even go so far as to suggest that the fundamentalist voluntarily suspends his imagination: for, as Chambers's decision to open anticommunist books reminds us, once one imagines that events or beliefs could be different, one is already risking heresy. David Hartman, the Israel-based religious philosopher, puts it this way:"A monolithic framework does not create a critical mind. . . . Where there is only one self-evident truth, nothing ever gets challenged and no sparks of creativity ever get generated."[25]

It is difficult to escape such an all-encompassing environment. Yet a large proportion of the sect—perhaps as many as half of the persons raised in fundamentalist communities—break away from that way of thinking. By far, the most likely to leave are adolescents. Unlike younger children who are mired in the concrete reality around them, adolescents become able to think in terms of different explanatory systems, drawn from politics, science, or religion, and many of them realize that what they have regarded as Gospel is just one of many ways of making sense of the world. Moreover, it is a way of thinking that cuts them off from some of the most lively, vibrant, and meaningful aspects of experience and from many of the most scintillating peers.

Nearly all of us need to have some core beliefs. We differ from one another in how coherent these beliefs need to be, and how willing we are to consider changing them. The appeal of a strong set of beliefs shared by all around one is clear; but especially in a pluralistic society, the costs involved in cutting oneself off from all other perspectives are patent. In the battle over faith, then, one witnesses the conflicting pulls of *reason, resistance, resonance,* and the *realities* of daily experience. Quite possibly, powerful descriptions of a desirable life exert an enormous influence on whether one takes up and adheres to a fundamentalist frame of mind.

CHANGES OF MIND IN THE SCHOLARLY SPHERE

Thus far in this chapter we've seen how changes of mind in the political sphere typically reflect an analysis of what has happened in world affairs. The rapid fall of communism, for example, caused many individuals to question the viability of that form of government. We've also seen how changes of mind in the religious sphere reflect one's emotional life and one's relation to the Almighty and, in theologian Paul Tillich's evocative phrase, to "ultimate concerns."[26] The promptings of one's own heart convince one person to return to her faith, another to shift to a new one, a third to become an agnostic or atheist.

When it comes to a change of mind in the scholarly realm, however, yet another set of forces come into play. Scholars are in the business of developing systems of ideas that offer explanations of the world: Scientists seek to explain the physical and biological world; humanists try to explain the world of human experience; philosophers offer explanations of, or at least reflections on, the puzzles of life, death, and the nature of reality and experience.

Unlike the other realms discussed in this chapter, then, where mind changes came as a surprise—and usually after considerable struggle—scholars open to new ideas can reasonably expect to change their minds. (Indeed, as we noted in chapter 6, the business of artists, scientists, scholars, and other "indirect" leaders *is* to change the minds of others.) New evidence alters beliefs. Following the experiments of Albert Michelson and Edward Morley and the theoretical work of Albert Einstein, physicists no longer believed in the existence of the ether. German philosopher Immanuel Kant read the Scottish philosopher David Hume on the nature of causal explanation and was "awakened" from his "dogmatic slumbers." Unanticipated trends in the world's marketplace challenge the economist's model and causes her to change its parameters. Yet at the same time, scholars—building on the past and living largely in their own minds—place a great value on consistency and continuity. As is the case in contemporary U.S. politics, it is considered by many a sign of scholarly weakness to announce that one has changed one's mind significantly. And, as we noted with intellectuals (who are not necessarily scholars, or vice versa), many individuals do not like to change their views publicly—witness the two following examples.

Sigmund Freud once gave a lecture where he expressed his view on a topic. After the lecture, a student approached the Master and pointed out timidly that he had contradicted what he had written a few years earlier. Deeply skeptical, Freud demanded the evidence. The student was able to find the relevant text and showed it to Freud. Freud read through the text, looked directly at the student, and responded sharply "*that* was right *then*." Linguist Noam Chomsky is famous for introducing a revised theory of linguistics every five to ten years, and thereby confounding his students, who had been promulgating the previous theory as if it were the last word of the master. Yet Chomsky insists—and I suppose he believes—that there are deep continuities in his theory and that the changes represent only a surface reflection of the same basic scientific program, pursued doggedly for the last half-century.

It is thus of considerable interest when a scholar makes a major shift in perspective and acknowledges it as such. One of the most striking instances of this phenomenon is the change in the writing of the Austrian-English philosopher Ludwig Wittgenstein. The major work that Wittgenstein produced in the first years of his life was the *Tractatus Logico-Philosophicus*. In this work, Wittgenstein presented a severe view of the nature of knowledge: Knowledge is based on a belief in facts, accurately described in language and logic; whereof individuals cannot speak, they are enjoined to remain silent. An explicit relation obtains among the objects of the world, the words of language, and the thoughts of one's mind.

But in subsequent years, Wittgenstein rejected this approach. He instead came to see language as a set of practices carried out within a community. Rather than looking to science, mathematics, and logic as the firm foundation of knowledge, Wittgenstein came to believe that the puzzles of life are entailed in our use of language; if we understand with some acuity our uses of language, we will be able to dissolve (rather than solve) philosophical problems. This difference was so striking that the Early Wittgenstein (as he came to be called) had a different set of supporters than the Later Wittgenstein. Early Wittgensteinians continued to focus on language as a picture of the world as it is; Later Wittgensteinians saw language as creating the cognitive worlds in which we are enmeshed.

Interestingly, while the change in his thinking was obvious to everyone (including Wittgenstein), he did not dwell on it. He restricted himself to brief comments like this:"Four years ago, I had occasion to reread my first book and to explain its ideas to someone. It suddenly seemed to me that I should publish those old thoughts and the new ones together; and that the latter could be seen in the right light only by contrast with and against the background of my old way of thinking. For since beginning to occupy myself with philosophy again, sixteen years ago [i.e., in 1929], I have been forced to recognize grave mistakes in what I wrote in that first book." [27]

In terms of our seven *R*s, Wittgenstein's change of mind came about through *reason*—his logical analysis of his own previous work—but without much explanation as to how it came about. Indeed, rare as an announced change of mind may be, it is even rarer when a scholar explicitly expands on a change of mind and the reasons that prompted it. [28] The French philosopher and anthropologist Lucien Lévy-Bruhl did just that, after a change of mind that resulted from another of our seven levers: *research*.

Lévy-Bruhl became famous for a series of books in the early years of the last century. [29] In these influential writings, he expounded the profound differences between the mind of the primitive and the mind of modern advanced human beings. The early Lévy-Bruhl (as I will dub him) claimed that primitives could not think logically and that they exhibited a weird phenomenon called "participation" in which an object could become a part of another—for example, an animal could be both itself and a part of the human spirit. Lévy-Bruhl was roundly criticized for making such stark statements, especially by anthropologists who noted that he had never met a so-called primitive and who claimed that he had misread the data on which his interpretations were built.

Faced with such stinging criticism, most scholars would do one of the following: move to a wholly new topic, stick stubbornly to their guns, or introduce subtle changes in the argument without explicitly conceding the validity of criticisms. To his credit, Lévy-Bruhl spurned these customary moves. Instead, in subsequent writings, he openly discussed places where he had gone too far and had overinterpreted the data; he actually admitted learning from his critics and took on a far more nuanced position.

More remarkably, in a set of notebooks that he maintained in the last years of his life, he explicitly discussed his own ambivalences, changes of mind, and errors of interpretation and argument.[30] Consider four of his "backtracking" comments:

- *It would in fact be an advance if, instead of presupposing these "mental habits" in primitive men, we abandon the idea, at least provisionally, in order to examine the facts.*[31]
- *I renounced the idea of participation. I know much more and I analyze much better than thirty years ago.*[32]
- *I will no longer express myself in this manner. Above all, I will no longer place, so to speak, on an equal level the two fundamental characteristics of the primitive mentality, prelogical and mystical. It now appears that there is a single fundamental characteristic.*[33]
- *The step which I have just taken, and hope is decisive, consists, in a word, in abandoning a badly proposed problem which resulted in some inextricable difficulties and in confining myself to a question the terms of which are suggested by the facts alone.*[34]

Clearly, Lévy-Bruhl was far more candid than most scholars in talking about his own mind changes and their bases in reason and research. And yet it is worth noting that these discussions did not appear in his last premortem publications but rather in notebooks that were published some years after his death. Whether, in published writings, he would have been as candid to the rest of the world as he was to himself will never be known.

In earlier chapters I spoke of paradigm shifts that occur from time to time in a science. Most individual scholars are born and die within a paradigm. A few, like Darwin or Einstein, create a new paradigm that comes to be accepted, more or less rapidly, by the younger persons in the domain. The cases in which an individual develops one paradigm and then abandons it for quite another one are strikingly few. Wittgenstein qualifies as one, Lévy-Bruhl as another. As suggested by the case of Whittaker Chambers, two different tipping points seem to be at work: one involves one's own change of mind, the other the willingness to announce that change of mind publicly and live with the consequences.

"ORDINARY" CHANGES IN "ORDINARY" FOLKS

Yet another kind of mind change within individuals warrants exploration here. While less likely to be covered in newspapers or recorded in textbooks or encyclopedias, the rest of us ordinary folk also change our minds. By virtue of one or more of the seven levers expounded here, we change our minds about politics, religion, and other spheres that we care about. Let me use myself as an example. Yes, I am a scholar, and in a moment I will touch on changes of mind I've experienced in my academic pursuits. But I'll begin with a brief summary of how, in my role as an ordinary citizen, I've changed my mind in some fundamental ways.

Born in Scranton, Pennsylvania, in the middle of World War II, I grew up in the time of the weekly news magazines issued by the likes of publisher Henry Luce. Like others of my generation, I was subjected to a steady stream of American triumphalism and Cold War propaganda. Accordingly, I saw the United States as the vessel of freedom in the world, and, as a white male, I assumed that members of my group would continue to hold the power indefinitely. (As a child of Jewish refugees from Nazi Germany, I also felt more marginal than most and had more sympathy with disadvantaged and marginal groups.) But the shocks attending the Vietnam War and the Watergate scandals severely shook my faith in the institutions of the U.S. government. The Vietnam War convinced me that U.S. foreign policy could be deeply flawed. At the same time, while not deeply involved in the protests of the 1960s, my views about the status and possibilities of women, blacks, and other minorities also shifted notably. The partial failure of Lyndon Johnson's Great Society convinced me that the problems of America's inner cities were far more intractable than I had thought. The assassinations of John F. Kennedy, Robert Kennedy, and Martin Luther King Jr.—and the reactions to these murders—convinced me that the hatred in American society was much more pervasive and deeply rooted than I had imagined. Finally, any lingering thoughts that I had about America's unique status in the world were forever shaken by the attack in 2001 on the twin towers and the subsequent reactions throughout the rest of the world.

Each of these changes of mind is significant. And if I compared my beliefs in 1950, 1975, and 2000 the differences would loom large. Yet it is important to state that these differences occurred gradually, often almost unnoticed, from one month or year to the next. I did not have an experience like Paul did on the road to Damascus. Nor did I feel a need to renounce my support of Stalinist Russia, as Ignazio Silone did, or to admit an intellectual shift, as occurred with the transition from the Early Wittgenstein to the later incarnation. Remember what Nicholson Baker said: What characterizes mind changing under ordinary circumstances is that it occurs largely beneath the surface; unless one has a keen memory or a well-documented journal, one may be surprised to discover that one ever held a contrary point of view. Moreover, when one's changes of mind co-occur with changes that have simultaneously occurred in the minds of millions of one's fellow citizens, they are unlikely to be noticed at all—they blend into the gradually evolving "conventional wisdom" or Zeitgeist.

But what of the areas in which I have devoted my greatest attention? What of my work as a psychologist who has for close to forty years studied the human mind? Surely I can point to changes of emphasis over the years. At one time, I thought of all of the arts as similar to one another, and of creativity as occurring similarly across various art forms. Nowadays, I am far more likely to emphasize the differences across art forms, and to see creativity as having distinctive characteristics in each particular art, science, and vocational or avocational calling. At one time, I favored a progressive approach to early childhood education, where play and exploration were essential and needed to occur before the development of skills kicked in. But after spending a good deal of time in China during the 1980s, I decided that it was less important that one's education begin with a strong immersion in play and exploration; it is equally valid to begin, Chinese-style, with the acquisition of skills. I came to see that what is important is an *oscillation* between periods of relatively free exploration, on the one hand, and the careful cultivation of discipline and skill, on the other. Moreover, at one time, I thought that there was a best approach to American education. After spending over a decade in school reform, however, I have come to the conclusion that this aspiration is an illusion. Americans differ far too deeply from one another in educational philosophy ever to agree on "one best system": indeed, how could we ever please Jesse Jackson, Jesse Helms, *and* Jesse Ventura with a single curriculum? Far better to offer choices, though I personally believe that the number of choices should be limited.

When it comes to my take on specific scholarly ideas, changes of mind have been less dramatic. For example, while I now see the defects in Freud and Piaget, I have never felt the need to make an open break with their legacies. As one who has thought intensively about multiple intelligences, I am more aware than most of the deficiencies in that theory; yet I am far from declaring that my own theory has been refuted or that I have adopted a new holistic, unitary, or genetically determined view of the human intellect. I did not like behaviorism at the start, and I always liked the cognitive view; and while I can now mount something of a defense of behaviorism and a critique of cognitivism, I am scarcely disposed to revert to the orthodoxies of 1950.

Which leads, finally, to issues of temperament and themata. We owe the concept of themata to Gerald Holton, a physicist and historian of science at Harvard University.[35] Even though paradigms in science can change, Holton insists that deep underlying motifs tend to characterize a person (and sometimes a field's) approach to issues over time. In his words, *themata* are "fundamental presuppositions, notions, terms, methodological judgments and decisions . . . which are themselves neither indirectly evolved from, nor resolvable into, objective observation on the one hand, or logical, mathematical, and other formal analytical ratiocination on the other hand."[36] One thema concerns an assumption that the world is continuous; a contrasting or antithema holds that the world is discontinuous. Other themata center on the question of whether everything is explicable, whether everything can be expressed in mathematical terms, whether all knowledge can be reduced to the simplest units, or whether at least some knowledge is better thought of as emergent, and so on.

Using myself again as an example, I am a person who tends to see validity in a range of positions and, when possible, seeks to reconcile or synthesize them. My temperament is conciliatory rather than confrontational, my scholarly disposition is synthetic, rather than analytic. I love to examine the same issue from multiple perspectives, including the lenses provided by various scholarly disciplines. It is hard for me to see myself ever becoming a diehard anything—in politics, religion, academe, or the personal sphere—or to see myself fully engaged over decades in the analysis of one particular issue or concept. I would sooner or later step back and try to place the issue in a broader, more synthetic context . . . or simply move onto another puzzle or problem. I am sensitive to resistances on both sides of an issue. However, I am not content to create the typology or taxonomy and leave it there. I also possess a unifying and synthesizing impulse that stimulates me to try to connect these component parts into a more coherent whole. In the Holton scheme of things, I emerge as a splitter or analyst who wants ultimately to be a lumper; in the more poetic language, which philosopher Isaiah Berlin borrowed from the seventh-century Greek poetic Archilochus, I am a "fox" that aspires to be a "hedgehog."[37] And in the language of this book, positions that feature both analysis and integration resonate the most with me.

Changing minds on issues of consequence is never easy; proclaiming that one has changed one's mind is even more difficult. When such changes of mind occur, they are most likely to entail issues that are readily articulated and categorizable: "I used to be a Democrat but from now on I am going to vote Republican," or "I am finally convinced that behaviorism will never explain language acquisition and so I am taking Chomskian vows." It is difficult to recognize the themata to which one has a deep and often unconscious affiliation, and hence even more difficult for individuals to change their fundamental assumptions about the nature of experience. In the terms of my analysis, what resonates with our psyche is what we most cherish and are least likely to abandon.

Indeed, only those whose defining trait is fickleness or fluidity find it easy to change their minds and to announce that they have done so. But then, we don't take those changes of mind seriously because they reveal more about the person than about his ideas. People like Whittaker Chambers, Ludwig Wittgenstein, or Lucien Lévy-Bruhl stand out because they appear to be serious, dogged, passionate about one point of view and yet end up embracing a point of view that is strikingly different from the original one. When changes of mind matter mightily, when resistances melt and a new set of resonances takes over, the rest of us take note.

CHAPTER 10

Epilogue: The Future of Mind Changing

OF ALL OF THE SPECIES ON EARTH, we human beings are the ones who specialize in voluntary mind change: we change the minds of others, we change our own minds. We have even crafted various technologies that allow us to extend the sweep of mind change: powerful mechanical artifacts like writing implements, televisions, and computers; and equally powerful human contrivances like the teaching strategies, curricula, and tests that we associate with schools. In the coming decades, mind changing will continue and, in all probability, accelerate. I believe that new forms of mind changing will emerge in three areas—in what I'll call wetware, dryware, and goodware.

WETWARE

We are born into this world with many reflexes and proclivities, but the knowledge that we begin to construct is based on the experiences that we undergo. Each organism must build up its understanding of the world from scratch. If all the faces that we encounter happened to have but one eye, we would see the world as Cyclopean; if the only language we heard was Esperanto, that is what we would speak; if all surfaces were rough (or smooth or a checkerboard hybrid thereof), that is the texture that we would learn to feel. And because all of this newly acquired knowledge is

stored in the brain, cortical and subcortical areas that serve those perceptions would become our windows on the world.

Sometimes, of course, glitches in brain development emerge. For
example, a small percentage of the population—say 5 percent to 10 percent—will exhibit genuine difficulties in learning how to read alpha-
betic texts. We might hypothesize that these individuals have an underlying
deficit—perhaps in processing the sounds of language quickly enough
(so that they can reliably discern the difference between *pat* and *bat* in
the course of ordinary speech) or in connecting isolated sounds (*puh*)
to particular squiggles (*p,* rather than *q, d,* or *b*). Fifty years ago these
individuals would have been considered stupid; one hundred years ago
they might have gotten expelled from school. Nowadays, however, we
realize that the problem of dyslexia is often a specific (rather than general) disorder, reflecting difficulties in making certain kinds of neural
connections that (fortunately) prove unproblematic for a large majority
of the population.

Faced with this situation, what are the options? Until recently, the education of individuals with reading problems has been largely an art.
Some teachers are gifted at figuring out the problems of individual
youngsters and contriving an appropriate set of rehabilitative experiences. With the advent of neuroimaging techniques, however, the treatment of dyslexia is evolving into a science: It should be possible to
identify at ever-earlier ages those children who are "at risk" for reading
disability. Distinctive patterns of neural anomaly should indicate *which*
kinds of interventions are likely to be appropriate and at what ages. Then,
once the intervention has been introduced, the same imaging techniques
can detect the effect on neural organization of the intervention and
whether the requisite reading skills are accordingly falling into place.

The result of such strategic intervention on our brains—or our
"wetware"—of course, is "mind change" in the most literal sense. When
one treats the brain as a black box, interventions necessarily operate
purely at the behavioral level: They may work, or they may fail, but
much of the endeavor remains guesswork. Once we begin to understand
in greater detail what is actually happening in the brain, we can attack
the problem more directly. We can specify the structures that are at risk;
we can attempt to bolster them or to develop alternative routes; and we

can observe what is happening in the brain as reading improves or fails to improve. The links between brain changing and mind changing become a matter of knowledge, rather than speculation, prayer, luck, or idiosyncratic artistry.

Improving one's capacity to read is an intervention that affects an important skill. Should one's reading improve dramatically, one has available a powerful means of encountering, and perhaps mastering, the concepts, stories, and theories of one's culture. I think it is premature to think about interventions that directly affect the neural representations of stories and theories. The first successful attempts to change the *contents* of minds through neurological interventions are likely to involve concepts, and particularly those concepts that prove difficult for a certain group of individuals to master. Perhaps, for example, interventions will help autistic individuals understand concepts having to do with human social interactions.

In such speculating, we move from the present to the future. I anticipate three different approaches to changing minds that directly involve the wetware. One is through *behavioral training* that affects the brain and that we will be able to observe directly through imaging. The second is through frank *neural intervention*. Perhaps in the future, changes in the brain will be brought about directly—either through neural transplants or through the use of drugs or hormone therapy that effect specifiable alterations in neural connections. Say we have determined that a certain group of dyslexic individuals has difficulty in developing neural networks in the cross-modal cortical regions that ordinarily connect arbitrary auditory and arbitrary visual signals. This part of the brain could be fortified. The third approach is through the *manipulation of genes*. We might discover that dyslexic individuals have mutations on genes situated on chromosomes 1, 2, 6, and/or 15.[1] Rather than the indirect methods of behavioral or neural manipulation, one might attempt therapy on the flawed genes—either repairing or replacing them.

I am not comfortable with proposals for direct brain and genetic experiments to correct cognitive defects. Yet I have little doubt that these neural enhancements—as they are now called—will be attempted.[2] Moreover, if these interventions prove successful and do not have noticeable side effects, most people—perhaps including me—will come to embrace them. The danger, of course, is the slippery slope. If, tomorrow, we accept such interventions to correct reading problems, will we try to raise IQ or interpersonal intelligence in the same way? And, to bring us closer to the subject of this book, will we attempt ever more blatant efforts at Mind Control and Mind Change, courtesy of our increased knowledge of how the brain and mind work? Neuroscientist Martha Farah reminds us how quickly the range of tools has expanded: "Twenty years ago, it would have seemed implausible that neuroscientists would have even candidate brain indices of truth vs. lie, veridical vs. false memory, the likelihood of future violent crime, styles of moral reasoning, the intention to cooperate, and even the specific contents (visualizing houses versus faces). What might we have in another twenty years or fifty?"[3]

While one cohort of scholars concerned with the Human Mind has approached understanding through a study of brains and genes, another has proceeded with equal gusto through the study of information systems and artificial intelligence: "dryware," as I've termed it.

DRYWARE

Thanks to brilliant efforts by mathematicians Alan Turing, Norbert Wiener, and Claude Shannon, who laid forth in the 1930s the basic laws of computing and information processing, high-speed computers are now ubiquitous in our lives. They aid us in all sorts of tasks, from doing our taxes to handling our airplane reservations to guiding our missiles. Speculative thinkers, like computer experts Ray Kurzweil and Hans Moravec, see both the programming software and the robotic hardware as gaining intelligence with each passing year.[4] They believe that artifacts will surpass humans in intelligence sometime in this century and that it remains an open question whether such artifacts will work for us, whether we will work for them, or whether human beings will become increasingly irrelevant.

But even those who adopt a deflationary view of computers—such as virtual reality expert Jaron Lanier, who believes that computing systems have been unduly "hyped"[5]—must concede that such systems will become ever more intertwined with our mental lives and better able to produce mind change. Much of our interaction takes place nowadays with computer systems with which we "converse" in order to carry out various tasks. Young children play with toys that can react in emotionally convincing ways to the behaviors of the child. Lifelike entities also offer advice to adults, and many adults gain palpable solace from conversation with computers that are following relatively simply postulates.[6] The clunky teaching machines of fifty years ago have been replaced by alluring educational software. One can learn a great deal by surfing the Web, becoming engaged with hypermedia and hypertexts, and participating in distance learning as part of school or work training.

Fast-forward just a few years, and the merging of human and artifactual cognition is likely to be more pervasive. As machines become better at producing and understanding natural language, far more of our daily needs and wishes will be satisfied without the need for human interface. Tim Berners-Lee, the inventor of the World Wide Web, believes that within a few years, new computational systems will be capable of understanding ideas, of full-blown semantic processing.[7] One will tell a Semantic Web just what one wants to know; like a competent librarian, the Web will provide the answer and explain why it corresponds to what was requested. Already, amazon.com does a better job at suggesting books that fit my wife's tastes, based on her previous patterns of scanning and purchasing, than would anyone except a close friend. It is as likely that our psychic needs for love, support, and motivation can also increasingly be met by well-designed and smartly programmed artifacts, from prosthetics that help handicapped people navigate the physical world to artifacts that minister to people with emotional hangups. Perhaps at some future time a troubled seminarian will be "treated" by a program called EHErikson or a difficult negotiation will be aided by a program called PresProf.

We can even extend the use of artificial intelligence to multiple intelligences—in which smart programs can increasingly help people in those areas of intelligence where they have weaknesses. For example, I am not skilled at solving spatial tasks. Ask me to fold and refold sheets of paper in my mind and I soon have a headache. Knowing of this weakness, however, I can make use of software that represents publicly those spatial operations that I have difficulty carrying out in the privacy of my mind. With a little drill-and-practice I become as "smart" as a skilled mental imager. Clearly, then, knowledge of my own "MI profile" should be helpful to any entity that seeks to interact with my mind. If such a hypothetical entity is trying to teach me something or sell me something, it can provide information in ways that fit the current contents and favored formats of my mental representations. Conversely, if I am trying to communicate information to such an entity, it should be able to take information from me in ways that are comfortable for me, and its mind—if you will permit this attribution—should accordingly be affected by the contents that I am transmitting. And to the extent that such artifacts become concerned with emotional and motivational life, they will have to speak to our personal intelligences—whether or not they strike us in appearance or approach as plausible members of "our" species. (On a recent visit to Sony's futuristic Media World in Tokyo, I noted that the newest robots look and behave increasingly like domestic pets, if not little human children.)

I am again moving in the direction of future science, if not science fiction. That point conceded, artificial intelligence is already engaged in changing our minds and will doubtless do so to a much greater degree in the future. I fully expect the enterprise of dryware—artificial intelligence of one sort or another—to become far more enmeshed with our own present wetware. Interfaces are being created between silicon-based hardware and primate neural tissue.[8] This transformation will occur even if the critics are right in their essential claims that machine intelligence is not of the same order or variety as human intelligence and will remain— at least for the foreseeable future—fundamentally different from, and subservient to, human intelligence. In fact, it has become clear that the whole universe can be thought of as an information system: computer programming information and genetic information are just two instances of the same genre. Just as computational science and neuroscience have combined in computational neuroscience, we now have genetic algorithms, artificial life, and other compounds that straddle the gulf between "bits" and "molecules."[9] No doubt this blurring of boundaries between "wet" and "dry" will continue, and changes of mind will entail the reordering of information of both sorts in the human psyche.

All of which begs the question of value judgment: Is changing minds through such boundary blurring a "good" or "bad" thing?

GOODWARE

Clearly, neither science nor technology is good or bad in itself. Einstein's understanding of the relationship between mass and energy can be drawn on to create nuclear power plants or thermonuclear weapons. A pencil can be used to write beautiful sonnets, to poke out the eye of an enemy intentionally, or to puncture one's skin accidentally. Computer programs can calculate the medicine needed to save the lives of children in a distant land or guide a missile so that it hits a hospital filled with handicapped children.

Accordingly, the kinds of mind change discussed in this book can serve a variety of ends. Much of what I've discussed has been value-neutral. A leader like Napoleon can inspire his nation to make war; a leader like Nelson Mandela can bring about an epochal change of political regime through peaceful means. Religious training can induct Islamic (or Christian or Jewish) youths to undertake a holy war against infidels or to lead a peaceful life in a pluralistic society. And even intimate mind changing within families, therapy, or love relations can proceed in ways that are constructive or destructive for those in their circle or for the individuals themselves.

Influential thinkers in the West have done an admirable job of cleaving apart excellence in technique from distinction in morality. We appreciate that a person can be highly skilled without being moral in the least; that a person can be ethical without having the requisite competence; and that many of us stand out neither in terms of excellence nor social responsibility. We have come to realize that most experts represent an amalgam of ethical and nonethical conduct: How does one weigh the courage and heroism of the young Mao Zedong against the dastardly behavior of the aging tyrant? Or, to use more local examples, how do we balance the ethical scales as we pass judgment on complex political figures of the 1960s such as Lyndon Johnson or Malcolm X?

Looking forward, we may ask whether it may be possible to change minds so that excellence and ethics are more closely allied. Recently, Mihaly Csikszentmihalyi, William Damon, and I have been studying what we term GoodWork—work that is at once technically excellent and that seeks outcomes that are ethical, moral, and responsible. There are Good-Workers in every profession and domain. Among the individuals of recent memory whom I admire are publisher Katharine Graham, cellist Pablo Casals, ecological writer Rachel Carson, scientist Jonas Salk, ballplayer Jackie Robinson, and American public figure John Gardner (no relation!) to whom my colleagues and I dedicated our 2001 book *Good Work: When Excellence and Ethics Meet*.[10] Though the ethical quotient for any individual may be contested, there is clearly a difference between individuals who strive to be accountable on the ethical dimension and those for whom only monetary or worldly success or power matter.

How does one become a GoodWorker, and how does one remain such in the face of various temptations? Our studies suggest a number of factors, including the development in childhood of a strong moral code (often through religious training), the milieu of one's early training (e.g., clubs in school, professional school), and the kind of peer support and mentoring received at one's first job. Yet even in the case of such early supportive factors, an individual may slip. Temptations are rampant; new or altered work environments may honor work that is bad or compromised; conditions in a domain may change so cataclysmically that it is not clear any longer just what is, and is not, GoodWork. Accordingly, it is important for workers to achieve periodic booster shots, such as powerful experiences that underscore the continuing need for GoodWork and demonstrate how it might be carried out.

How does a person determine whether he or she is a GoodWorker? We propose a threefold process, conveniently designated by three *M*s: mission, models, and mirror test.

First, it is important to recognize and confirm the *mission* of one's profession. Why did one enter the profession, what is its contribution to society, how does one personally conceive of the domain? I am a teacher, for example. I believe that the mission of teaching has three facets: (1) to introduce students to the best thinking of the past; (2) to prepare their minds for an uncertain future, where knowledge will be drawn on or transformed in ways that are difficult to anticipate; and (3) to model aspects of civility in the treatment of the individuals and the materials of work. It is not enough for me to commit to memory an oath or mission statement crafted by someone else. I need to review this mission from time to time, personalize it, revise it if necessary, and monitor critically whether I am fulfilling aspects of the mission.

Next, one needs to look for and acknowledge *models*. Some of these models will be admirable: individuals whom one respects and to whom one looks for guidance in one's work. One also learns from negative role models—we call these antimentors or tormentors. Such individuals serve as cautionary tales—whatever I do, I don't want to be like Xc#!vYz@!

Finally, there is the *mirror test*. Every worker needs regularly to look into the mirror and pose the personal questions: "Am I a GoodWorker? Am I proud of the work that I do? And if not, what I can do to become a GoodWorker?" The mirror is useless, of course, if one lies to oneself; that's why it helps to check your self-perception (in my terms, your intrapersonal intelligence) in light of evaluations by individuals whose opinion you trust. The personal mirror test can then be complemented with a broader one: "Am I proud of the way in which my fellow professionals are carrying out their work? Is my profession currently marked by GoodWork?" If a gulf obtains between the personal and the professional mirror tests, this is a clarion call, a sign that all is not well. To aid an ailing profession, we've identified a special role of "trustee": the self-imposed assignment of such senior figures is to help maintain quality work throughout the domain. As the playwright Jean-Baptiste Molière acutely pointed out, "We are responsible not only for what we do but for what we don't do."

Let me spell out the link between GoodWork and mind changing. Many of us in the contemporary world consider our work as an area for professional excellence. And some of us believe that morality has no place in the workplace, though certainly we have the option of being charitable in person or on the weekends or in our will, as we shuttle off expectantly to heaven. The concept of GoodWork directly challenges such a bifurcation of experience. My colleagues and I hold that a society needs GoodWorkers, and especially so at a time when things are changing rapidly, our sense of time and space is being radically altered by technology, and market forces are tremendously influential, with few counterforces of equal power.

The achievement of GoodWork, then, involves two orders of mind change. First, it requires a belief that GoodWork is an important part of life, a phenomenon too vital to be left to chance or to others. Making this point is a job for direct leaders, like presidents and CEOs, and for aspiring indirect leaders, such as my scholarly colleagues and me. Second, it requires the creation of experiences that are likely to increase the incidence of GoodWork. The above trio of recommendations—early ethical belief systems, peer and mentor support in training and at the first workplace, periodic "booster experiences"—represent efforts to create and keep GoodWork front and center. And the three practical monitors—mission, model, and mirror—are convenient ways to assess how one is faring as a worker.

If there is such a thing as GoodWork, there is, alas, also the phenomenon of bad or compromised work. Every day one reads in the newspaper or sees on television portrayals of individuals who besmirch the core values of a profession: journalists who distort or even invent facts, scientists who overlook discrepant data in order to publish first, physicians who only serve those who can pay high fees, and so on. In such cases, one hopes to change the minds (and practices!) of these bad workers and to influence those who witness and may be tempted by these malpractices.

We should not assume that mind changing is always desirable. It is not always "good" to attempt to change minds; it is not always "bad" to remain in the same mental place. In every instance, individuals with the capacity and the opportunity to change the minds of others need to ask about whether this is the right course to follow. And while there are no formulas, the three measures that I suggested—mission, models, and mirror tests—can help us to determine which instances of mind changing are GoodWork and which run the risk of encouraging poor or compromised work.

MIND CHANGE, ONE LAST TIME

By now, I hope that the curiosity that motivated you to read this book has been satisfied. As our inquiry draws to a close, allow me to review the skeleton of the argument that I have developed; I encourage you to flesh out this précis not only by recalling the examples that I used but also by bringing to bear instances from your own experiences—and to consider whether your own mind has been altered by what you have read.

Generically, mind change entails the alteration of mental representations. All of us develop mental representations quite readily from the beginning of life. Many such representations are serviceable, some have notable charm, others are misleading or flatly wrong. Mental representations have a *content:* we think of these contents as ideas, concepts, skills, stories, or full-fledged theories (explanations of the world). These contents can be expressed in words—and in a book, that medium is customarily used. However, nearly all contents can be expressed in a variety of *forms,* media, symbol systems: these systems can be exhibited publicly as marks on a page and can also be internalized in a "language of the mind" or a particular "intelligence."

We also encountered a paradox of mind changing. Mind changing occurs all the time, especially among the young, and until death we cannot stop the process. Yet certain ideas develop very early in life and prove surprisingly refractory to change. The trick in "psychosurgery" (i.e., mind changing) is to accept the changes that will happen anyway, acknowledge that certain other changes may be impossible, and concentrate one's efforts on those changes of mind that are important, won't occur naturally, but can be achieved with sufficient effort and motivation.

With this generic view of mind changing as background, I teased out a number of crucial dimensions. These can serve as a checklist when one is considering candidates for mind changing:

1. Present Content and Desired Content

One should begin by determining what is the present (current) content—be it an idea, a concept, a story, a theory, a skill—and what is the desired content. Once the desired content has been identified, the various competing countercontents must be specified. The more explicitly one can lay these out, the more likely that one can arrive at a strategy suitable for mind changing in the particular instance. Both contents and countercontents may be presented in various formats.

2. Size of Audience

The challenge of mind change is quite different depending on whether one is dealing with a large audience or a tiny audience. Large audiences are affected chiefly by powerful stories, rendered by individuals who embody their stories in the lives that they lead; intimate audiences can benefit from approaches that are much more individually contextualized. Of special interest are the changes that take place in one's own mind, involving the most intimate kind of conversation with oneself.

3. Type of Audience

When one is dealing with an audience that is large and heterogeneous, one is dealing with the unschooled mind. Expertise cannot be assumed. Simple stories work the best. On the other hand, when one is dealing with individuals who share knowledge and expertise, one can assume a mind that is schooled and relatively homogeneous with respect to other minds in the group. Stories or theories related to such groups can be more sophisticated, and counterarguments can and should be addressed directly.

4. Directness of Change

Political, business, and educational leaders bring about change through the messages that they convey directly to their respective audiences. Creative and innovative individuals bring about change indirectly, through the symbolic products—art works, inventions, scientific theories—that they fashion. In general, mind changes due to indirect creations take longer, but their effects have the potential to last for a far longer period of time. In general, we remember the artistic creators of bygone civilization far more vividly than we recall the political leaders.

5. Levers of Change and Tipping Points

Classically, change takes place through compulsion, manipulation, persuasion, or through some combination thereof. In this book I have directed attention to deliberate and open attempts at mind change. I have also stressed the classic forms of persuasion: talk, teaching, therapy, and the creation and dissemination of new ideas and products. We must recognize, however, that in the future, these low-tech agents may well be supplanted by new forms of intervention: some will be biological, involving transformation of genes or brain tissue; some will be computational, entailing the use of new software and new hardware; and some will represent increasingly intricate amalgams of the biological and the computational realms.

Perhaps the greatest challenge is to determine when the desired content has in fact been conveyed and whether it has actually been consolidated. Alas, there are no formulas for this step: each case of mind changing is distinctive. It is helpful to bear in mind that most mind change is gradual, occurring over significant periods of time; that awareness of the mind change is often fleeting, and the mind change may occur prior to consciousness thereof; that individuals have a pronounced tendency to slip back to earlier ways of thinking; but that when a mind change has become truly consolidated, it is likely to become as entrenched as its predecessor.

Every example of mind changing has its unique facets. But in general, such a shift of mind is likely to coalesce when we employ the seven levers of mind change: specifically, when *reason* (often buttressed with *research*), reinforcement through multiple forms of *representation, real world events, resonance,* and *resources* all push in one direction—and *resistances* can be identified and successfully countered. Conversely, mind changing is unlikely to occur—or to consolidate—when resistances are strong and most of the other points of leverage are not in place.

6. The Ethical Dimension

As Niccolò Machiavelli pointed out dramatically, skills in bringing about change need not (in fact, he argued, *should* not) have a moral dimension. Indeed, most of the processes outlined in this book can be carried out for amoral ends, for immoral ends, or for impressively moral ends.

Given the complexity of forces in the world, it is tempting to throw up one's hands and to declare that the possibilities for positive, deliberate changes of mind are modest. That may be true. But unless one is willing to become a full determinist—and no one ever leads his or her own life that way—we must continue to believe that the will is free and that individuals can make a difference. The human mind is a human creation, and all human creations can be changed. We need not be a passive reflector of our biological heritage or our cultural and historical traditions. We can change our minds and the minds of others around us. The cognitive perspective provides a way of thinking and an array of tools. It is up to us whether we choose to use these, and whether we do so in ways that are selfish and destructive or in ways that are generous and life-enhancing.

Appendix

A FRAMEWORK FOR ANALYZING
CASES OF MIND CHANGING

In this chart I apply the analytic framework introduced in the first three chapters to major cases discussed in the remainder of the book. The chart can be read independently but is best understood in conjunction with the related text.

LEGEND:

Type of Idea: Concept/story/theory/skill (see chapter 1)

Desired content: The mind change being sought

Countercontent: The idea(s) that run counter to the desired content

Type of audience/arena: Large/small; diverse (heterogeneous)/uniform (homogeneous)

Format: Intelligences, media, symbol systems by which content is conveyed

Levers of change/tipping point factors: The most germane of the seven levers, and considerations that determine whether a tipping point is reached

CHAPTER I

Nicholson Baker's Furniture
  Idea: Concept/image

  Content: New ways of furnishing apartment seats

  Countercontent: Usual seating arrangements

  Audience: Self

  Format: Imaginary experiments, models, daydreaming

  Levers/tipping point: Unknown, "something happened"

The 80/20 Principle
  Idea: Concept

  Content: Uneven, perhaps lopsided, investment of resources

  Countercontent: Even investment of resources

  Audience: Varied (self/organization/general public)

  Format: Linguistic, graphic, humorous, other symbol systems

  Levers/tipping point: Reason, research, representational redescription, overcoming resistance

CHAPTER 2

Multiple Intelligences Theory
  Idea: Theory

  Content: Several relatively autonomous intelligences

  Countercontent: Standard view of intelligence, adequately captured by IQ tests

  Audience: Varied (scholars/public)

  Format: Scientific theory expressed in language and other symbol systems; powerful examples

  Levers/tipping point: Research, representational redescription, overcoming resistance, resonance with personal observations, experience

CHAPTER 3

Naturally Occurring Changes of Mind in Children
    Idea: Concepts/intuitive theories

    Content: More sophisticated understanding of the physical, biological, and human worlds

    Countercontent: Initial intuitive theories

    Audience: Child himself/herself

    Format: Explanations given to self, others, in various media and symbol systems

    Levers/tipping point: Real world experience (experimenting in the world to overcome the resistances embodied in earlier theories), representational redescription, resonance (with experiences of older peers and admired adults)

CHAPTER 4

Margaret Thatcher's Reorientation of Great Britain
    Idea: Story

    Content: Britain has lost its way, must become entrepreneurial again

    Countercontent: Post–World War II consensus: long live a partially socialized state

    Audience: Large, diverse

    Format: Linguistic, occasionally graphic, embodiment in one's own life

    Levers/tipping point: Resources to deploy, rhetoric (mobilizing reason, research, and resonance), real world events, overcoming resistance based on post-war consensus

Newt Gingrich's Failed Revolution
    Idea: Story

    Content: Government as problem, let markets regulate everything

    Countercontent: Government has its place, markets require regulation

    Audience: Large/diverse

Format: Linguistic, video, embodiment (nonembodiment) in one's own life

Levers/tipping point: On positive side: reason, resources; on negative side: lack of resonance (due to failure to embody), underestimating resistance, real world event (effectiveness of Clinton opposition), overheated rhetoric

Mahatma Gandhi's Peaceful Resistance

Idea: Concept (satyagraha)/story/practice

Content: Nonviolent engagement, peaceful resistance

Countercontent: Conflicts can only be resolved in a confrontational and aggressive manner

Audience: Large/diverse

Format: Powerful personal example, linguistic, use of news media

Levers/tipping point: Research with various methods, until they are fine-tuned; resonance with experience of population, longstanding traditions, and embodied skills; representational redescription (embodiment, dramatic encounters); real world events (Depression, world wars, decline of colonialism)

CHAPTER 5

James O. Freedman's New Vision for Dartmouth College

Idea: Story

Content: Dartmouth as more intellectual, tolerant, peaceful

Countercontent: Dartmouth of olden times, athletic, macho, politically conservative

Audience: Moderate size/relatively uniform

Format: Written and oral language, personal example, new visions and demonstrations

Levers/tipping point: Resonance (based on embodiment, redescriptions, and rhetoric), use of resources, research, reason, overcoming resistances

Robert Shapiro's Failed Attempt to Launch a Revolution in Genetically Modified Food

Idea: Story

Content: A new agricultural vision, featuring genetically modified food

Countercontent: Don't interfere with nature; any experimentation must be cautious and publicly debated

Audience: Homogeneous within corporation; large and diverse in the case of general public

Format: Language, demonstrations

Levers/tipping point: On positive side: reason (overreliance on), research, resources; on negative side: lack of resonance, underestimating resistance, organizing resources of opponents, excessive rhetoric

CHAPTER 6

Charles Darwin's Evolutionary Revolution

Idea: Theory

Content: Origin of species through natural selection over long periods of time

Countercontent: Religious accounts, intuitive theories of creationism

Audience: Initially, small and uniform; ultimately, larger and more diverse

Format: Linguistic argument in book form, corroborating evidence in fossils, flora, fauna

Levers/tipping point: Reason, research, representational redescription, overcoming resistances

Creators of the Modern Era (for example, Picasso, Stravinsky, T. S. Eliot, Martha Graham, Virginia Woolf)

Idea: Practices

Content: Overthrow of realism and romanticism; new modernist sensibility

Countercontent: Continued embrace of representational art, classical harmonic music, realistic writing

Audience: Initially, small and uniform; ultimately, larger and more diverse

Format: Different artistic symbol systems and media

Levers/tipping point: Effective, novel representational redescriptions; resonance with current trends and real world events; overcoming and also making judicious use of resistances

Jay Winsten Introduces the Designated Driver

Idea: Concept/practices

Content: Don't drink and drive

Countercontent: It's safe, we've done it before, we know what we are doing

Audience: Large, diverse

Format: Television plots, public service announcements, convincing embodiments

Levers/tipping point: Resonance (with characters, message), significant resources, representational redescription (through media), overcoming resistances

CHAPTER 7

New Disciplinary Understandings

Idea: Disciplinary concepts/theories/skills

Content: Disciplinary (and interdisciplinary) ways of thinking, often deeply nonintuitive

Countercontent: Common sense and common nonsense; reliance on intuition; memorization of factual information

Audience: Moderate size, varied, unschooled mind

Format: Classroom lessons, texts (primarily linguistic); practice in thinking in new ways; possible use of other symbol systems as entry points

Levers/tipping point: Representational redescriptions, reason, and research; understanding the power of resistances and showing their inadequacy

Changes at BP

Idea: Concepts/practices

Content: A nonhierarchical learning organization that is entrepreneurial, competitive, and cooperative

Countercontent: Comfortable lifelong employment; don't rock the boat

Audience: Moderate size, relatively uniform

Format: Messages conveyed linguistically, graphically, and through personal examples

Levers/tipping point: Reason, research, resources and rewards, real world events (competition), representational redescriptions

CHAPTER 8

Erik Erikson Treats a Seminarian

Idea: Image/story/practice

Content: An integrated viable identity that allows one to move forward with one's life

Countercontent: Continuing to feel distraught because there is little understanding of the various themes in one's life and therefore little hope of changing life conditions

Audience: Self (seminarian); therapist (as enabler)

Format: Dream analysis; psychotherapeutic encounter and accompanying interpretations

Levers/tipping point: Resonance (of interpretation with feelings), representational redescriptions (dreams), resources (time, rather than money), reasons (offered by therapist)

Lawrence Summers Confronts Cornel West

Idea: Concept/story/practice

Content: A university professor who focuses on scholarship and is centered on campus

Countercontent: A public intellectual who is in contact with the wider world of persons and ideas

Audience: One person

Format: Personal conversation

Levers/tipping point: On positive side: reason, resources; on negative side: lack of resonance, real world events (including competing offers and resources available to other party), underestimation of personal resistance

Jefferson and Adams Reconcile

Idea: Story/practice

Content: A restored friendship, based on recognition of ties and capacity to modulate differences

Countercontent: Years of political antagonism that had spilled over to the personal

Audience: Two people

Format: Written letters

Levers/tipping point: Restored resonance, real world events (end of presidencies, aging process), overcoming resistance through artful, highly motivated communication

CHAPTER 9

President George W. Bush's Changed Foreign Policy

Idea: Concepts (including self-concept)/stories

Content: Focus on foreign affairs, being well informed, making difficult decisions, searching for allies internationally

Countercontent: Isolationism; reliance on father and advisers

Audience: Self

Format: Briefings, meetings with staff and leaders, reflection in personal symbol systems

Levers/tipping point: Real world events, resources (to try out something new)

Whittaker Chambers Rejects Communism

Idea: Stories/theory (form of society); self-concept

Content: The unvarnished critical truth about the evils of communism, at the risk of self-ruination

Countercontent: (1) Own earlier embracing of communism; (2) letting the past simply disappear

Audience: Initially, self; ultimately, large and varied

Format: Reading, writing, oral argument, reflection

Levers/tipping point: Real world events, resonance, reason, and research

Becoming a Fundamentalist

Idea: Self-concept/story/theory/practice (kind of life)/self

Content: A coherent, enveloping approach to life, based on literal interpretation of the Bible and membership in a supportive religious community

Countercontent: Remaining in one's current social environment and belief system

Audience: Self

Format: Reading text; meetings and exchanges with supportive group; personal reflection

Levers/tipping point: Resonance (with supportive group); representational redescription, research

Rejecting Fundamentalism

Idea: Self-concept/story/theory/practice

Content: Opportunity to think matters through on one's own, live with uncertainty

Countercontent: A powerful and comfortable closed system, difficult to escape

Audience: Self

Format: Arguments with self, exposure to new sources of information

Levers/tipping point: Reason, research, representational redescription, and resonance (with realities of wider world)

Lucien Lévy-Bruhl Renounces His View on the Primitive Mind

Idea: Theory/concept

Content: Primitive mind not genuinely different from modern mind; willingness publicly to change one's mind

Countercontent: Primitive mind is fundamentally different; scholars should be consistent above all

Audience: Initially, self; ultimately, wider scholarly audience

Format: Reading and corresponding; private thoughts and notebook jottings

Levers/tipping point: Research, reason

Notes

Chapter 1

1. Nicholson Baker, "Changes of Mind," in *The Size of Thoughts: Essays and Other Lumber,* ed. Nicholson Baker (New York: Random House, 1982/1996), 5–9. I thank Alex Chisholm for this citation.
2. Ibid., 5.
3. Ibid., 9.
4. J. S. Bruner, *In Search of Mind* (New York: Harper, 1983); Howard Gardner, *The Mind's New Science: A History of the Cognitive Revolution* (New York: Basic Books, 1985).
5. Richard Koch, *The 80/20 Principle: The Secret of Achieving More with Less* (New York: Currency, 1998).
6. Michael Moss, "A Nation Challenged: Airport Security. U.S. Airport Task Force Begins with Hiring," *New York Times,* 23 November 2001, 21.
7. The expression "representational redescription" is taken from A. Karmiloff-Smith, *Beyond Modularity* (Cambridge: MIT Press, 1992).

Chapter 2

1. Howard Gardner, Vernon Howard, and David Perkins, "Symbol Systems: A Philosophical, Psychological, and Educational Investigation," in *Media and Symbols,* ed. D. Olson (Chicago: University of Chicago Press, 1974); Norman Geschwind, "Disconnexion Syndromes in Animals and Man," *Brain* 88 (1965): 237–285; Nelson Goodman, *Languages of Art* (Indianapolis: Bobbs-Merrill, 1968); Roger Sperry, "Some Effects of Disconnecting the Cerebral Hemispheres" (Nobel Prize lecture), in *Neuroscience,* eds. P. H. Abelson, E. Butz, and

Solomon H. Snyder (Washington: American Association for the Advancement of Science, 1985), 372–380.

2. Howard Gardner, *To Open Minds: Chinese Clues to the Dilemma of Contemporary Education* (New York: Basic Books, 1989), 84; see also Howard Gardner, *The Shattered Mind: The Person After Brain Damage* (New York: Knopf, 1975).

3. See also Jerry A. Fodor, *The Language of Thought* (New York: Thomas Crowell, 1975).

4. Albert Einsten, quoted in Brewster Ghiselin, *The Creative Process* (New York: Mentor, 1952), 43.

5. Howard Gardner, *Frames of Mind: The Theory of Multiple Intelligences* (New York: Basic Books, 1983/1993); *Multiple Intelligences: The Theory in Practice* (New York: Basic Books, 1993); *Intelligence Reframed: Multiple Intelligences for the Twenty-First Century* (New York: Basic Books, 1999).

6. For elaborations of the traditional view, see Hans J. Eysenck, "The Theory of Intelligence and the Psychophysiology of Cognition," in *Advances in Research on Intelligence,* ed. R. J. Sternberg (Hillsdale, NJ: Lawrence Erlbaum, 1986); Richard J. Herrnstein and Charles Murray, *The Bell Curve* (New York: Free Press, 1994); Arthur Jensen, *The "g" Factor: The Science of Mental Ability* (Westport, CT: Praeger, 1998).

7. Howard Gardner, *Leading Minds* (New York: Basic Books, 1995), 137; Alfred P. Sloan, *My Years at General Motors* (Garden City, NJ: Doubleday, 1972).

8. David Halberstam, *The Best and the Brightest* (New York: Random House, 1972).

9. Julian Stanley, "Varieties of Giftedness" (paper presented at the Annual Meeting of the American Educational Research Association, San Francisco, April 1995).

10. Rosamund Stone Zander and Benjamin Zander, *The Art of Possibility: Transforming Professional and Personal Life* (Boston: Harvard Business School Press, 2000).

11. I have been unable to verify this quote, but for comparable sentiments see Bill Bradley, *Life on the Run* (New York: Quadrangle, 1976), 87, 170.

12. Albert Einstein, quoted in Brewster Ghiselin, *The Creative Process* (New York: Mentor, 1952), 43.

13. Howard Gardner, *Intelligence Reframed*.

14. Daniel Goleman, *Emotional Intelligence* (New York: Bantam, 1995); Daniel Goleman, *Working with Emotional Intelligence* (New York: Bantam Books, 1998).

15. Daniel Goleman, Richard Boyatzis, and Annie McKee, *Primal Leadership: The Hidden Driver of Great Performance* (Boston: Harvard Business School Press, 2002).

16. Roger Fisher and William Ury, *Getting to Yes* (Boston: Houghton Mifflin, 1981).

17. M. Buckingham and D. O. Clifton, *Now, Discover Your Strengths* (New York: Free Press, 2001).

18. Peter Drucker, "Managing Oneself," *Harvard Business Review,* March–April 1999, 65–74.

19. See Howard Gardner, *Intelligence Reframed,* chapters 4 and 5, for the reasons that led to this conclusion. The eight criteria, elaborated on in Howard Gardner, *Frames of Mind,* chapter 4, are these: (1) Existence of a discrete symbol system; (2) evidence for specialized representation in the brain; (3) a distinctive evolutionary history; (4) a distinctive developmental pattern; (5) identifiable core psychological operations; (6) existence of special populations that highlight or lack a capacity; (7) patterns of results on psychometric measures of intelligence; and (8) patterns of transfer or lack of transfer across tasks that putatively involve a specific intelligence. An additional criterion, sometimes cited, is the existence of roles that foreground the intelligences in different cultures.

20. See Sharon Begley, "Religion and the Brain," *Newsweek,* 7 May 2001, 50ff.

21. Howard Gardner, Mihaly Csikszentmihalyi, and William Damon, *Good Work: When Excellence and Ethics Meet* (New York: Basic Books, 2001).

22. Stephen Wolfram, *A New Kind of Science* (Champaign, IL: Wolfram Media, 2002), 1177.

23. See, for example, Paul Lawrence and Nitin Nohria, *Driven: How Human Nature Shapes Our Choices* (San Francisco: Jossey Bass, 2002); Nigel Nicholson, *Executive Instinct* (New York: Crown, 2000).

24. For a historical-cultural approach to the growing industrial might of East Asia, see Charles Hampden-Turner and Fons Trompenaars, *Mastering the Infinite Game* (Oxford: Capstone, 1997).

Chapter 3

1. Philippe Ariès, *Centuries of Childhood* (London: Jonathan Cape, 1962).

2. See Howard Gardner, *The Quest for Mind,* 2d ed. (Chicago: University of Chicago Press, 1983); Jean Piaget, "Piaget's Theory," in *Handbook of Child Psychology,* vol. 1, ed. P. Mussen (New York: Wiley, 1983).

3. Sigmund Freud, *The New Introductory Lectures* (New York: Norton, 1933/1964).

4. Philip Sadler, *A Private Universe* (Washington, DC: Annenberg/CPB, 1987).

5. Howard Gardner, *The Unschooled Mind* (New York: Basic Books, 1991).

6. See ibid. and references therein.

7. During the first decades of cognitive science, the reigning metaphor for mind changing was the learning of a rule. These rules were considered to be more or less explicit. And so, a child on the edge of mastering conservation would in effect come to behave in accordance with a rule that says: "Water does not change in amount when it is poured into another container, so long as nothing is added or subtracted." Computers were also programmed in accordance with such strings of symbols. More recently, however, the reigning metaphor

has been a set of networked neurons, the strength of whose connections to one another is changed gradually as a result of experiences that accumulate over time. On this analysis, the child gradually shifts from a stage where he reliably associates height with amount to a stage where he reliably associates "lack of addition or subtraction" to identity of amount. There is no need for the formal statement of a rule—neither for the child nor for the computer. My own view is that most changes of mind (such as the apartment-furnishing scenario chronicled in chapter 1 by writer Nicholson Baker) are best described by the neural network metaphor, but that important changes may also be brought about by more explicit learning and mastery of rules. See Gerald Edelman, *Bright Air, Brilliant Fire* (New York: Basic Books, 1992); Gerald Edelman and G. Tononi, *A Universe of Consciousness: How Matter Becomes Imagination* (London: Penguin Press, 2001); Jeffrey Elman et al., *Rethinking Innateness* (Cambridge: MIT Press, 1996); Steven Pinker, *How the Mind Works* (New York: Norton, 1997); Manfred Spitzer, *The Mind Within the Net* (Cambridge: MIT Press, 1999).

8. Elliot Turiel, "The Development of Morality," in *Handbook of Child Psychology*, vol. 3, ed. W. Damon (New York: Wiley, 1997), 863–932.

9. Lev Semonovich Vygotsky, *Thought and Language* (Cambridge: MIT Press, 1962); *The Mind in Society* (Cambridge: Harvard University Press, 1978).

Chapter 4

1. For portraits of Thatcher's political career, see Howard Gardner, *Leading Minds* (New York: Basic Books, 1995); Margaret Thatcher, *The Downing Street Years* (New York: HarperCollins, 1993); Margaret Thatcher, *The Path to Power* (New York: HarperCollins, 1995); Hugo Young, *The Iron Lady* (New York: Farrar, Straus, and Giroux, 1989).

2. Thatcher, *Path to Power*, 440; Thatcher, *Downing Street Years*, 7.

3. Thatcher, *Downing Street Years*, 10.

4. Quoted in *Women's Own* magazine, 3 October 1987.

5. Thatcher, *Downing Street Years*, 4.

6. Ibid., 10.

7. See photo after page 114 in Young, *Iron Lady*.

8. Thatcher, *Downing Street Years*, 123.

9. Ibid., 264.

10. Thatcher, *Path to Power*, 416.

11. Thatcher, *Downing Street Years*, 755.

12. As reported in David Maraniss, *First in His Class: A Biography of Bill Clinton* (New York: Simon and Schuster, 1995), 282.

13. Joe Klein, *The Natural* (New York: Doubleday, 2002), 40.

14. For such critiques, see ibid.

15. For information about the career of Speaker Newt Gingrich, see David Maraniss and Michael Weiskopf, *Tell Newt to Shut Up* (New York: Touchstone, 1996); and Joan Didion, "Newt Gingrich, Superstar," in *Political Fictions* (New York: Knopf, 2001), 167–190.

16. On "hot" and "cool" personalities, see Marshall McLuhan, *Understanding Media* (New York: McGraw-Hill, 1974).

17. For fuller portrayals, see Howard Gardner, *Leading Minds,* 1995, and the references cited therein.

18. Nelson Mandela, *Long Walk to Freedom* (Boston: Little, Brown, 1994).

19. François Duchêne, *Jean Monnet: The First Statesman of Interdependence* (New York: Norton, 1994), 23.

20. Quoted in *Hansard,* May 13, 1940.

Chapter 5

1. The one exception is with young persons, who are often convinced by an argument that is slightly more sophisticated—particularly if it is voiced by someone who is older and more respected.

2. I spoke at length to James Freedman about these events and also reviewed newspaper clippings from his file.

3. Details about Freedman's struggle with the *Dartmouth Review* are found in the *Chronicle of Higher Education,* 6 April 1988; *New York Times,* 29 March 1988; "Freedman: It Was Time to Speak Out," *Valley News,* 1 April 1988; Sean Flynn, "Dartmouth's Right Is Wrong," *Boston Phoenix,* 15 April 1988.

4. Sean Gorman, telephone conversation with author, 20 November 2002.

5. James O. Freedman, *Idealism and Liberal Education* (Ann Arbor: University of Michigan Press, 1996/2001).

6. Robert Slater, *The Eye of the Storm: How John Chambers Steered Cisco Through the Technology Collapse* (New York: Harper Business, 2003), 16.

7. John McMillan, "Come Back, New Economy," *New York Times Book Review,* 26 January 2003, 27.

8. *Business Week,* 28 March 2002, 33.

9. Paul Krugman, "Clueless in Crawford," *New York Times,* 12 August 2002, A21.

10. Paul Abrahams, "Cisco Pays High Price for Low Revenue Growth," *Financial Times,* 10 May 2001, 32.

11. Slater, *Eye of the Storm,* 269.

12. Ibid., 248.

13. *New York Times,* 7 November 2002.

14. Slater, *Eye of the Storm,* 267.

15. Craig Benson, quoted in ibid., 147.

16. On Shapiro, see Michael Spector, "The Pharmageddon Riddle," *New Yorker,* 10 April 2000. Specter refers to Shapiro as "Johnny Appleseed."

17. C. Hoenig, *Wall Street Journal,* 3 May 2001; see also 26 October 1999.

18. Justin Gillis and Anne Swardson, "Crop Busters Take on Monsanto: Backlash Against Biotech Goods Exacts a High Price," *Washington Post,* 26 October 1999.

19. Erik H. Erikson, "Identity and the Life Cycle," *Psychological Issues* 1 (1959).

20. James McGregor Burns, *Leadership* (New York: Harper & Row, 1978); Howard Gardner, *Leading Minds* (New York: Basic Books, 1995); John Gardner, *On Leadership* (New York: Free Press, 1999).

21. Louis Schweitzer, personal communication, 1 February 2001.

Chapter 6

1. Howard Gruber, *Darwin on Man* (Chicago: University of Chicago Press, 1981), 162.

2. Janet Browne, *Charles Darwin* (London: Jonathan Cape, 1995).

3. Howard Gardner, *The Disciplined Mind* (New York: Penguin, 2000), chap. 7 and references therein.

4. Frank Sulloway, *Born to Rebel* (New York: Pantheon, 1996).

5. E. Margaret Evans, "Beyond Scopes: Why Creationism Is Here to Stay," in *Imagining the Impossible: Magical, Scientific, and Religious Thinking in Children,* ed. K. Rosengren, C. Johnson, and P. Harris (Cambridge: Cambridge University Press, 2000), 330–351.

6. Thomas Kuhn, *The Structure of Scientific Revolutions* (Chicago: University of Chicago Press, 1970).

7. Howard Gardner, *Creating Minds* (New York: Basic Books, 1993); Banesh Hoffmann, *Einstein* (St. Albans, England: Paladin, 1975); Arthur Miller, *Einstein/Picasso* (New York: Basic Books, 2000).

8. Sigmund Freud, *New Introductory Lectures* (New York: Norton, 1933/1964); Gardner, *Creating Minds*; Ernest Jones, *The Life and Work of Sigmund Freud,* edited and abridged by Lionel Trilling and Steven Marcus (New York: Basic Books, 1961).

9. Carol Gilligan, *In a Different Voice* (Cambridge: Harvard University Press, 1984).

10. Judith Rich Harris, *The Nurture Assumption* (New York: Free Press, 1998), and "What Makes Us the Way We Are: The View from 2050," in *The Next Fifty Years,* ed. John Brockman (New York: Vintage, 2002).

11. Dean Keith Simonton, *Greatness* (New York: Guilford, 1994).

12. Jacques Derrida, *Of Grammatology* (Baltimore: Johns Hopkins University Press, 1974).

13. Harry Collins and Trevor Pinch, *The Golem: What Everyone Should Know About Science* (Cambridge: Cambridge University Press, 1993); Stanley Fish, "Condemnation without Absolutes," *New York Times,* 15 October 2001, A19; Stanley Fish, "There Is No Such Thing as an Orientation to Understanding: Why

Normative Schemes Are Good for Nothing," unpublished paper, University of Illinois, Chicago Circle, 2002; Stanley Fish, "Don't Blame Relativism," *The Responsive Commmunity* 12, no. 3 (2002): 27–31; Donna Haraway, *Simians, Cyborgs, and Women: The Reinvention of Nature* (New York: Routledge, 1991); *Modest-witness, Second Millennium: Femaleman Meets Oncomouse; Feminism and Technoscience* (New York: Routledge, 1996); Charles Lemert, *Postmodernism Is Not What You Think* (Malden, MA: Blackwell, 1997); for a critique see Allan Sokal and Jean Bricmont, *Intellectual Imposters* (London: Profile, 1998).

14. Kuhn, *Structure of Scientific Revolutions.*

15. Jean-François Lyotard, *The Postmodern Condition* (Minneapolis: University of Minnesota Press, 1979/1984).

16. Jay Winsten, personal communications, 1999–2002.

17. W. De Jong and Jay Winsten, *The Media and the Message: Lessons Learned from Past Public Service Campaigns* (Washington, DC: National Campaign to Prevent Teen Pregnancy, 1998).

18. T. Mendoza, telephone conversation with author about the "Squash-It" campaign, 2 May 2002.

19. De Jong and Winsten, *Media and the Message.*

20. Malcolm Gladwell, *The Tipping Point* (Boston: Little, Brown, 1999).

21. Richard Lyman, "Watching Movies with Barry Levinson: Telling Complex Stories Simply," *New York Times,* 26 April 2002, E01.

22. David Feldman, Mihaly Csikszentmihalyi, and Howard Gardner, *Changing the World* (Greenwood, CT: Praeger, 1994).

Chapter 7

1. The argument presented here is elaborated on at greater length in Howard Gardner, *The Unschooled Mind* (New York: Basic Books, 1991), and *The Disciplined Mind* (New York: Penguin, 2000).

2. *Making Learning Visible: A Joint Publication of Harvard Project Zero and Reggio Children,* 2001, available from electronic bookstore at pzweb.harvard.edu; Sidney Strauss, Margalit Ziv, and Adi Stein, "Teaching as Natural Cognition and Its Relation to Preschoolers' Developing Theory of Mind," *Cognitive Psychology* 17 (2002): 1473–1487; Michael Tomasello, *The Cultural Origins of Human Cognition* (Cambridge: Harvard University Press, 1999).

3. David Olson, *The World on Paper* (New York: Cambridge University Press, 1994).

4. David Feldman, *Beyond Universals in Cognitive Development* (Norwood, NJ: Ablex, 1980/1994).

5. Gardner, *The Unschooled Mind,* chapters 2 through 5; Gardner, *The Disciplined Mind,* chapter 6.

6. Gardner, *The Disciplined Mind,* chapters 7 through 9.

7. For information about the changes at BP, see Sophie Barker, "America Helps BP Soar to Four Billion Dollar Record," *The Daily Telegraph,* 19 May 2001, 36; BP Annual Report, 1999; J. Guyon, "When John Browne Talks, Big Oil Listens," *Fortune,* 5 July 1999, 116–122; K. Mehta, "Mr. Energy: The Indefatigable John Browne," *World Link* (September–October 1999): 13-20; Steve Prokesch, "British Petroleum's John Browne," *Harvard Business Review* (September–October 1997), 146–168.

8. Prokesch, "British Petroleum's John Browne."

9. Barker, "America Helps BP Soar," 36.

10. BP Annual Report, 1999; *Economist,* 29 June 2002.

Chapter 8

1. Erik H. Erikson, *The Nature of Clinical Evidence*, 1964, quoted in Robert Coles, *The Erik Erikson Reader* (New York: Norton, 2000), l62–187.

2. Erik H. Erikson, *The Nature of Clinical Evidence*; Lawrence Friedman, *Identity's Architect* (New York: Scribner's, 1999); Leston Havens, *Coming to Life* (Cambridge: Harvard University Press, 1993); Peter Kramer, *Should You Leave?* (New York: Scribner, 1997); Robert Lindner, *The Fifty Minute Hour: A Collection of True Psychoanalytic Tales* (New York: Rinehart, 1955); Anthony Storr, *The Art of Psychotherapy* (London: Routledge and Kegan Paul, 1972/1990).

3. Storr, *Art of Psychotherapy*. I am indebted to my late friend Anthony Storr for many insights about effective psychotherapy.

4. Erikson, *Nature of Clinical Evidence,* 179.

5. Ibid., 170, 182.

6. Leston Havens, *Coming to Life* (Cambridge: Harvard University Press, 1993), 204–205.

7. For a sampling see John McWhorter, "The Mau-mauing of Harvard," *City Journal* (spring 2002): 67–73; Shelby Steele, "White Guild–Black Power," *Wall Street Journal,* 2002; Sam Tanenhaus, "The Ivy League's Angry Star," *Vanity Fair,* June 2002, 201–223; M. Van der Werf, "Lawrence Summers and His Tough Questions," *Chronicle of Higher Education,* 26 April 2002, A29; R. Wilson and S. Smallwood, "Battle of Wills at Harvard," *Chronicle of Higher Education,* 18 January 2002, 8; Karen Zernicke and P. Belluck, "Harvard President Brings Elbows to the Table," *New York Sunday Times,* 6 January 2002, 20.

8. Elliot Aronson, T. D. Wilson, and R. M. Eckert, *Social Psychology,* 3d ed. (New York: Longman, 1999); Robert Cialdini, *Influence: Science and Possibility* (Boston: Allyn and Bacon, 2001); Roger Fisher and William Ury, *Getting to Yes* (Boston: Houghton Mifflin, 1981); Philip Zimbardo and Michael R. Leippe, *The Psychology of Attitude Change and Social Influence* (Philadelphia: Temple University Press, 1991).

9. In this account, I have relied principally on four recent books: Joseph Ellis, *American Sphinx: The Character of Thomas Jefferson* (New York: Knopf, 1997); Joseph Ellis, *Founding Brothers* (New York: Knopf, 2000); Francis Jennings, *The Creation of America Through Revolution to Empire* (New York: Cambridge University Press, 2000); David McCulloch, *John Adams* (New York: Simon and Schuster, 2001).

10. McCulloch, *John Adams,* 312–313.

11. Ibid., 317.

12. Ibid., 361.

13. Ibid., 431.

14. Ibid., 448.

15. Ibid., 465

16. Ibid., 488.

17. Ellis, *Founding Brothers,* 220–222.

18. Ibid., 223.

19. Ibid., 228.

20. Ibid., 230.

21. Ibid., 231.

22. Ibid., 238, 242.

23. McCulloch, *John Adams,* 632.

24. Sigmund Freud, *New Introductory Lectures* (New York: Norton, 1933/1964); Jerome Kagan, "The Concept of Identification," *Psychological Review* 65 (1958): 296–305.

25. Judith Rich Harris, *The Nurture Assumption* (New York: Free Press, 1998).

26. For details about the relation between Sakharov and Bonner, see Richard Lourie, *Sakharov: A Biography* (Waltham, MA: Brandeis University Press, 2002); Andrei Sakharov, *Memoirs,* trans. Richard Lourie (New York: Knopf, 1990).

27. *Anna Karenina,* part VI, chap. 3, quoted in Lev Vygotsky, *Thought and Language,* trans. A. Kozulin (Cambridge: MIT Press, 1986), 238.

Chapter 9

1. Both quoted in Steve Thomma, "Growing on the Job," *Miami Herald,* 12 December 2001.

2. Quoted in David Shribman, "From Change of Mind, Bush Gains Major Turning Point," *Boston Globe,* 7 June 2002, A38.

3. Howard Fineman and Martha Brant, "This Is Our Life Now," *Newsweek,* December 2001, 22.

4. Thomma, "Growing on the Job."

5. Jessica Matthews, Carnegie Endowment Policy Brief #18, 2002.

6. Alan Murray, "Bush Agenda Seeks to Remake World Without Much Help,"

Wall Street Journal, 5 June 2003, A4. See also David Sanger, "Middle East Mediator: Big New Test for Bush," *New York Times,* 5 June 2003, A14; Richard Norton Smith, "Whose Side Is Bush On?" *New York Times,* 7 May 2003, A29.

7. David Brooks, "Whatever It Takes," *New York Times,* 9 September 2003, A31.

8. *Business Week,* 16 September 2002.

9. Fineman and Brant, "This Is Our Life Now."

10. Sam Tanenhaus, *Whittaker Chambers* (New York: Random House, 1997), 55.

11. Whittaker Chambers, *Witness* (New York: Random House, 1952).

12. Ibid., 25.

13. Tanenhaus, *Whittaker Chambers,* 220, 408.

14. Richard Crossman, *The God that Failed* (New York: Harper, 1950).

15. Quoted in Ari Goldman, "Junius Scales, Communist Sent to a Soviet Prison, Dies at 82" (Obituary), *New York Times,* 7 August 2002, C23.

16. Ignazio Silone, *Emergency Exit* (New York: Harper and Row, 1965), 89.

17. See, for example, Martin Malia, *Russia Under Western Eyes* (Cambridge: Harvard University Press, 2000); Juluis Muravchik, *Heaven on Earth: The Rise and Fall of Socialism* (San Francisco: Encounter Books, 2002).

18. Karlheinz Stockhausen, quoted in "The Difficult Mr. Stockhausen," *Art Journal,* 30 September 2001.

19. David Brock, *Blinded by the Right: The Conscience of an Ex-Conservative* (New York: Crown Publishers, 2002).

20. Rudolph Giuiliani, "Global Agenda," (speech to the World Economic Forum, Davos, Switzerland, January 2003), 50.

21. Eric Hoffer, *The True Believer* (New York: Harper 1951).

22. Nancy Ammerman, *Bible Believers: Fundamentalists in the Modern World* (New Brunswick, NJ: Rutgers University Press, 1987); Ellen Babinski, *Leaving the Fold: Testimonies of Former Fundamentalists* (Amherst, NY: Prometheus Books, 1995); James D. Hunter, *American Evangelicism: Conservative Religion and the Quandary of Modernity* (New Brunswick, NJ: Rutgers University Press, 1983); Chandra Ullman, *The Transformed Self: The Psychology of Religious Conversion* (New York: Plenum, 1989).

23. Ullman, *Transformed Self,* 19.

24. Quoted in Babinski, *Leaving the Fold,* 84.

25. Quoted in Thomas Friedman, "Cuckoo in Carolina," *New York Times,* 28 August 2002, A19.

26. Paul Tillich, *The Essential Tillich,* ed. F. Forrester (Chicago: University of Chicago Press, 1999).

27. Ludwig Wittgenstein, *Philosophical Investigations* (New York: Macmillan 1953), x.

28. In a recent example, Professor Mark Taylor renounced deconstructionism, a doctrine that he had supported for twenty years. "It's not every day that a professor issues a public apology to his students for leading them astray intellectually," noted Joshua Glenn in "The Examined Life," *Boston Globe,* September 2003.

29. Lucien Lévy-Bruhl, *How Natives Think* (London: George Allen and Unwin, 1910/1926); *Primitive Mentality* (London: George Allen and Unwin, 1923).

30. Lucien Lévy-Bruhl, *The Notebooks on Primitive Mentality* (New York: Harper and Row, 1945/1979).

31. Ibid., 30.

32. Ibid., 60.

33. Ibid., 37.

34. Ibid., 90.

35. Gerald Holton, *Thematic Origins of Scientific Thought* (Cambridge: Harvard University Press, 1988).

36. Ibid., 41.

37. Isaiah Berlin, *The Hedgehog and the Fox: An Essay on Tolstoy's View of History* (London: Weidenfeld and Nicolson, 1953/1966).

Chapter 10

1. Albert Galaburda, ed., *From Reading to Neurons* (Cambridge: MIT Press, 1989); See Sally Shaywitz, in Barbara Guyers and Sally Shaywitz, *The Pretenders: Gifted People Who Have Difficulty Learning* (Homewood, IL: High Tide Press, 2002).

2. For an excellent discussion of neural enhancement, see Martha Farah, "Emerging Ethical Issues in Neuroscience," *Nature Neuroscience* 5, no. 11 (2003): 1123–1129.

3. Ibid., 1128.

4. Ray Kurzweil, *The Age of Spiritual Machines: When Computers Exceed Human Intelligence* (New York: Viking, 1999); Hans Moravec, *Mindchildren* (Cambridge: Harvard University Press, 1988).

5. Jaron Lanier, "The Complexity Ceiling," in *The Next Fifty Years,* ed. John Brockman (New York: Vintage, 2002).

6. Sherry Turkle, *Life on the Screen* (New York: Simon & Schuster, 1995).

7. Tim Berners-Lee, "Next Up: Web of Data Time: Berners-Lee Wants His Newest Creation to Reach Its Full Potential," *Boston Globe,* 20 June 2002, C1.

8. "Spare Parts for the Brain," *Economist Technology Quarterly,* 21 June 2003.

9. *Economist,* 22 September 2001.

10. Howard Gardner, Mihaly Csikszentmihalyi, and William Damon, *Good Work: When Excellence and Ethics Meet* (New York: Basic Books, 2001). See also Wendy Fischman, Becca Solomon, Deb Greenspan, and Howard Gardner, *Making Good: How Young People Cope with Moral Dilemmas at Work* (Cambridge: Harvard University Press, 2004).

Index

About the Author

HOWARD GARDNER is the John H. and Elisabeth A. Hobbs Professor of Cognition and Education at the Harvard Graduate School of Education. He also holds positions as Adjunct Professor of Psychology at Harvard University, Adjunct Professor of Neurology at the Boston University School of Medicine, and Senior Director of Harvard Project Zero.

Gardner is best known in educational circles for his theory of multiple intelligences, a critique of the notion that there exists but a single human intelligence that can be assessed by standard psychometric instruments. During the past two decades, he and colleagues at Project Zero have been working on the design of performance-based assessments; education for understanding; the use of multiple intelligences to achieve more personalized curriculum, instruction, and assessment; and the nature of interdisciplinary efforts in education. In recent years, in collaboration with psychologists Mihaly Csikszentmihalyi and William Damon, Gardner has embarked on a study of GoodWork—work that is at once excellent in quality and also socially responsible. The GoodWork Project includes studies of outstanding leaders in several professions—among them journalism, law, science, medicine, theater, and philanthropy—as well as examinations of exemplary institutions and organizations.

Gardner is the author of several hundred articles and twenty books translated into twenty-two languages, including *Good Work: When Excellence and Ethics Meet; The Disciplined Mind: Beyond Facts and Standardized Tests, the K–12 Education That Every Child Deserves; Intelligence Reframed: Multiple Intelligences for the Twenty-First Century;* and *Making Good: How Young People Cope with Moral Dilemmas at Work* (with Wendy Fischman, Becca Solomon, and Deborah Greenspan).

Among numerous honors, Gardner received a MacArthur Prize Fellowship in 1981. In 1990, he was the first American to receive the University of Louisville's Grawemeyer Award in Education, and in 2000 he received a Fellowship from the John S. Guggenheim Memorial Foundation. He has received honorary degrees from twenty colleges and universities, including institutions in Ireland, Italy, and Israel.